# FEARLESS COOKING FOR COMPANY

# FEARLESS COOKING FOR COMPANY

*Michele Evans'*
*Most Requested Recipes*

*by*

## MICHELE EVANS

𝕿imes
BOOKS

Published by TIMES BOOKS, The New York Times Book Co., Inc.
130 Fifth Avenue, New York, N.Y. 10011

Published simultaneously in Canada by Fitzhenry & Whiteside, Ltd.,
Toronto

Library of Congress Cataloging in Publication Data

Evans, Michele.
  Fearless cooking for company.

  Includes index.
  1. Cookery.   I. Title.
TX715.E884   1984        641.5        83-40088
ISBN 0-8129-1100-8

Coordinating Editor: Rosalyn T. Badalamenti

MANUFACTURED IN THE UNITED STATES OF AMERICA

84 85 86 87 88 5 4 3 2 1

*For Susan Angel*

# Acknowledgments

Thanks go to Helen Abbott, Clita Illene Allen, Ellie and Jack Ashworth, Mary and Dick Auletta, Frances and Stanley Bangel, Jeff Barr and his mother the late Lili Barr, Emilie Bartok, Jane, Melanie, Wendy, and Larry Cohen, Nancy Dussault, Kitty Freydberg, Bobbe and Donn Hart, Norman Hodgson, Emily and Edward McCormack, Cathy O'Neill and Richard Reeves, Phyllis and Robbie Robinson, Vicki, Nicholas, and Charles Sopkin, Diane Terman, Ann and C. C. Wong and Mrs. M. T. Wong, who either contributed recipes or their discriminating palates during the writing of this book.

Special thanks, as always, to Tully Plesser and Esther Newberg, and to my editors, Kathleen Moloney and Rosalyn T. Badalamenti, who were encouraging, supportive, and incredibly patient.

# Contents

# Introduction

The serious cook is always delighted when company applauds a meal with words like "superb, delicious, and bravo," but the ultimate compliment received at any table is the question: "May I have a copy of that recipe?" How to cook fearlessly for company came to me many years ago one evening after a dinner party when a departing guest paid me that ultimate compliment, and requested copies of the recipes for several of the dishes I'd served. I closed the door, exhilarated. It was then I realized that cooking for company could always be rewarding and fearless for the cook if most of the dishes served were selected from an exclusive collection of "requested" recipes: recipes that could be *counted* on.

This book includes ten years of "most requested" recipes, my own and those of family, friends, and gracious chefs in restaurants from around the world who have all generously shared their secrets. Now I always ask for the recipe for an outstanding dish, no matter where the setting or what the circumstance. At worst, you flatter the cook, and, at best, you gain both a friend and a new addition to your kitchen library. Some of these most requested recipes are adaptations from the works of talented food enthusiasts and professionals who have inspired me over the years with their extraordinary creativity and skillful executions. Some are based on references to foods, cooking styles, and techniques of different countries and periods in the pages of novels, historical literature, and travel books. But as a cooking instructor at the London Cordon Bleu once suggested, we often find our most prized recipes by being "open" to food wherever we are. From my earliest cooking experiences in Great Bend, Kansas, where I was born, to Texas, Istanbul, Peking, Kyoto, and Venice—and to Southampton, New York, and St. Thomas in the United States Virgin Islands, where I do much of my writing and testing—staying "open" to food has been a constant source of education and pleasure. Some of the best cooking ideas are found as we travel. Exposure to different styles and cultures, the mood of adventure, a more leisurely approach to dining—all bring us in contact with foods that can serve as perfect highlights when cooking for company. All it takes is a healthy curiosity and a notebook.

In St. Thomas recently, I discovered *Roti* at a lunch wagon parked next to the old fort in Charlotte Amalie. Roti is a flat bread from Trinidad. It has evolved into a dish of a spicy thick curried ragout, which is rolled up in a giant crêpe and served with chutney. I tasted one and asked the native St. Thomian cook of that rolling restaurant for the recipe. He beamed with pride and gave me an oral account. After some experimentation, his recipe for this unusual delicacy developed into one of the most "requested" recipes in this book.

The tendency to assume that cooking for company is always elaborate and time-consuming is unfortunate and often inhibiting. The fearless cook never shrinks from a special dish that requires careful planning and skilled preparation, but many dishes that please company most are both easy and quick.

This collection ranges from nearly instant dishes made from fresh and some prepared foods to elaborate presentations that require time and totally fresh ingredients. In either case, never look the other way when a short cut allows you to save time and effort without sacrificing taste and quality. We can be as proud of the food processor and canned whole cranberries as we can of the fresh fruits and vegetables that we plant, pick, and peel ourselves.

Included is a special section of cooking for crowds, with recipes and menus that serve 12 or 24. Cooking for crowds often dictates the serving of roasts, baked hams, and salads, but there are other unusual and tempting crowd-pleasers.

All entrées in the book are accompanied by serving suggestions, *with capital letters* signifying recipes that are in the book.

Some recipes may appear basic, but they are included to remind the reader of fundamental procedures, techniques, and timing. For example, the recipe for the classic Cooked Asparagus is included to remind cooks that asparagus must be peeled before cooking, and usually cooked no longer than 6 minutes.

The first chapter, *Mise en Place* (or putting everything in its place), suggests ways of organizing the preparation of a recipe in the most efficient manner possible. Organization is as important to the home cook as it is to the chef in the largest restaurant kitchen, and it is one of the critical keys to good anxiety-free cooking for company.

Whether you entertain often, only on special occasions, or whenever the mood strikes you, I hope that these recipes will become part of your own treasured collection—recipes that your "company" will ask for, and that you will pass on with pleasure.

# FEARLESS COOKING FOR COMPANY

# Mise en Place

The French phrase *mise en place* means, literally, putting things in their place. Chefs often use the term when assembling the food, equipment, and utensils and completing any procedure necessary before beginning to cook a dish. "Let's do the *mise en place*," they'll say.

Organization is vital in efficient good cooking. In the end it always saves time and, inevitably, affects the quality of the dish. Every recipe in this cookbook—or any cookbook—should be completely read through before shopping, *mise en place*, and cooking a dish.

The *mise en place* includes setting out all the ingredients in proper amounts, getting the pots, pans, knives, bowls, utensils, and equipment needed ready and close at hand to use. If an ingredient needs to be chilled, softened, or heated in advance of the actual cooking, that's *mise en place*. Plates and bowls might require chilling or warming or a baking sheet may need to be greased. *Mise en place* also means dicing, slicing, cubing, chopping, husking, seeding, shelling, grating, and grinding. When a recipe reads "Melt the butter and add the chopped onions," the onions should already have been chopped.

In short, *mise en place* in the kitchen means having everything ready as directed in the recipe just before actually beginning to cook and assemble the dish.

I've used the recipe for Chocolate Mousse on the following page to illustrate exactly what I mean by *mise en place*.

# Chocolate Mousse

## Serves 8

| | |
|---|---|
| 8 ounces semisweet chocolate, cut into small pieces | 2 tablespoons Cognac or brandy |
| 1 tablespoon butter | 2 teaspoons freshly grated orange rind |
| 3 large eggs, separated | 2 cups heavy cream |
| ½ cup sugar | |

1. Melt the chocolate with the butter in the top of a double boiler over simmering water.

2. Meanwhile, in a large bowl, beat the egg yolks with the sugar until light and fluffy. Add the brandy and orange rind and combine well.

3. Whip the cream and stir in half. Fold in the remaining half of the cream.

4. Beat the egg whites until stiff but not dry and fold into the mixture.

5. Turn the mousse into a large chilled dessert bowl, cover, and chill thoroughly.

### Mise en Place:

1. Chill the dessert bowl in the refrigerator.

2. Place all the equipment and utensils to be used in the recipe in the work area: chopping knife, measuring spoons, double boiler, 2 small bowls for separating the eggs, measuring cup, grater, 2 large bowls for beating the cream and then the egg whites, an electric mixer, wooden spoon, and a spatula. (A serving spoon for the dish can be put out when you set the table.)

3. Place all the ingredients in the work area. Measure the ingredients in the proper amounts if it saves time: Coarsely chop the chocolate. Measure the butter and place it in the top of the double boiler. Separate the eggs into the 2 small bowls. Measure the sugar in a measuring cup and set it aside. The Cognac can be poured directly from the bottle into the measuring spoon and added directly to the dish when called for . . . no need to have to wash an extra bowl. Grate the orange rind onto a small saucer or a piece of wax paper.

4. Put the water in the bottom of the double boiler and bring it to a boil, then lower the heat to a simmer.

That's the *mise en place.* Now the recipe is ready to be cooked.

# Hors d'Oeuvres

Hors d'oeuvres are taste-teasers. The French call them *amuse gueules*—to amuse the palate. An hors d'oeuvre is meant to only pique or wake up the appetite, so the amount served should be minimal and should not conflict with the rest of the meal. Hors d'oeuvres cannot make the meal, but they can stimulate your company's anticipation and appreciation of whatever follows. An hors d'oeuvre can be a plate of small crisp radishes, thin slices of cooked sausage, or sautéed almonds. There is no need for extravagance, but the subtlety required to stimulate the appetite calls for the best quality of food. The presentation of the hors d'oeuvre is especially important. Not long ago I was served a simple hors d'oeuvre of small black Niçoise olives piled high in a red ceramic bowl; it left such a strong impression that now whenever I think of hors d'oeuvres, I automatically recall that colorful combination.

# Hot Hors d'Oeuvres

## Shrimp Toast Coins

### Serves 10 to 12    Makes 48

1 pound shrimp, shelled
and deveined
2 scallions, minced
½ cup minced water
chestnuts
1 large egg, lightly beaten
1 tablespoon soy sauce
(light, if possible)
1 teaspoon grated fresh
ginger
1 tablespoon sesame oil

1 tablespoon cornstarch
½ teaspoon salt
12 slices firm sandwich
bread
Unseasoned bread
crumbs
1 tablespoon sesame seeds
Peanut oil
Snipped fresh chives

1. Grind the shrimp in the food processor, but don't over grind. The shrimp should be ground but not paste-like.

2. In a large bowl combine the shrimp with the next 8 ingredients.

3. Trim the crusts off the bread and cut each square into 4 circles, using a small round 1¼-inch cutter.

4. Spread the mixture evenly over the bread rounds and dust them with the bread crumbs. Sprinkle lightly with the sesame seeds.

5. Heat ¾ inch of peanut oil in a large frying pan and cook the coins shrimp side down over medium-high heat until they are golden brown. Cook only about 8 to 10 at a time. Turn the coins and brown them on the bread side. Remove and drain on paper towels. Cook the remaining shrimp coins.*

6. Put all the shrimp coins on a baking sheet and heat in a preheated 350-degree oven for 10 minutes. Garnish each with the snipped chives.

*At this point, the shrimp coins can be cooled, wrapped in foil, and frozen. To reheat, place on a baking sheet in a preheated 350-degree oven for about 20 minutes.

# Shrimp-filled Fried Wontons with Hoisin Sauce

*Serves 10   Makes 30*

This recipe can easily be doubled to serve 20 to 24 people.

## SHRIMP FILLING

1   pound shrimp, shelled, deveined, and coarsely ground
½   cup finely chopped water chestnuts
2   scallions, minced
1   tablespoon Oriental sesame oil

1   tablespoon dry sherry
1½   tablespoons soy sauce
1   tablespoon cornstarch
1   large egg yolk
½   teaspoon salt
Freshly ground black pepper

30   wonton wrappers
Water
3   cups peanut oil

1   cup hoisin sauce (available in Oriental grocery stores)

1. In a large bowl combine the filling ingredients well.

2. Lightly moisten a ¼-inch border of 2 adjoining sides of 1 wonton wrapper with a finger. Place a rounded teaspoon of the filling in the center of the wonton and fold it over. Press the edges together firmly. Fold the center flap down against the middle and press the two corners, one moistened lightly with water, together. Prepare the remaining wontons in the same manner.

3. Heat the oil to 375 degrees in a wok or large frying pan. Fry the filled wontons, about 10 at a time, until they are golden brown all over, stirring often. Drain well on paper towels and serve with the hoisin sauce.

## Sautéed Bay Scallop Kebabs

*Serves 4 to 6    Makes 12 hors d'oeuvres*

| | | | |
|---|---|---|---|
| 48 | bay scallops, about 1½ pounds | | All-purpose flour |
| | Salt and freshly ground black pepper | 3 | tablespoons butter |
| | | 3 | tablespoons peanut or vegetable oil |

1. Season the scallops with salt and pepper and coat them with the flour. Thread 4 scallops onto each of 12 rounded wooden toothpicks.

2. Heat the butter and oil in a large frying pan and brown the scallop kebabs over medium-high heat for about 3 minutes per side, or until they are golden brown. Drain and serve. Serve with lemon or lime wedges, if desired.

## Anchovy and Apple Tidbits

*Serves 12    Makes 28*

| | | | |
|---|---|---|---|
| 1 | 2-ounce can anchovies, drained | 1 | sheet frozen puff pastry, thawed |
| ¾ | cup unpeeled minced apple | 4 | tablespoons butter, melted |
| 3 | tablespoons mayonnaise | | |
| 2 | teaspoons fresh lemon juice | | |

1. Soak the anchovies in cool water to cover for 5 minutes, then drain and pat dry. Chop the anchovies very fine and combine them in a bowl with the apple, mayonnaise, and lemon juice.

2. Preheat the oven to 350 degrees.

3. On a lightly floured surface, roll out the sheet of pastry to approximately 8 by 12 inches. Cut the sheet into 4 2-inch lengths.

4. Spoon ½ teaspoon of the mixture at ½-inch intervals in the center of each strip. Fold the strips over crosswise and press the ends together and the space between each filling.

5. Cut the strips into 12 filled tidbits* and brush with the melted butter. Place on a baking sheet and bake for about 15 minutes, or until puffed and golden.

*The tidbits can be wrapped up and frozen at this point, if desired.

# Potato Shells with Tarragon Lobster Salad

### Serves 6   Makes 12

6  small baking potatoes
   (about 3 inches in length)
2  tablespoons butter, melted

Salt and freshly ground
black pepper

## TARRAGON LOBSTER SALAD

2½  cups chopped cooked
    lobster
½  cup mayonnaise
2  teaspoons fresh lemon
   juice
1  tablespoon chopped
   fresh tarragon, or 1
   teaspoon dried tarragon

1  tablespoon chopped
   fresh parsley leaves
1  scallion, minced
   Salt and freshly ground
   black pepper

1. Preheat the oven to 400 degrees.

2. Prick each potato once and bake them in the oven for about 30 minutes, or until they are tender.

3. Meanwhile, combine the salad ingredients in a bowl and set them aside.

4. Cut each potato in half lengthwise and scoop out the potato pulp with a teaspoon. Leave a border of about ⅛ inch of potato attached to the skin. (Use the pulp for potato pancakes, croquettes, or another use.) Brush the insides of each potato shell with the butter and sprinkle them with salt and pepper.

5. Place the shells on a baking sheet under the broiler for a few minutes until they are golden brown.

6. Stuff the shells with equal amounts of the salad and serve immediately.

*Variation:* Crabmeat can be substituted for the lobster and 2 teaspoons of diced radish or red, yellow, or green pepper can be added.

# Sardine and Chutney Canapés

*Serves 4 to 6   Makes 16 canapés*

Sardines too often are forgotten by hosts and hostesses as an hor d'oeuvre or for any course. Here's an unusually delicious sardine starter.

| | | | |
|---|---|---|---|
| 1 | 2¾-ounce can boned and skinned sardines, well drained and chopped | 1 | tablespoon fresh lemon juice |
| ½ | cup chutney, chopped fine | 16 | ½-inch-thick slices French bread |
| 1 | scallion, minced | | Chopped fresh parsley leaves |

1. Preheat the broiler.
2. Combine the first 4 ingredients in a bowl.
3. Spread equal amounts of the mixture on the bread slices.
4. Put the canapés on a baking sheet and broil for a few minutes until the tops sizzle and the bread crusts are golden brown. This will only take 3 or 4 minutes, so watch carefully. Sprinkle lightly with parsley and serve.

# Chinese Cattails

*Serves 6 to 8   Makes 18 cattails*

| | | | |
|---|---|---|---|
| 1½ | pounds boneless pork shoulder, cut into 1-inch cubes | | Pinch of freshly ground black pepper |
| ½ | cup unseasoned bread crumbs, plus bread crumbs for coating the cattails | 1 | tablespoon cornstarch |
| | | 1 | tablespoon rice wine or dry white wine |
| 3 | large eggs | | All-purpose flour |
| 1 | teaspoon salt | 1½ | cups peanut oil |
| ½ | teaspoon five spice powder | 1 | bunch scallions |

1. Grind the pork cubes and put the ground pork in a large bowl. Add the ½ cup bread crumbs, 1 egg, salt, five spice powder, pepper, cornstarch, and wine. Combine well.

2. Divide the mixture into 18 equal-sized pieces. Roll each between the palms of your hands to form a cylinder resembling the shape of the top of a cattail.

3. Beat the 2 remaining eggs. Put the flour and bread crumbs for coating on separate pieces of wax paper.

4. Roll each cattail first in flour, then in the beaten 2 eggs, and finally in the bread crumbs.

5. Heat the oil in a wok or large frying pan and fry the cattails until golden all over and thoroughly cooked. Drain. Stick the end of an 8-inch wooden skewer through a single green leaf of a scallion and weave it on for 3 inches of the skewer. Stick the top end of the skewer halfway into the cattail lengthwise. Repeat the procedure for the remaining cattails. If desired serve the cattails with hot Chinese mustard.

## Oven-fried Cornish Game Hen Pieces

*Serves 2 to 4   Makes 16*

| | |
|---|---|
| 2   **Cornish game hens (fresh, if possible)** | 6   **fresh parsley sprigs tied together** |
| ¼   **cup mayonnaise Italian-style dry bread crumbs** | |

1. Preheat the oven to 400 degrees.

2. Cut each Cornish game hen into 8 pieces, in the same manner as a chicken. Discard the wing tips and backbones. Rub each piece of game hen lightly with mayonnaise and coat the pieces with bread crumbs.

3. Put the breaded pieces on a baking sheet and bake for about 20 minutes, or until crisp and tender. Serve in a napkin-lined basket garnished with the parsley bouquet. An empty bowl will be necessary to dispose of the bones.

# Stuffed Chicken Pojarsky Balls with Lemon–Curry Dip

*Serves 24   Makes about 60 balls*

## LEMON–CURRY DIP

2   cups mayonnaise
1½  tablespoons curry powder
2   tablespoons fresh lemon juice
3   tablespoons canned cream of coconut

1   teaspoon black sesame seeds (found in Oriental grocery stores)
1   teaspoon chopped fresh chives

## CHICKEN POJARSKY BALLS

½   cup heavy cream
¼   cup milk
2   tablespoons dry white wine
4   slices firm white bread, crusts trimmed and coarsely cubed
4   large chicken breasts, boned, skinned, and cut into 1½-inch pieces
1   teaspoon salt
    Freshly ground white pepper to taste
6   tablespoons butter, softened

1   tablespoon chopped fresh parsley leaves
    Few gratings of nutmeg
12  ounces Fontina cheese, cut into ½-inch cubes
2   cups all-purpose flour
5   large eggs, well beaten
2   tablespoons water
3   cups unseasoned dry bread crumbs
    Peanut or vegetable oil for frying

1. First prepare the dip by putting all the ingredients, except for the sesame seeds and chives, in a bowl. Use a wire whisk to combine them well. Turn the dip into a serving dish and sprinkle half the surface with sesame seeds and the other half with the chives. Cover and refrigerate.

2. In a bowl combine the heavy cream, milk, and wine. Add the bread cubes and stir. Soak for 5 minutes.

3. Grind the chicken in a food processor or meat grinder. Put the ground chicken in a large bowl. Squeeze the liquid from the bread and add the bread to the chicken along with the salt, pepper, butter, parsley, and nutmeg. Combine thoroughly. Cover and refrigerate for 30 minutes.

4. Take a rounded teaspoon of the chicken mixture and shape it into a ball around 1 cube of cheese. Roll each chicken ball in flour and put the balls on wax paper. When all the chicken mixture is used, dip the flour-coated balls in the combined beaten eggs and water and coat with the bread crumbs.

5. Heat ½ inch of the oil in a large frying pan and fry the balls until golden brown all over. Cook only about 12 balls at a time. As the chicken balls are cooked, drain them on paper towels. Put the cooked chicken balls on a baking sheet and heat in a 350-degree oven for 15 minutes. Serve with the Lemon–Curry Dip.

*Variation:* Eliminate the cheese from the recipe and make about 72 small plain chicken balls, substituting 1 teaspoon dried tarragon for the parsley in the recipe.

NOTE: The cooked Chicken Balls can be cooled and frozen in a covered container for up to a month. To reheat the frozen Chicken Balls, put them on a baking sheet and warm in a preheated 325-degree oven for about 25 minutes.

# Fried Chicken Breast Cubes with Scallion–Marmalade Dip

### Serves 8

3 large chicken breasts, boned, skinned, and cut into 1-inch cubes
Salt and freshly ground black pepper

All-purpose flour
3 tablespoons peanut oil
3 tablespoons butter

## SCALLION–MARMALADE DIP

1½ cups orange marmalade
½ cup drained crushed pineapple
2 minced scallions

1½ teaspoons sesame seed oil
2 tablespoons soy sauce

1. Heat the oven to low.
2. Season the chicken cubes with salt and pepper and coat them with the flour. Shake off any excess flour.
3. Heat the oil and butter in a large frying pan and brown the chicken cubes on each side until they are tender, cooking about 16

pieces at one time. Keep the cooked pieces warm on a platter in the oven.

    4. Combine the Marmalade Dip ingredients in a bowl and serve with the crisp cooked chicken cubes.

# Sausage Balls with Jalapeño Hot Cheese Dip

*Serves 12    Makes 48*

| | |
|---|---|
| 1 **pound bulk sausage** | ⅔ **cup herbed-seasoned** |
| 1 **large egg, lightly beaten** | **bread crumbs** |
| 2 **tablespoons grated onion** | |

## JALAPEÑO HOT CHEESE DIP

| | |
|---|---|
| ⅔ **cup scalded milk, or as needed** | 2 **scallions, cut into ½-inch lengths** |
| 12 **ounces cubed Monterey Jack cheese** | 1 **tablespoon cornstarch** |
| 4 **jalapeño chili peppers, seeded and coarsely chopped** | ¼ **cup diced sweet green or red pepper** |

    1. In a bowl combine the sausage, egg, onion, and bread crumbs well. Shape into 48 small balls.

    2. Sauté the balls in a large frying pan, half a batch at a time, until they are evenly browned. Drain well and keep warm in a low oven.

    3. Put the cheese, jalapeño peppers, scallions, and cornstarch in a food processor or blender. Turn the machine on and pour the hot milk through the feed tube or the top of the blender and run for 15 seconds.

    4. Transfer the mixture to a saucepan and stir in the sweet pepper. The mixture should be thick enough to coat a spoon and stir easily. If not, add a little more hot milk. Heat the mixture over medium heat, stirring constantly, for about 5 minutes. Transfer to a bowl on a serving platter and surround the bowl with the sausage balls. Serve with toothpicks.

# Gougère Puffs

*Serves 12   Makes about 3 dozen puffs*

Gougère is cream puff pastry with cheese added. When baked in the shape of little balls it becomes an elegant and savory hors d'ouvre, or an alternative to bread that can be served with any meal, even breakfast.

| | |
|---|---|
| 1   cup water | 1   cup sifted all-purpose |
| ½   cup (1 stick) butter, plus | flour |
| butter for greasing the | 4   large eggs |
| baking sheet | ¾   cup grated Gruyère |
| ¼   teaspoon salt | cheese |

1. Preheat the oven to 400 degrees.

2. Combine the water, butter, and salt in a large saucepan and bring to a boil. Remove from the heat and add the flour all at once. Beat vigorously with a wooden spoon until the mixture rolls off the side of the pan and forms a ball. Beat in 1 egg at a time until each is well incorporated into the mixture. Beat in the cheese.

3. Spoon the mixture into a pastry bag fitted with a round tube. Make 1 inch balls about 2 inches apart on a greased baking sheet. Bake for 18 to 20 minutes, or until the puffs are golden. Turn off the oven and remove the baking sheet. Prick each puff with the sharp point of a small knife. Return the Gougère to the oven, leaving the door slightly ajar, for 15 minutes. This procedure helps dry out the moist centers. Serve immediately.

*Variations:* Gougère Puffs may also be cooked, cut in half, and stuffed with fillings such as Fresh Salmon Salad. Grated Swiss or Cheddar or crumbled Gorgonzola or Roquefort can be substituted for the Gruyère.

# Tortilla Pizza Rolls

*Serves 4 to 6*

| | | | |
|---|---|---|---|
| ½ | pound ground chuck | 1½ | cups shredded Monterey |
| 2 | scallions, thinly sliced | | Jack or Cheddar cheese |
| 1 | tablespoon chili powder | 16 | stuffed green olives |
| 4 | 8-inch flour tortillas | | |
| ½ | cup fresh or canned | | |
| | tomato sauce | | |

1. Put the ground chuck, scallions, and chili powder in a frying pan and cook over medium-high heat, stirring often, for about 10 minutes.

2. Preheat the broiler.

3. Put the tortillas on a baking sheet. Spread equal amounts of the tomato sauce over each tortilla. Sprinkle the tops with equal amounts of the meat mixture and the cheese. Run under the broiler until the cheese sizzles. Cut each pizza into 4 equal-sized wedges and roll each up from the pointed end. Secure each with a toothpick and top each toothpick with an olive. Serve immediately.

# Sun-dried Tomato and Mozzarella Canapés with Fried Capers

*Serves 8    Makes 32 canapés*

| | | | |
|---|---|---|---|
| 3 | tablespoons large capers, well drained and patted dry (see Note) | 16 | sun-dried tomatoes, drained and patted dry |
| 1 | cup peanut oil | 6 | ounces mozzarella, shredded |
| 8 | slices toast, crusts trimmed and cut into 4 squares each | | |

1. Preheat the broiler.

2. Heat the oil in a heavy saucepan and fry the capers, stirring often, until the flowers open and the capers crisp. Drain and set aside.

3. Place the toast squares on a baking sheet. Top each with half a sun-dried tomato. Sprinkle with equal amounts of the cheese.

4. Run under the broiler until the cheese sizzles. Top each canapé with 2 or 3 fried capers. Serve immediately.

NOTE: Sun-dried tomatoes are available in specialty food stores or Italian markets.

## French Pizza Canapés

*Serves 10 to 12    Makes about 36 canapés*

Olive oil
1½ cups well-drained finely chopped canned tomatoes
4 tablespoons tomato paste
6 anchovy fillets, drained and finely chopped
2 tablespoons drained capers
½ teaspoon dried oregano
½ teaspoon dried thyme
Freshly ground black pepper to taste
1 long loaf French bread (ficelle, the thin loaf, is best), cut into ½-inch slices
12 ounces mozzarella, thinly sliced and cut to fit the bread slices
Freshly grated Parmesan cheese

1. Preheat the broiler.
2. Combine 2 tablespoons of olive oil, the tomatoes, tomato paste, anchovy fillets, capers, oregano, thyme, and pepper. Spread the mixture over each bread slice and top each with a slice of mozzarella. Sprinkle the canapés lightly with Parmesan cheese and drizzle a few drops of olive oil over each.
3. Put the canapés on a baking sheet and run under the broiler until the cheese melts and the tops sizzle. Serve immediately.

# Cold Hors d'Oeuvres

## *Fruit Crudités*

Many of us enjoy a first course of fruit, so I can see no reason on earth why fresh-cut fruit can't be served as a cold hors d'oeuvre. Select fruits of complementary flavors, textures, and colors and arrange them attractively on a platter. Serve with toothpicks and napkins if including grapefruit or orange sections. Decorate the platter with fresh mint leaves if they are available, and serve with the suggested dip, if desired. One pound of cut fruit serves 4 to 5 people. Fresh Fruit Crudités served as dessert can be accompanied with flavored whipped cream using sugar, vanilla, and the liqueur of your choice, or scoops of sherbet or ice cream. Here's a list to select from depending on the season of the year:

Grannie Smith or Delicious apples, cored and cut into slices, wedges, or rings
Apricot halves
Banana slices, with lemon juice squeezed over
Blackberries on toothpicks
Blueberries on toothpicks
Cantaloupe, sliced or cut into balls or cubes
Figs, peeled and quartered
Grapefruit sections
Seedless green or red grapes
Honeydew melon, sliced or cut into balls or cubes
Kiwi fruit, peeled and cut into wedges
Mango slices
Nectarines, quartered
Orange sections
Papaya slices or cubes
Pears, cored and cut into wedges
Peaches, cut into quarters
Pineapple slices
Plums, cut in half or quartered, depending on size
Raspberries on toothpicks
Large strawberries
Watermelon fingers, seeded

# Caribbean Curried Mayonnaise

*Makes about 2 cups*

1 cup mayonnaise
1 tablespoon curry powder
1 tablespoon fresh lemon
   juice

1 small banana, sliced
3 tablespoons cream of
   coconut

Combine the ingredients in a food processor or blender. Transfer to a bowl, cover, and chill until ready to serve.

# Vegetable Crudités

The following list of vegetables serves as a reminder for those of us who prefer only crisp fresh raw vegetables as an hors d'oeuvre. Today there is certainly a cornucopia of vegetables to select from our local farmers' markets or our own gardens. A pound of crudités serves 4 to 5 people. Serve with any of the suggested dips.

Asparagus stalks, ends trimmed
Broccoli flowerets
Carrot sticks or diagonal slices
Cauliflower flowerets
Celery sticks
Cherry or yellow pear tomatoes
Cucumber slices or sticks
Endive leaves
Fennel sticks
Mushrooms, small to medium, whole
Green, red, or yellow pepper strips or rings
Red radishes, trimmed
Scallions
Snow pea pods, ends trimmed and strings removed
String beans, ends trimmed
Zucchini or yellow squash, slices or sticks

# Aïoli

*Makes about 1½ cups*

2  large garlic cloves, crushed
2  large egg yolks
1  tablespoon fresh lemon
   juice

1  cup olive oil
   Salt and freshly ground
   black pepper

In a shallow bowl beat together the garlic and egg yolks until pale yellow. Beat in the lemon juice. Drop by drop whisk in the olive oil and season to taste with salt and pepper. Cover and chill until ready to serve.

# Cottage Cheese Diet Herb Dip

*Makes about 1½ cups*

1  cup cottage cheese
2  tablespoons mayonnaise
1  tablespoon white wine
   vinegar or fresh lemon
   juice
3  tablespoons chopped fresh
   parsley leaves

1  tablespoon chopped fresh
   basic, or 1 teaspoon
   dried basil
½  teaspoon dried tarragon
1  scallion, thinly sliced
   Salt and freshly ground
   black pepper to taste

Combine the dip ingredients in a food processor or blender. Transfer to a bowl, cover, and chill until ready to serve.

# Green Goddess Dip

*Makes about 1½ cups*

1 cup mayonnaise
1 3-ounce package cream
  cheese, softened
1 teaspoon dried tarragon
4 to 6 anchovy fillets,
  drained and chopped

2 tablespoons tarragon or
  white wine vinegar
2 tablespoons chopped fresh
  parsley leaves

Combine the dip ingredients in a food processor or blender. Transfer to bowl, cover, and chill until ready to serve.

# Guacamole and Toasted Pine Nuts in Cherry Tomatoes

*Serves 12   Makes 36*

1 large ripe avocado, cut
  in half, pitted and
  cubed
1 tablespoon fresh lemon
  juice
1 large garlic clove,
  crushed

  Salt and freshly ground
  black pepper
36 cherry tomatoes
2 tablespoons olive oil
½ cup pine nuts

1. Purée the avocado, lemon juice, and garlic in a food processor or blender. Season with salt and pepper to taste.

2. Cut ¼ inch off the side opposite the stem end of each tomato. (This makes it easier to balance the tomatoes on a tray.) Scoop out the pulp and seeds of each tomato with a teaspoon and discard. Stuff the tomatoes with the Guacamole.

3. Heat the olive oil in a frying pan and lightly brown the pine nuts. Drain well on paper towels and place several nuts on top of each stuffed tomato.

# Salmon Mousse with Red Salmon Caviar and Fresh Dill

*Serves 12 as appetizer, or 6 to 8 as first course*

1   16-ounce can salmon, well drained
2   tablespoons (2 envelopes) unflavored gelatin
1/3   cup coarsely chopped scallions
1/2   teaspoon crushed garlic
1/2   cup boiling water
2½   tablespoons fresh lemon juice
1/2   teaspoon paprika
2   dashes of Tabasco sauce
1   tablespoon chopped fresh dill, plus 8 sprigs for garnish (Use 1 teaspoon dried dill if fresh is unavailable and omit the garnish.)

1/4   teaspoon freshly ground black pepper
3   ounces cream cheese, softened
1   cup heavy cream
2   ounces red salmon caviar, well-chilled
1   tablespoon vegetable oil

1. Put the salmon in a large bowl and remove and discard all the bones and skins.

2. Put the gelatin, scallions, garlic, and boiling water in the container of a blender. Purée until the gelatin dissolves. Add the lemon juice, paprika, Tabasco sauce, chopped dill, pepper, and salmon. Purée until well blended.

3. In a bowl beat the cream cheese until it is light and fluffy and add it to the blender and mix thoroughly. Pour the mixture into a large bowl and let it cool for 5 minutes.

4. Add the red caviar to the salmon mixture and combine well.

5. Whip the heavy cream. Fold the whipped cream into the mixture.

6. Brush the sides and bottom of a 9-inch cake pan with the oil. Turn the salmon mousse mixture into the pan. Refrigerate for several hours, or until the mousse is firm; overnight is best.

7. Invert the mousse onto a round serving dish and, holding the plate and pan firmly, shake once with vigor. This should release the mousse. Garnish the dish by surrounding the mousse with the sprigs

of dill and placing a sprig or two on the top. Serve with pumpernickel bread slices, toast triangles, or crackers.

NOTES: Canned salmon is used in this recipe because it has a stronger flavor than fresh salmon and it is also less expensive. Fresh salmon's delicate flavor should not be tampered with by the addition of too many potent flavors. The discriminate use of butter, fresh lemon juice, herbs, salt, and pepper enhances cooked fresh salmon.

A cake pan is used in this recipe to give the mousse more surface area than a traditional mold would allow. Some of the red salmon caviar sinks to the bottom of the mold creating an attractive dotted pattern on the top of the mousse after it is unmolded. The red salmon caviar and green dill make a particularly appealing dish at Christmas or any holiday.

To make a first-course dish, brush vegetable oil on the sides and bottoms of 6 to 8 individual soufflé dishes or molds and fill them with equal amounts of the mousse. Place the filled dishes on a small baking sheet and refrigerate until firm or overnight. Unmold each mousse on a first-course plate as described in the recipe and garnish each with a sprig of dill and several slices of pumpernickel bread or toast points.

## Herring in Mushroom Caps

### Serves 8

1   pound medium-sized fresh mushrooms
¾  cup sour cream
2   tablespoons minced scallion
1   8-ounce jar wine-marinated herring, well-drained and cut into ¾-inch pieces

Chopped fresh parsley leaves

1. Remove the stems from the mushrooms. (Use the stems for stock or soup.)
2. Bring 1 quart of water to a boil in a saucepan and add the mushroom caps. Simmer for 5 minutes. Drain well, stem side down.
3. Combine the sour cream and scallions and spoon a teaspoon into each mushroom cavity. Top each with a piece of herring. Sprinkle with parsley.

# Country Pâté

*Serves 8   Makes 1 loaf*
*(Preparation begins the night before)*

| | | | |
|---|---|---|---|
| 1 | cup cooked chopped fresh spinach, well drained and cooled | 1 | medium-sized onion, minced |
| 1½ | pounds ground beef | ½ | teaspoon dried thyme |
| ½ | pound ground pork | ½ | teaspoon dried rosemary |
| ½ | pound ground veal | | |
| ½ | pound bulk sausage | 1 | tablespoon chopped fresh parsley leaves |
| 1 | large egg | ½ | teaspoon salt |
| ½ | cup unseasoned dry bread crumbs | ¼ | teaspoon freshly ground black pepper |

1. Preheat the oven to 350 degrees.

2. Combine all the ingredients well and transfer to a 9- by 5- by 3-inch loaf pan.

3. Put the loaf in a larger pan filled with 1½ inches of boiling water or enough to reach halfway up the side of the loaf pan. Bake for 1½ hours.

4. Remove from the oven and drain off the fat. Cool the pâté for 1 hour.

5. Cover loosely with plastic wrap and place a weight, such as a foil-covered brick, on top of the pâté. Refrigerate overnight. Unmold and cut into ½-inch-thick slices. Serve with mustard, cornichon pickles, radishes, French bread, and unsalted butter.

# Chicken Liver Pâté with Cognac with a Parsley Topping

## Serves 6 to 8

This recipe can be easily doubled to serve 12 to 16 people.

| | |
|---|---|
| 2 tablespoons olive oil | 3 tablespoons Cognac |
| 10 tablespoons butter | ½ cup chopped fresh |
| 1 cup coarsely chopped | parsley leaves |
| onion | Salt and freshly ground |
| 1 pound chicken livers, cut | black pepper |
| into 1-inch pieces | French bread |

1. Heat the olive oil and 2 tablespoons of the butter in a large frying pan. Add the onions and sauté for 5 minutes, stirring often. Add the chicken livers and cook over medium heat, stirring occasionally, for about 12 minutes, or until the livers are cooked through. Pour in the Cognac, stir, and cook for 1 minute. Remove from the heat and stir in ¼ cup of the parsley.

2. Purée for 10 seconds in a food processor fitted with a steel blade.

3. Quarter the remaining stick of butter and add it to the mixture. Turn on the processor and purée *only* until thoroughly combined.

4. Turn the mixture into a bowl and season it with salt and pepper to taste.

5. Transfer the pâté to a 3-cup glass bowl, if possible, and smooth the top with the back of a spoon. Sprinkle the remaining ¼ cup of parsley evenly over the top. Cover and refrigerate for at least 4 hours. Ideally, prepare the pâté in the morning and serve it in the evening. Serve the pâté with ¼-inch-thick slices of fresh French bread.

NOTE: To use up any extra pâté make open-faced sandwiches on pumpernickel bread. Garnish the tops with sautéed sliced mushrooms and/or crisp-cooked bacon strips and red onion rings.

# Antipasto Kebabs in a Bread Basket

### Serves 12   Makes 36 kebabs

1½ pounds Genoa salami in one piece, cut into ¾-inch cubes

1½ pounds mozzarella, cut into ¾-inch cubes

36 small Marinated Mushrooms (see recipe page 212 or use commercial brand)

36 stuffed green olives, well drained

1 large round loaf Italian or French bread

6 sprigs fresh parsley

Olive oil

1. Put 1 cube of salami, 1 cube of cheese, 1 mushroom, and 1 olive, in that order, on each of 36 rounded toothpicks.

2. Cut off 1 inch from the top of the loaf of bread and pull out the bread in the center of the loaf. Put the Antipasto Kebabs in the hollowed-out loaf.

3. Make a small (⅓-inch) hole in the center of the top of the loaf you cut off. Hold the parsley sprigs together and thread their stems through the hole. Serve the bread basket on a platter with the parsley-topped lid to the side. Just before serving, sprinkle the kebabs lightly with olive oil.

# Brie with Helen Abbott's Pepper Jelly

*Serves 6 to 8*
*(Preparation begins the day before)*

## PEPPER JELLY

2 cups diced seeded sweet red and green peppers
¼ cup finely diced hot chili peppers

6½ cups sugar
1½ cups white or cider vinegar
4 ounces Certo

1 pound wedge ripe Brie
Sliced French bread
and/or crackers

1. First, make the jelly: Put the peppers, sugar, and vinegar in a large enamel-coated flameproof casserole or saucepan. Bring to a boil, stirring occasionally. Immediately remove from the heat and let stand for 15 minutes.

2. Bring the mixture back to a boil and boil for 2 minutes. Remove from the heat and stir in the Certo. Let cool for 30 minutes, stir, and fill sterilized bottles or jars the size of your choice.

3. When the jelly is completely cool, pour about ¼ inch of melted paraffin over the top of the jelly, cover tightly, and refrigerate overnight. (This recipe makes about 1½ quarts of jelly, and only 1 cup will be needed for this recipe. Use the rest of the jelly with lamb, pork, or chicken.)

4. Put the Brie on a serving dish. Spoon 1 cup of jelly over the cheese and serve with the bread or crackers.

# Celery Sticks with Roquefort–Cream Cheese Spread

### Serves 6   Makes 24

Celery sticks stuffed with cream cheese are hardly innovative or that interesting, but the addition of Roquefort cheese, sour cream, and lemon juice to the cream cheese brings a new and delicious dimension to an old standby. Several variations follow:

| | | | |
|---|---|---|---|
| 8 | ounces cream cheese, softened | | Salt and freshly ground black pepper |
| ½ | cup sour cream | 8 | celery stalks, cut into 3-inch lengths |
| 3 | ounces Roquefort cheese, crumbled (about ¾ cup) | | Paprika |
| 1 | teaspoon fresh lemon juice | | |

1. In a large bowl beat the cream cheese until it is light and fluffy. Add the sour cream, Roquefort, and lemon juice and combine thoroughly. Season with salt and pepper to taste.

2. Spread the mixture onto the center of the celery sticks. Sprinkle lightly with paprika.

*Variations:* Fresh fennel sticks or cored apple slices can be substituted for the celery. One tablespoon of chopped fresh parsley leaves can be added and/or ¼ cup chopped walnuts or almonds. The spread can be served on small pumpernickel rounds and garnished with julienne strips of salami or ham.

# Hearts of Palm Rolled in Ham

*Serves 6 to 8   Makes about 32*

1   13¾-ounce can hearts of
    palm, drained
4   ounces cream cheese,
    softened

2   scallions, minced
2   teaspoons fresh lemon
    juice
8   thin slices boiled ham

1. Pat the hearts of palm dry with paper towels and set them aside.

2. In a bowl beat the cream cheese until it is light and fluffy. Add the scallions and lemon juice and combine.

3. Carefully spread the cream cheese mixture over each slice of ham. Place a heart of palm at the short end of each ham slice and roll it up. Repeat the procedure for the remaining slices of ham and hearts of palm.

4. Cover and chill in the refrigerator for at least 1 hour. To serve, cut crosswise into 1-inch-thick pieces and place, cut side down, on a serving platter.

# Jumbo Black Olives Stuffed with Walnut Cream Cheese

*Serves 6 to 8   Makes about 28 stuffed olives*

1   15¾-ounce can jumbo
    pitted black olives, well
    drained
4   ounces cream cheese,
    softened

¼   cup minced scallions
1   tablespoon chopped fresh
    parsley leaves
⅓   cup chopped walnuts

1. Slit each olive lengthwise on one side.

2. In a bowl combine the remaining ingredients well.

3. Spread the olives open, one by one, and stuff each with about 1 teaspoon of the mixture. Serve on a lettuce-lined flat dish.

*Variations:* Add 1 teaspoon curry powder to the cream cheese, and/or ¼ cup diced apple with the skin.

# Hummus with Toasted Almonds on Endive Leaves

*Serves 8 to 10*

2   cups well drained
    canned chick-peas
1   large garlic clove
    Juice of 1 lemon
½   cup tahini (sesame seed
    paste, available in health
    or gourmet shops)
    Salt and freshly ground
    black pepper

    Olive oil
2   tablespoons butter
½   cup chopped slivered
    almonds
5   endives, stemmed and
    leaves separated
1   lemon, cut in a fluted
    pattern

1. In a food processor purée the chick-peas with the garlic, lemon juice, tahini, salt and pepper to taste, and ¼ cup olive oil. Continue adding olive oil as needed until the purée is the consistency of creamy peanut butter. Set aside.

2. Melt the butter in a frying pan and lightly brown the almonds over medium heat. Drain well.

3. Place 1 rounded teaspoon of the Hummus at the stem end of each endive leaf and sprinkle each with the toasted almonds. Place the stuffed endive leaves on a platter and garnish with the fluted lemon halves.

# Curried Tuna and Hearts of Palm Canapés

*Serves 6 to 8   Makes 24 canapés*

1   *7-ounce can white meat tuna, well drained and flaked*
3   *tablespoons mayonnaise*
1   *3-ounce package cream cheese, softened*
2   *teaspoons sesame seed oil*
2   *tablespoons soy sauce*
1   *tablespoon curry powder*

1   *14-ounce can hearts of palm, well drained and cut into ⅓-inch-thick slices*
24   *¼-inch-thick slices French bread (ficelle, the thin loaf, if possible)*
1   *large pimiento, cut into thin strips*

1. In a bowl combine the tuna, mayonnaise, cream cheese, sesame seed oil, soy sauce, and curry powder.

2. Spread the mixture evenly over the 24 bread slices and place a slice of hearts of palm in the center of each. Garnish each hearts of palm slice with a pimiento strip.

# Sliced Eggs and Caviar Canapés

*Serves 6 to 8   Makes 24 canapés*

3   *tablespoons butter, softened*
24   *small slices pumpernickel bread*
4   *hard-boiled large eggs, sliced with an egg cutter*
½   *cup sour cream*
½   *cup mayonnaise*

1   *tablespoon minced scallion or onion*
2   *teaspoons grated lemon rind*
1   *tablespoon chopped fresh parsley leaves*
3   *ounces red salmon caviar*

1. Spread butter lightly on one side of each slice of pumpernickel. Top each with an egg slice.

2. In a bowl combine the sour cream, mayonnaise, scallion, lemon rind, and parsley.

3. Spread 1 rounded teaspoon of the mixture over the center of each egg yolk. Top with ½ teaspoon of red caviar.

# Red Salmon Caviar Canapés

*Serves 8    Makes 24 canapés*

½ cup sour cream
6 ounces cream cheese, softened
1 teaspoon fresh lemon juice
1 celery stalk, finely chopped
1 scallion, finely chopped

2 tablespoons chopped fresh parsley leaves
4 ounces red salmon caviar
24 cocktail pumpernickel rounds
Freshly ground black pepper

1. In a bowl combine the sour cream, cream cheese, lemon juice, celery, scallion, and parsley well. Fold in 2 ounces of the caviar.

2. Spread the mixture evenly over the slices of pumpernickel. Garnish each with the well-drained remaining 2 ounces of caviar and a light sprinkle of pepper.

# Smoked Chicken Canapés

*Serves 6 to 8    Makes 24 canapés*

¼ cup (½ stick) butter, softened
¼ cup cream cheese, softened
1 tablespoon chopped fresh dill, or 1 teaspoon dried dill
1 teaspoon Dijon mustard

24 melba toast rounds
3 smoked chicken breasts, thinly sliced and cut into circles the same size as the melba toasts
8 cornichon pickles, cut lengthwise into 3 slices each

1. In a bowl combine thoroughly the butter, cream cheese, dill, and mustard.

2. Spread the melba toasts with the mixture and top with 1 slice of smoked chicken. Garnish each canapé with 1 slice of cornichon.

# First Courses

When you hear someone say, "This first course is so good, I could stop right here," you can interpret the comment two very different ways. The first course may be delicious but too filling for its role as a preliminary before a main event; or it may be a contender for use as a main dish at some time in the future.

To avoid first courses that overpower instead of enhancing the dishes to follow, review the different flavors, textures, and quantities that will be served during the course of the meal. The Belgian Leeks might offer a perfect balance to a sautéed sole main dish, but it would be excessive if followed by a more substantial Beef Carbonnade.

From time to time, the appeal of exotic first courses in small portions can become irresistible to the undecided diner in a fine restaurant. On many occasions in the past at restaurants like Voile d'Or in St. Jean Cap Ferrat, Carol's in Southampton, or Hotel 1829 in St. Thomas, I have ordered my entire dinner from the first course selection of the menu. Bewildered waiters and chefs are always won over when you explain that everything looks and sounds so good, you just can't limit yourself to only one. Perhaps it was from such requests that *dégustation* menus were born.

The same rule applies when entertaining at home. On the right occasion, a sensational first course at one meal can easily qualify as the perfect main dish at another. The Belgian Leeks that scored so well as the prelude to the sole would make a perfect main dish by itself if a light dinner was in order. And two first-course dishes, such as Gruyère, Mushroom, and Celery Salad with Walnut Oil Dressing and Coquilles St. Jacques offer an excellent balance as a combined main dish at lunch or for a late supper.

Considering the fact that guests are always hungrier when they eat their first course than when they reach the main dish, don't be surprised if the exclamations of approval peak early in the meal.

# Hot First Courses

## Coquilles St. Jacques

### Serves 6

1 cup bottled clam juice
1 cup dry white wine
2 tablespoons minced
  shallots
1 tablespoon chopped
  fresh parsley leaves
1¼ pounds bay scallops
½ pound fresh mushrooms,
  thinly sliced
3 tablespoons butter, plus
  extra for buttering the
  shells

3 tablespoons all-purpose
  flour
1 cup milk
½ cup heavy cream
2 teaspoons fresh lemon
  juice
  Salt and freshly ground
  black pepper
¾ cup grated Gruyère or
  Swiss cheese

1. Put the clam juice, wine, shallots, and parsley in a large enamel-coated or nonstick saucepan. Bring the mixture to a boil and add the scallops and mushrooms, lower the heat and simmer for 5 minutes.

2. Use a slotted spoon to transfer the scallops and mushrooms to a strainer and drain. Over high heat reduce the liquid in the pan to ½ cup. Strain and reserve.

3. Preheat the oven to 375 degrees.

4. In a clean saucepan melt the butter and whisk in the flour. Cook over medium heat for 1 minute, whisking constantly. Add the reduced broth and the milk. Whisk until the sauce boils and is smooth and has thickened. Whisk in the heavy cream and lemon juice. Season with salt and pepper to taste. Add the scallops and mushrooms and the cheese. Combine well.

5. Spoon equal amounts of the mixture into 6 lightly buttered scallop shells or ramekins. Place the filled shells on a baking sheet and bake for 12 minutes. Turn on the broiler and place the baking sheet with the shells about 6 inches from the heat and broil for only a moment to lightly brown the tops. Serve immediately.

# Steamed Mussels Marinated in Fresh Herb and Shallot Sauce

*Serves 6*

| | | | |
|---|---|---|---|
| 2 | medium-sized onions, quartered | 1 | sprig fresh thyme |
| 4 | sprigs fresh parsley | 2 | cups dry white wine |
| 1 | bay leaf | 2 | quarts mussels, well scrubbed and bearded |

## FRESH HERB AND SHALLOT SAUCE

| | | | |
|---|---|---|---|
| 1 | cup olive oil | 2 | tablespoons fresh lemon juice |
| 1 | large garlic clove, chopped | | Salt and freshly ground black pepper to taste |
| 1/3 | cup chopped fresh parsley leaves | | |
| 2 | tablespoons chopped shallots | | |

1. Put the onions, parsley, bay leaf, thyme, and wine in a large pot. Bring the mixture to a boil, add the mussels, cover, and cook for 8 minutes, or until the mussels open. Discard any mussels that do not open.

2. Break off the empty half of each mussel shell and discard. With a small sharp knife separate each mussel from its shell but leave it in the shell. Put an equal number of mussels on 6 first-course plates in circles with the pointed ends of the shells facing out.

3. Combine the sauce ingredients in a blender or food processor.

4. Spoon the sauce over the mussels. Cover the plates with plastic wrap and marinate at room temperature for 1 hour before serving.

# Sole à la Normandy

*Serves 6*

| | | | |
|---|---|---|---|
| 6 | sole fillets, each about 6 ounces | ¼ | cup Calvados |
| | Salt and freshly ground black pepper | 1½ | cups heavy cream |
| | | 6 | sprigs fresh parsley |
| 2 | tablespoons fresh lemon juice | | |

1. Sprinkle the skin side of each fillet with salt and pepper. Roll up, skin side inside, and set aside.

2. Heat the lemon juice in a frying pan over high heat until only about 1 teaspoon remains. Add the Calvados and reduce to half over high heat, stirring occasionally. Pour in the cream and cook over high heat for 1 minute.

3. Put the rolled fillets in the frying pan seam side down and spoon some cream over each fillet. Cover and simmer for 12 minutes. Garnish each serving with a sprig of parsley.

# Spiedini

*Serves 4*

| | | | |
|---|---|---|---|
| 8 | firm slices white bread | 3 | large eggs, lightly beaten |
| 8 | thin slices Fontina cheese | 1½ | cups peanut oil |
| | All-purpose flour | | |

### ANCHOVY–CAPER SAUCE

| | | | |
|---|---|---|---|
| 3 | tablespoons sweet butter | ¾ | cup dry white wine |
| 8 | anchovy fillets, drained and finely chopped | 1 | tablespoon fresh lemon juice |
| 2 | tablespoons drained capers | | |

1. Cut the crusts from the bread slices and cut each slice into 4 squares.

2. Cut the cheese slices into pieces the same size as the bread squares.

3. Stack 8 squares of bread together and insert 6 slices of the cheese between the inner slices of bread. Push an 8-inch wooden

skewer through the bread and cheese stack. Repeat the procedure for the remaining 3 spiedini. Set aside.

4. To prepare the sauce, melt the butter in a saucepan. Stir in the anchovies and capers and cook over medium-high heat for 1 minute. Add the remaining sauce ingredients, stir, and simmer over very low heat until used.

5. Meanwhile, dust the brochettes with flour and dip in the eggs. Coat again with flour.

6. Heat the oil in a large frying pan and fry the brochettes until golden brown all over. Drain.

7. Place each brochette on a warmed first-course plate and remove the skewers. Spoon equal amounts of the sauce over the brochettes and serve immediately.

# Herb-breaded Fried Sardines

### Serves 4

| | |
|---|---|
| 2 $4\frac{3}{8}$-ounce cans imported skinless and boneless sardines packed in olive oil, drained | 2 tablespoons chopped fresh parsley leaves |
| All-purpose flour | $\frac{1}{2}$ teaspoon dried oregano |
| | $\frac{1}{2}$ teaspoon salt |
| 1 large egg, lightly beaten | $\frac{1}{2}$ cup peanut oil |
| $\frac{3}{4}$ cup unseasoned fresh bread crumbs | 1 lemon, cut into 4 wedges and seeded |

1. Carefully dust the sardines with flour, coat with egg, and roll in the combined bread crumbs, parsley, oregano, and salt.

2. Heat the oil in a frying pan and fry the sardines over medium heat until golden brown all over. This will only take a few minutes.

3. Divide the sardines among 4 warmed first-course plates and serve each with a lemon wedge.

*Variation:* Combine 2 tablespoons fresh lemon juice with 2 tablespoons drained capers and 2 tablespoons olive oil and spoon equal amounts onto each of the 4 plates alongside the sardines.

# Chicken Oysters and Morels in Mustard Cream Sauce

*Serves 4*

Chicken oysters are the delectable small pieces of meat found in the concave bones at the lower back—two per chicken. When cooked they are extremely tender and succulent, perhaps the tastiest meat of the chicken. It is remarkable that these pieces of meat are so often discarded or used only in stock-making. Buy the backs, remove the oysters and freeze the backs for stock.

| | | | |
|---|---|---|---|
| 16 | chicken backs, oysters removed with a small sharp knife | 2 | tablespoons minced shallots |
| | Salt and freshly ground black pepper | 1 | teaspoon Dijon mustard |
| | | 1 | tablespoon Cognac or brandy |
| 4 | ounces dried morels, soaked in lukewarm water for 30 minutes (available in speciality food stores) | 1 | cup heavy cream |
| | | 1 | teaspoon Bouvril |
| | | 4 | slices toast, crusts trimmed |
| 3 | tablespoons butter | | Chopped fresh parsley leaves |

1. Pat the chicken oysters dry and season them with salt and pepper.

2. Drain the morels and pat them dry with paper towels. Cut each morel in half.

3. Melt the butter in a frying pan and add the chicken oysters and morels. Cook over medium-low heat for 4 minutes. Add the shallots and turn the chicken oysters and morels. Cook for about 4 minutes. Transfer the oysters and morels to a dish.

4. Mix together the mustard, Cognac, cream, and Bouvril. Add to the pan and whisk over high heat for 5 minutes, or until the sauce thickens. Season with salt and pepper to taste. Return the oysters and morels to the sauce and heat through.

5. Spoon the mixture in equal amounts over each of 4 slices of toast on 4 first-course course plates. Sprinkle with parsley and serve immediately.

# Fried Sweetbreads with Dill Sauce

*Serves 4*
*(Preparation begins the night before)*

1½   pounds sweetbreads
     Salt and freshly ground
     black pepper to taste
     All-purpose flour

4   tablespoons peanut or
     vegetable oil
4   tablespoons sweet butter

## DILL SAUCE

½   cup mayonnaise
½   cup sour cream
¼   cup finely chopped fresh
     dill, or 1 tablespoon
     dried dill
¼   cup chopped fresh parsley
     leaves

1   minced scallion
2   teaspoons fresh lemon
     juice
     Salt and freshly ground
     black pepper to taste

1. Place the sweetbreads in a bowl and cover them with cold water. Cover and refrigerate overnight.

2. Combine the sauce ingredients.

3. When ready to cook remove the sauce and sweetbreads. Drain the sweetbreads and place them in a saucepan and cover with cold water. Bring to a boil, lower the heat, and simmer for 8 minutes. Drain and cool. Remove any membranes or tough outer portions.

4. Cut the sweetbreads into 1½-inch-thick slices and season with salt and pepper. Coat the pieces with flour, shaking off any excess.

5. Heat the oil and butter in a large frying pan and cook the sweetbreads over medium-high heat until they are golden brown on each side, about 4 minutes per side. Serve with the sauce spooned over.

# Mini Roman Omelets with Tomato Coulis

*Serves 4*

## TOMATO COULIS

3 tablespoons butter
3 tablespoons minced
shallots
1 large garlic clove,
minced
1½ cups peeled, seeded, and
finely chopped ripe
tomatoes

1 teaspoon chopped fresh
parsley leaves
¼ teaspoon sugar
Salt and freshly ground
black pepper to taste

## OMELETS

2 tablespoons butter
8 large eggs
Salt and freshly ground
black pepper
4 ¼-inch-thick slices
mozzarella, cut into
julienne strips and
arranged in separate piles

4 parsley flowerets
8 slices toasted French
bread

1. First prepare the Tomato Coulis: Melt the butter in a heavy saucepan. Add the shallots and garlic and sauté over medium-low heat for about 4 minutes, stirring often. Add the remaining ingredients and simmer over low heat, stirring often, for about 25 minutes, or until the liquid evaporates.

2. Meanwhile, warm 4 plates.

3. For each omelet heat 1½ teaspoons of the butter in an omelet pan. In a bowl beat 2 eggs with a whisk and season lightly with salt and pepper. Add the eggs to the pan and cook over medium-high heat, stirring with a fork, until the eggs begin to set. Spread the eggs over the bottom of the pan and place one quarter of the julienned slices of mozzarella in the center of the eggs. Tilt the pan and, at the elevated end of the pan, begin to turn the eggs over the cheese. Turn the omelet out onto a warm plate. Cook the remaining 3 omelets in the same manner.

4. With a small sharp knife make a 4-inch slit in the center of each omelet, lengthwise, exposing the melted cheese. Spoon about 3 generous tablespoons of the Tomato Coulis crosswise over the center of each omelet and about 1 inch over each side onto the plate. Place a parsley floweret on the center of each omelet. Serve with toasted French bread.

# Miniature Puff Pastry Pizzas Niçoise
*Serves 4*

These small and crisp pizzas never fail to please, and they are remarkably easy to prepare. I often serve them as a first course with either a pasta or chicken entrée, plus a simple green salad. However, the pizzas provide a perfect light lunch or supper, whether cooking for oneself or for many.

| | |
|---|---|
| 4 *frozen puff pastry patty shells, thawed* | 8 *anchovies, drained and coarsely chopped* |
| 1 *cup fresh Marinara Sauce (see recipe page 170) or canned tomato sauce* | $\frac{1}{4}$ *cup coarsely chopped black olives* |
| 1 *tablespoon olive oil* | $1\frac{1}{2}$ *tablespoons drained capers* |
| $\frac{1}{2}$ *teaspoon dried oregano* | 10 *ounces mozzarella, shredded* |
| $\frac{1}{2}$ *teaspoon dried basil* | *Freshly grated* |
| 1 *teaspoon chopped fresh parsley leaves* | *Parmesan cheese* |

1. Preheat the oven to 450 degrees.

2. Combine the Marinara Sauce, oil, and herbs in a bowl.

3. On a lightly floured board, roll out each patty to a 7-inch circle. Place the circles of dough on 1 large or 2 baking sheets.

4. Spoon about $\frac{1}{4}$ cup of the sauce over each and smooth the sauce with the back of a spoon to reach $\frac{1}{2}$ inch from the outer edge of the dough. Top each with equal amounts of the anchovies, black olives, and capers. Sprinkle the tops with the mozzarella and lightly with the Parmesan cheese.

5. Place the pizzas in the oven and lower the oven temperature to 400 degrees. Bake for 20 minutes. Transfer the pizzas to warmed serving dishes and serve immediately.

NOTE: Double the ingredients for 8 pizzas, and bake in 2 batches, because the oven won't hold all 8 pizzas on the lower shelf.

*Variations:* Thin slivers of boiled ham, onion, and green or yellow peppers can be substituted for the anchovies, olives, and capers, in slightly larger amounts. The pizzas can be made with just the combined Marinara Sauce, oil, and herbs, topped with the cheese for a plainer version. Or, to each of the latter versions, add a few tablespoons of cooked crumbled Italian sweet sausage over the Marinara Sauce with the oil and herbs, and top with the cheese.

# Belgian-style Leeks

*Serves 6*

You can double the recipe to serve 12 people.

|  |  |  |  |
|---|---|---|---|
| 6 | large equal-sized leeks | 6 | thin slices baked or |
| ½ | cup grated Gruyère |  | boiled ham |
|  | cheese | 3 | tablespoons seasoned |
| 12 | ½-inch-thick slices |  | bread crumbs |
|  | French bread | 12 | sprigs watercress |

## GRUYÈRE MORNAY SAUCE

|  |  |  |  |
|---|---|---|---|
| 4 | tablespoons butter | ¾ | cup grated Gruyère |
| 3 | tablespoons all-purpose |  | cheese |
|  | flour |  | Salt and freshly ground |
| 1¾ | cups milk |  | black pepper to taste |

1. Cut off the root end and the green part of each leek. Make a crisscross cut ½ inch deep into the root end of each leek. Open the ends gently by spreading them apart with the fingers and wash away the grit and sand thoroughly under cold running water.

2. Bring 2 inches of water to a boil in a large frying pan and add the leeks. Cook the leeks over medium heat for 10 minutes, or until they are tender.

3. Meanwhile, combine the ½ cup of grated Gruyère cheese and the bread crumbs and set aside.

4. Now prepare the sauce. In an enamel or stainless steel saucepan melt the butter and whisk in the flour. Cook over medium heat, whisking constantly, for 1 minute. Add the milk, whisking continually until the sauce boils, thickens, and is smooth. Stir in the remaining cheese and whisk until it melts. Season with salt and pepper to taste. Cover the pan and turn off the heat.

5. Toast the bread on each side under the broiler and set aside. Do not turn off the broiler.

6. Drain the cooked leeks well and pat them dry. Roll each leek up in 1 slice of the ham and place in a lightly greased au gratin dish.

7. Reheat the sauce over high heat, whisking constantly for 30 seconds. Spoon the sauce over the ham–leek rolls, covering them completely. Sprinkle the cheese and bread crumb mixture evenly over the top.

8. Run under the broiler for about 4 minutes, or just until the cheese melts and the top turns golden brown. Garnish each serving

with 2 sprigs of crisp watercress and 2 slices of the grilled French bread. Serve immediately.

*Variation:* Substitute large trimmed equal-sized endives for the leeks. Cook the endives in simmering water about the same amount of time as the leeks, but test for tenderness with the tip of a small sharp knife. Over-cooking endives makes them bitter.

# Baked Italian-style Mushrooms in Scallop Shells

*Serves 4*

| | | | |
|---|---|---|---|
| ½ | pound mushrooms | 3 | tablespoons olive oil |
| ½ | cup pitted black olives | 1 | large garlic clove, minced |
| ½ | cup jarred roasted red peppers | 1 | cup chopped undrained canned tomatoes |
| 4 | anchovy fillets, drained | ¼ | teaspoon dried rosemary leaves |
| 3 | tablespoons freshly grated Parmesan cheese Salt and freshly ground black pepper | 4 | teaspoons butter Chopped fresh parsley leaves |

1. Coarsely chop the mushrooms, olives, red peppers, and anchovies.

2. Combine the mixture in a bowl with the Parmesan cheese and season with salt and pepper to taste. Divide the mixture among 4 scallop shells, smooth the tops, and set aside.

3. Heat the olive oil in a saucepan and add the garlic. Cook over low heat for 5 minutes, stirring often. Add the tomatoes and rosemary and simmer for 10 minutes.

4. Meanwhile, preheat the oven to 375 degrees.

5. Season the tomato sauce with salt and pepper to taste. Spoon the sauce over the mushroom mixture in the shells and dot each portion with 1 teaspoon of the butter.

6. Transfer the filled shells to a baking sheet and bake for 15 minutes. Garnish with the parsley before serving.

# Sizzling Mushrooms Stuffed with Snails and Basil–Garlic Butter

*Serves 4*

½ pound (2 sticks) sweet butter, softened

¼ cup finely chopped fresh basil (do not substitute dried basil)

1 tablespoon finely chopped fresh parsley leaves

2 tablespoons minced shallots

3 large garlic cloves, crushed

1 teaspoon salt

Freshly ground black pepper

2 dozen canned snails, drained

2 dozen fresh medium-to-large mushroom caps

1 lemon, cut into 4 wedges and seeded

1 loaf crusty French bread, sliced

1. Preheat the oven to 400 degrees.

2. In a bowl combine the first 7 ingredients well.

3. Place a snail in each mushroom cap and top with equal amounts of the butter.

4. Put the stuffed mushrooms in a shallow baking pan. Bake for 10 minutes. Place 6 of the sizzling mushrooms on each of 4 warmed first-course plates and spoon equal amounts of the butter from the pan over the tops of the mushrooms. Garnish each serving with a lemon wedge. Pass the bread separately.

# Broiled Stuffed Mushroom Caps with Spinach Purée

*Serves 4*

16 large fresh mushrooms, stems removed (save for another use)
4 tablespoons butter, melted
1½ cups well-drained hot cooked spinach
1 tablespoon butter, plus extra to spread over the toast
⅓ cup sour cream
Freshly grated nutmeg
Salt and freshly ground black pepper to taste
1 pimiento, cut into 16 strips
4 slices buttered toast, crusts removed

1. Preheat the broiler.
2. Brush the mushrooms' stem sides with half of the melted butter. Put the mushrooms on a baking sheet, stem side up, and cook under the broiler for about 3 minutes. Turn the mushrooms and brush with the remaining 2 tablespoons of butter. Cook for 3 minutes and remove from the oven.
3. In a food processor fitted with the steel blade purée the hot cooked spinach with 1 tablespoon of butter, the sour cream, and nutmeg and salt and pepper to taste. (You can also force the mixture through a food mill.)
4. Spoon equal amounts of the purée into the mushroom caps. Garnish each with a strip of pimiento. Place 4 stuffed mushrooms on a slice of buttered toast for each serving.

# Wilted Spinach and Bacon Salad "Hotel 1829"

### Serves 4

My favorite restaurant in St. Thomas is the restaurant at Hotel 1829. The building, once a nineteenth-century townhouse, is a national historic landmark and one of the few restaurants with true old island ambience. The dining areas are located either in a charming stone-walled open-air room or along a lengthy flower- and plant-lined gallery, where it's always cool in the evening. Chef Hoffman turns out superbly executed fresh grouper dishes, a fine garlic and parsleyed rack of lamb—enough for two really—and many more good dishes. At tableside though, it's Hans, a skilled cook and waiter, who prepares this delectable salad. Here is my adapted version.

| | | | |
|---|---|---|---|
| 1 | quart fresh spinach, washed, dried, and broken into bite-sized pieces | 1 | tablespoon butter |
| | | 8 | strips crisp-cooked bacon, chopped |
| 1/4 | pound fresh mushrooms, thinly sliced | 1 | tablespoon Cognac or brandy |
| 1 | medium-sized red onion, thinly sliced and separated into rings | 2 | tablespoons Cointreau |
| | | 2/3 | cup Herbed Dressing (see recipe page 242) |
| 1/3 | cup freshly grated Parmesan cheese | | |

1. Put the spinach, mushrooms, onion rings, and Parmesan cheese in a large salad bowl.

2. Melt the butter in a large frying pan and stir-fry the bacon for 2 minutes over medium-high heat.

3. Standing well back, add the Cognac and Cointreau and ignite it. When the flame goes out stir in the Herbed Vinaigrette. Heat thoroughly and pour the mixture over the salad. Toss and serve immediately.

# Cold First Courses

## Shrimp Wrapped in Prosciutto with Pimiento Mayonnaise

*Serves 4*

### PIMIENTO MAYONNAISE

¼ cup well-drained chopped pimiento

¾ cup mayonnaise
1 teaspoon fresh lime juice

### SHRIMP WRAPPED IN PROSCIUTTO

16 large boiled shrimp, shelled and deveined
16 very thin slices prosciutto

20 watercress sprigs
2 teaspoons snipped fresh chives

1. Combine the Pimiento Mayonnaise ingredients in a food processor or force through a fine sieve. Transfer to a jar, cover, and refrigerate for several hours before serving.

2. At dinnertime wrap each shrimp in a slice of prosciutto and set aside.

3. Place 5 watercress sprigs on each of 4 first-course plates. Arrange 4 wrapped shrimp in a fan shape across each watercress-lined plate. Spoon equal amounts of the Pimiento Mayonnaise at the bottom of the shrimp and sprinkle each with ½ teaspoon of chives.

# Diane Terman's Shrimp in Dill Sauce
## (with thanks to Mary Auletta)

*Serves 12 as a first course, or 6 as entrée salad*

2½ pounds medium-sized shrimp, shelled and deveined
¼ cup Dijon mustard
½ cup fresh lemon juice
½ cup olive oil
1 tablespoon sugar
2 tablespoons red wine vinegar

2 tablespoons chopped fresh dill
1½ cups thinly sliced radishes
1 tablespoon chopped fresh parsley leaves
French bread

1. Cook the shrimp in 1½ quarts of rapidly boiling water for exactly 5 minutes. Drain well and put into a large bowl.

2. In a small bowl mix together the mustard, lemon juice, and oil with a fork. Dissolve the sugar in the vinegar and add to the oil mixture. Stir in the dill and pour over the shrimp and toss. Cover and refrigerate for at least 5 hours or, preferably, overnight.

3. One hour before serving add the radish slices to the mixture and combine. Sprinkle with the parsley. Serve with thin slices of French bread.

# Avocado and Prosciutto

*Serves 4*

2 large ripe avocados, halved and pitted
1 lemon, halved
⅓ pound very thinly sliced prosciutto

Freshly ground black pepper

Cut each avocado half into thin slices and arrange across each of 4 first-course plates. Sprinkle the lemon juice over the avocado slices. Top each plate of sliced avocado with equal amounts of the sliced prosciutto. Pass the peppermill.

# Avocado with Curried Beef

*Serves 4*

⅓ pound thinly sliced
cooked roast beef, cut
into thin strips about ⅛
by 1½ inches

3 tablespoons orange juice

1 teaspoon soy sauce

1 tablespoon curry powder

1 scallion, thinly sliced

½ cup chopped chutney

2 tablespoons currants or
raisins

2 ripe avocados

2 teaspoons fresh lemon
juice

1. Put the beef strips in a bowl.

2. In another bowl combine the orange juice, soy sauce, and curry powder. Stir in the scallion, chutney, and currants. Pour the mixture over the beef and toss. Cover and chill thoroughly.

3. At serving time halve and pit the avocados. Sprinkle ½ teaspoon of the lemon juice over each avocado half and spoon equal amounts of the mixture into the avocado centers. Serve immediately.

# Roast Beef with Red Pepper Coulis

*Serves 4*

¼ cup olive oil

4 large red peppers,
stemmed, seeded, and
cut into thin strips

1 teaspoon fresh lemon
juice
Salt and freshly ground
black pepper

12 thin slices medium-rare
roast beef

2 tablespoons chopped
fresh parsley leaves

8 slices toasted French
bread

1. Heat the olive oil in a large frying pan. Add the peppers, cover, and cook over low heat for 30 minutes, stirring occasionally. Don't let the peppers brown.

2. Purée the peppers and oil in a food processor half a batch at a time. (Or you can force the mixture through a food mill.) Add the lemon juice and season with salt and pepper to taste.

3. Spread 3 slices of the beef over each of 4 plates. Spoon equal amounts of the pepper coulis over the beef and sprinkle each with ½ tablespoon of the parsley. Serve with toasted French bread.

# Individual Composed Salads

*Serves 4*

| | |
|---|---|
| 2 medium-sized firm ripe tomatoes, seeded and cut into small dice | 1 cup diced celery |
| 2 scallions, chopped | 1 cup grated Gruyère |
| 1 cup drained canned chick-peas | ¾ cup quartered pitted large black olives |
| ¼ pound Genoa salami, cut into julienne strips | |

## CREAMY TARRAGON VINAIGRETTE

| | |
|---|---|
| 1 teaspoon Dijon mustard | ½ teaspoon dried tarragon |
| 1 egg yolk | Salt and freshly ground black pepper to taste |
| ½ cup olive oil | |
| ½ cup vegetable oil | |
| 1½ tablespoons tarragon vinegar, or to taste | |

1. Combine the tomatoes and scallions in a bowl.

2. On each of 4 salad plates arrange the combined tomatoes and scallions, chick-peas, salami, celery, Gruyère, and olives in equal amounts in single rows just touching each other.

3. Prepare the vinaigrette: In a shallow bowl beat together the mustard and egg yolk with a whisk. Drop by drop add the olive and vegetable oils, whisking constantly until it is all combined. Beat in the remaining ingredients. Serve the dressing with the salads.

*Variations:* Obviously this salad lends itself to inventive combinations using any small bits of meat, fish or shellfish, cheese or vegetables. Diced hard-boiled eggs can also be used as well as cooked lentils or beans. Make sure that the ingredients complement each other in taste, texture, and color.

# Scallop, Mushroom, and Avocado Salad with Dill Vinaigrette

*Serves 4*

½  cup dry white wine
1  cup homemade chicken stock or canned broth
1½  pounds sea scallops
1  medium-sized avocado, halved, pitted, peeled, and cut into bite-sized pieces

¼  pound fresh mushrooms, thinly sliced
1  bunch watercress, washed, dried, and stems removed
8  cherry tomatoes

## DILL VINAIGRETTE

½  cup olive oil
1½  tablespoons fresh lemon juice

2  teaspoons fresh dill
Salt and freshly ground black pepper to taste

1. First prepare the dressing by combining the ingredients in a jar; cover tightly and shake well. Leave at room temperature for 1 hour.

2. Pour the wine and broth into an enamel coated or nonstick saucepan and bring to a boil. Add the scallops and simmer for 8 minutes. Drain well.

3. When the scallops are cool enough to handle, slice each cross-wise into 3 equal-sized pieces. Put the scallop slices in a large bowl with the remaining salad ingredients, except for the watercress and tomatoes. Shake the dressing well and pour over the salad. Toss gently.

4. On each of 4 salad plates arrange a bed of equal amounts of the watercress. Top with equal portions of the salad and garnish each with 2 cherry tomatoes.

# Papaya Stuffed with Chinese Waldorf Salad

*Serves 4*

1   medium-sized Delicious
    apple, cored and cubed
¾  cup mandarin oranges
1   celery stalk, diced
8   snow pea pods, cut into
    thin strips crosswise on
    the diagonal
¼  cup thinly sliced water
    chestnuts

¼  cup chopped walnuts
½  cup mayonnaise or as
    needed
2   ripe papayas, halved and
    seeded
1   lime, quartered and
    seeded

1. Combine the apple, mandarin oranges, celery, snow pea pods, water chestnuts, and walnuts in a large bowl. Add the mayonnaise and toss. Add a little more mayonnaise, if needed.

2. Squeeze a lime wedge over each papaya half and spoon equal amounts of the salad into the center of each papaya.


# Hearts of Palm Salad

*Serves 6*

2   14-ounce cans hearts of
    palm, chilled
3   cups washed and dried
    mixed lettuce pieces
    (romaine, Boston, and
    watercress for example)

1   large pimiento, cut into
    thin strips

## CREAMY VINAIGRETTE DRESSING

2   tablespoons white wine
    vinegar
1   teaspoon Dijon mustard
¾  cup olive oil
    Salt and freshly ground
    black pepper

2   tablespoons Crème
    Fraîche (see recipe page
    277)

1. Drain the hearts of palm.

2. Prepare the dressing by whisking the vinegar and mustard together in a bowl. Add the olive oil drop by drop, whisking constantly. Season with salt and pepper to taste and whisk in the Crème Fraîche.

3. Line 6 plates with equal amounts of the lettuce. Top with equal amounts of the hearts of palm in rows. Spoon equal amounts of the dressing over the hearts of palm and garnish each salad with the pimiento strips crisscrossed over the hearts of palm.

# Antipasto Salad

### Serves 6

½ cup olive oil
3 tablespoons white wine vinegar
1 tablespoon finely chopped shallots
2 teaspoons fresh lemon juice
½ teaspoon dried oregano
½ teaspoon dried basil
¾ cup drained jarred sliced marinated mushrooms
¾ pound thinly sliced mortadella, cut into ⅓- by 2-inch strips and separated

¾ pound thinly sliced Genoa salami, cut into ⅓- by 2-inch strips and separated
½ pound thinly sliced Provolone, cut into ⅓- by 2-inch strips and separated
¼ cup well-drained diced pimiento
¼ cup sliced cornichon pickles
6 Boston or red leaf lettuce leaves
12 large stuffed green olives

1. In an enamel or stainless steel saucepan bring the olive oil, vinegar, and shallots to a boil. Simmer for 2 minutes. Remove from the heat and stir in the lemon juice, herbs, and mushrooms.

2. Put the meat, cheese, pimiento, and cornichons in a large bowl. Pour the sauce over the mixture. Toss gently.

3. Place a leaf of lettuce on each of 6 first-course plates and top with equal amounts of the salad. Garnish each salad with 2 of the olives.

# Gruyère, Mushroom, and Celery Salad with Walnut Oil Dressing

*Serves 6*

1¼ cups shredded Gruyère
½ pound fresh mushrooms, thinly sliced
1¼ cups thinly sliced hearts of celery

4 small heads Bibb lettuce, separated, washed, and dried
Chopped fresh parsley leaves

## WALNUT OIL DRESSING

½ teaspoon dry mustard
⅓ cup vegetable oil
3 tablespoons walnut oil
1 tablespoon white wine vinegar

Salt and freshly ground black pepper to taste

1. In a large bowl gently combine the cheese, mushrooms, and celery.

2. Use a whisk to mix the dressing ingredients together in a bowl. Pour the dressing over the salad and toss.

3. Arrange the lettuce leaves over 6 salad plates and top with equal portions of the salad. Sprinkle each lightly with chopped parsley.

# Soups

The word "soup" lacks precision. It can mean chowder, bisque, consommé, or broth, hot or cold, and it can contain everything from sausage, shellfish, and croutons to a dollop of sour cream with avocado cubes.

The best way to define soups is to classify them according to their purpose. Pea soup with chunks of meat so thick your spoon can stand alone in the bowl serves as a meal in itself in cold weather. The cold soups of summer are designed to be light refreshment, and to complement the other light dishes on the menu. Bisques and broths are often perfect introductions to more intense flavors and seasonings that will follow in the main course—hints of the good things to come.

The right approach to selecting a soup course, then, is first to decide its function and how it relates to the other courses surrounding it. Then review the availability of high-quality fresh ingredients, which are as important in soup as in any other dish.

# Hot Soups

## Venetian Pinto Bean and Pasta Soup

*Serves 8*

| | |
|---|---|
| 1 pound dried pinto beans | 2 tablespoons tomato paste |
| 1 cup coarsely chopped onion | 2 teaspoons salt |
| 1 cup sliced celery | 1½ cups ditali (small macaroni) |
| 1 large garlic clove, minced | ½ cup olive oil |
| 2 quarts homemade chicken stock or canned broth | Salt and freshly ground black pepper |
| 1½ cups water | ¼ cup chopped fresh parsley leaves |
| 1 teaspoon dried basil | Freshly grated Parmesan cheese |
| 1 bay leaf | |

1. Rinse the beans and soak them overnight covered with 2 inches of cool water.

2. Drain the beans and put them in a large heavy pot with the onion, celery, garlic, stock, water, basil, and bay leaf. Slowly bring to a boil; immediately lower the heat and simmer for 2½ hours stirring every half hour. Add the tomato paste, stir, and continue to simmer.

3. Bring 2½ quarts of water to a boil in a large saucepan and add the salt, stir, and add the ditali. Stir and cook for 6 minutes.

4. Meanwhile, remove 2 cups of the soup and purée it in a blender. Return the purée to the soup and stir. Drain the pasta well and add to the soup. Stir and simmer for 10 minutes, adding a little water, if necessary. Stir in the olive oil, season with salt and pepper to taste, and add the parsley. Serve with freshly grated Parmesan cheese.

*Variation:* Add 1 pound of sliced cooked sweet or hot Italian sausages to the soup with the pasta and follow the recipe from that point on in the directions.

# Black Bean Soup with Sherry, Sour Cream, and Avocado

*Serves 4*

Here is a nearly instant soup which is made from a good-quality canned product, Goya black beans.

| | |
|---|---|
| 2 16-ounce cans Goya black beans | ½ cup sour cream, at room temperature |
| 3 tablespoons olive oil | 1 firm ripe avocado, peeled, pitted, and cubed |
| 1 scallion, thinly sliced | |
| 3 tablespoons dry sherry | |

1. Pour the beans and their liquid into a saucepan. Add the olive oil, scallions, and sherry and bring to a boil. Lower the heat and simmer for 10 minutes. If necessary, add a small amount of canned chicken broth.

2. Spoon equal amounts of the soup into 4 soup bowls and top with dollops of the sour cream and the avocado cubes.

# Succotash and Ham Bisque

*Serves 6*

| | |
|---|---|
| 1 10-ounce package frozen corn kernels | 1 cup cubed smoked ham |
| 1 10-ounce package frozen baby lima beans | ½ teaspoon dried thyme |
| 2½ cups homemade chicken stock or canned broth | 1 tablespoon chopped fresh parsley leaves |
| 2 tablespoons butter | 1 cup heavy cream |
| 1 small onion, minced | Salt and freshly ground black pepper |

1. Put the corn, lima beans, and stock in a large saucepan or pot and bring to a boil. Lower the heat to a low boil and simmer for 10 minutes.

2. Meanwhile, melt the butter in a frying pan and cook the onion and ham for 5 minutes, stirring often. Add the mixture to the soup with the thyme, parsley, and cream and bring to a boil. Lower the heat and simmer for 10 minutes. Season with salt and pepper to taste.

# Broccoli and Broken Spaghetti Soup

*Serves 4*

Scant ¼ pound spaghetti
1 teaspoon minced garlic
¼ cup minced onion
¼ cup olive oil
1 quart homemade chicken stock or canned broth

1½ cups finely chopped fresh broccoli stalks (peel stems before chopping)
1 medium-sized carrot, scraped and diced
Freshly ground black pepper

1. In a large bowl break up the spaghetti into about ½-inch pieces. This is easily accomplished by first breaking all the pieces in half, then in half again. Using the fingers pick up a fist of spaghetti and squeeze it. Repeat until the spaghetti is the correct size. (There should be just under a cup of broken spaghetti.)

2. Put the garlic, onion, and oil in a heavy saucepan. Cook over medium-low heat for 5 minutes, stirring. Don't let the garlic brown.

3. Meanwhile, bring 1½ quarts of water to a boil in another saucepan or pot.

4. Add the stock, broccoli, and carrot to the onion and garlic mixture. Slowly bring to a boil.

5. Add the spaghetti to the boiling water, stir, and cook it for 6 minutes.

7. When the broccoli mixture reaches a boil, lower the heat to medium.

8. Drain the spaghetti well and add it to the soup. Cook the soup over low heat for 8 minutes, stirring occasionally. Season with pepper to taste. (No salt is required since the stock should have the amount of salt required.)

*Variations:* Herbs such as basil and oregano and/or 1 tablespoon of chopped fresh parsley leaves may be added if desired.

# Cream of Carrot Soup

*Serves 6*

| | | | |
|---|---|---|---|
| 3 | tablespoons butter | 1 | cup heavy cream |
| 1 | pound carrots, scraped and thinly sliced | ½ | teaspoon dried chervil |
| | | ½ | teaspoon paprika |
| 1 | cup drained canned tomatoes, chopped | | Salt and freshly ground black pepper |
| 1 | medium-sized onion, chopped | | Chopped fresh parsley leaves |
| 3 | cups homemade chicken stock or canned broth | | |

1. Melt the butter in a heavy saucepan and add the carrots, tomatoes, and onion, stir and cover. Simmer for 5 minutes. Add the stock and bring to a boil. Lower the heat and simmer, partially covered, for 20 minutes.

2. Purée the mixture, a few cups at a time, in a food processor or blender. Return the mixture to a clean saucepan. Add the cream, chervil, and paprika. Season with salt and pepper to taste. Simmer for a few minutes until very hot. Garnish each serving with parsley.

*Variation:* For more texture, simmer ¾ cup of diced fresh carrots in 2 cups of water for 5 minutes. Drain and stir into the soup with the cream, or garnish the soup with butter-fried croutons.

# Chinese Velvet Corn Soup

### Serves 4

3½ cups homemade chicken stock or canned broth

1 teaspoon soy sauce

1 10-ounce package frozen corn, thawed and drained

1½ tablespoons cornstarch, dissolved in a little water

Salt and freshly ground black pepper

2 large egg whites

3 tablespoons heavy cream
Chopped fresh parsley leaves

1. Bring the stock and soy sauce to a boil in a large saucepan. Add the corn and bring to a boil again. Sir in the dissolved cornstarch and season with salt and pepper to taste.

2. In a bowl beat the egg whites until frothy, but not stiff. Beat in the cream.

3. Remove the saucepan from the heat and stir in the egg white mixture, stirring only to combine the ingredients. Serve immediately, garnishing each serving with parsley.

# New England Haddock Chowder

### Serves 4

2 pounds fish bones, skins, and heads

1½ quarts water

3 tablespoons diced salt pork

1 medium-sized onion, finely chopped

3 tablespoons butter

1 tablespoon all-purpose flour

½ cup milk

1 cup heavy cream

¾ pound haddock fillets, cut into bite-sized pieces

1 cup cooked diced potatoes
Salt and freshly ground black pepper

1 tablespoon chopped fresh parsley leaves

1. Put the fish bones, skins, and heads in a saucepan. Add the water and bring to a boil. Simmer for 45 minutes. Strain and reserve 3 cups of the liquid.

2. Heat the salt pork in a large saucepan and render the fat over medium-low heat for 5 minutes. Discard the pork fat pieces. Add the

butter and stir in the flour. Cook for 1 minute, stirring. Slowly pour in the fish stock, whisking constantly until it is boiling. Add the milk and cream and bring to a boil. Add the fish and potatoes and simmer for 5 minutes. Season with salt and pepper to taste. Sprinkle each serving with parsley.

# Curried Leek Soup with Sherry
### Serves 4

This recipe is one of the few in this collection not made from scratch; it's included because it's quick and delicious. I created it several years ago while sailing with a friend in the Virgin Islands. There were few supplies on board and only a butane two-burner stove plus a fantail barbecue to cook on. Steaks were being grilled on the fantail and potatoes were sautéing over one of the burners when two unexpected guests arrived. We halved the steaks, cooked an extra batch of potatoes and made up for the small portions of meat with this "in a pinch" soup. Dessert was fresh papaya slices with a mist of lime juice. (The soup proved just as good on land.)

1   *2¾-ounce package Knorr leek soup mix*
½   *cup heavy cream or milk*
2   *teaspoons curry powder*
2   *tablespoons dry sherry*
½   *cup sour cream*

1   *large unpeeled Delicious apple, cut into ½-inch cubes*
  *Freshly ground black pepper*

    1. Follow the package directions for preparing the soup using 4 cups of water and ½ cup of cream or milk and add the curry. When the soup is done add the sherry and cook over medium-high heat for 3 minutes, stirring often. Off the heat, stir in the sour cream.

    2. Place the apple cubes on a plate and sprinkle them with pepper. Garnish each bowl of soup with the peppered apple cubes.

# Cream of Celery Soup with Puff Pastry Topping

*Serves 6*

3   tablespoons butter
3   cups chopped celery
3   scallions, sliced
3   cups homemade chicken
    stock or canned broth
1   cup heavy cream

Few gratings of nutmeg
Salt and freshly ground
black pepper to taste
2   10-ounce packages frozen
    patty shells

1. Melt the butter in a large saucepan and add the celery and scallions. Cook over medium heat for 5 minutes, stirring often. Add the stock and bring to a boil. Lower the heat, partially cover, and simmer for 30 minutes, or until the celery is tender.

2. Purée the soup, a few cups at a time, in a blender or food processor.

3. Pour the purée into a large bowl and stir in the cream, nutmeg, and salt and pepper. Ladle the soup in equal amounts into 6 ovenproof soup crocks or bowls.

4. Preheat the oven to 400 degrees.

5. On a lightly floured surface, roll 2 patty shells on top of each other into a circle that hangs 1 inch over the rims of the soup bowls. The dough should be about ⅛ inch thick. Repeat the procedure until all 6 are rolled out. Cut a small circle in the center of each piece of dough. With a finger, wet the rim of one side of the dough with water.

6. Lay 1 piece of dough over each soup-filled bowl and press the water-brushed edges against the outer edges of the bowls. Place the soup bowls on a baking sheet and bake for about 20 minutes, or until the pastry puffs and is golden brown.

# Red Lentil Soup

*Serves 6*

6 strips crisp-cooked
bacon, crumbled
(reserve 2 tablespoons
of the drippings)
1 medium-sized onion,
finely chopped
1 large garlic clove,
minced
2 carrots, scraped and
thinly sliced
1 celery stalk, thinly
sliced
1 cup chopped, peeled,
and seeded tomatoes

1 tablespoon chopped
fresh parsley leaves
1½ cups red lentils (about
¾ pound), picked over,
washed, and drained
3½ cups homemade beef
stock or canned broth
1 cup tomato juice
1 tablespoon fresh lemon
juice
Salt and freshly ground
black pepper

1. Heat the bacon drippings in a large pan. Add the onion, garlic, carrots, celery, and tomatoes and stir. Simmer for 5 minutes. Add the parsley, lentils, stock, tomato juice, and lemon juice, stir and bring to a boil. Lower the heat and simmer for about 30 minutes, or until the lentils are tender.

2. Purée the mixture in a blender or food processor, a few cups at a time, and return to a clean pan. Heat thoroughly and season with salt and pepper to taste. Garnish each serving with the crumbled bacon.

# Bobbe Hart's Fresh Mushroom and Three-Cheese Soup

*Serves 4*

| | | | |
|---|---|---|---|
| 3 | tablespoons butter | ¼ | teaspoon dried thyme |
| 1 | cup chopped onion | ½ | cup dry white wine |
| 1 | garlic clove, minced | | Freshly ground black |
| 12 | ounces fresh mushrooms, thinly sliced | | pepper |
| | | 1 | cup grated Swiss cheese |
| 3 | cups homemade chicken stock or canned broth | 1 | cup grated Cheddar cheese |
| ⅓ | cup chopped fresh parsley leaves | ⅔ | cup grated Parmesan cheese |
| ¼ | cup ketchup | | |

1. Melt the butter in a large heavy saucepan. Add the onion and garlic and sauté over medium-low heat for 5 minutes. Add the mushrooms, stock, parsley, ketchup, and thyme and bring to a boil. Add the wine and cook for 1 minute. Lower the heat, cover, and simmer for 6 minutes. Season with pepper to taste.

2. Combine the cheeses and divide the mixture evenly among 4 soup bowls. Ladle the hot soup over the cheese and serve immediately.

# Dal
## (East Indian Yellow Split Pea Soup)

*Serves 6 to 8*

2 cups dried yellow split peas, picked over, washed, and drained

2 medium-to-large onions, finely chopped

2 celery stalks, diced

1½ quarts water

1 quart homemade chicken stock or canned broth

6 tablespoons butter

1 large garlic clove, crushed

1 tablespoon ground cumin

2 teaspoons ground coriander

½ teaspoon ground cardamon

1 teaspoon chili powder

1 teaspoon ground turmeric

½ teaspoon ground cinnamon

½ teaspoon ground allspice

1 tablespoon fresh lemon juice

Salt and freshly ground black pepper

8 pitted dates

1. Put the split peas, 1 finely chopped onion, celery, water, and stock in a large heavy pot. Bring to a boil, lower the heat, and simmer for 45 minutes.

2. Melt the butter in a frying pan and add the remaining finely chopped onion and the garlic. Cook over medium heat for 5 minutes, stirring often. Add all the spices and the lemon juice. Stir and cook for 1 minute. Set aside.

3. When the soup has cooked for 45 minutes, add the onion mixture to the soup, stir, and season with salt and pepper to taste. Simmer the soup for 15 minutes longer, or until the peas are tender.

4. Purée 2 cups of the soup in a blender or food processor and return it to the pot. Combine well. Garnish each serving with 1 chopped date.

# Sweet Potato Soup

*Serves 6*

| | |
|---|---|
| 2 tablespoons butter | 1 cup heavy cream |
| ¼ cup chopped shallots | Salt and freshly ground |
| 2 celery stalks, sliced | black pepper |
| 1 quart homemade chicken stock or canned broth | ½ cup chopped walnuts |
| 1½ pounds sweet potatoes, peeled and cut into 1-inch pieces | |

1. Melt the butter in a large heavy saucepan. Add the shallots and celery and cook over medium-low heat for 5 minutes, stirring often. Add the chicken stock and sweet potatoes. Bring to a boil, lower the heat, and simmer for 25 minutes, or until the potatoes are tender.

2. Purée 2 cups of the mixture at a time in a blender or food processor until smooth. Return the purée to a clean saucepan. Add the heavy cream, stir, and season with salt and pepper to taste. Heat thoroughly. Garnish each serving with equal amounts of chopped walnuts.

*Variation:* This soup may also be served well chilled.

# Cream of Watercress Soup

*Serves 4*

3 tablespoons butter
1 medium-sized onion,
  chopped
2 bunches watercress,
  leaves and stems
  chopped, save 4 sprigs for
  garnish
2 tablespoons all-purpose
  flour

Few gratings of nutmeg
2 cups milk
1 cup homemade chicken
  stock or canned broth
2 large egg yolks
½ cup heavy cream
  Salt and freshly ground
  black pepper

1. Melt the butter in a heavy saucepan. Add the onion and watercress. Stir, cover, and cook over low heat for 8 minutes. Sprinkle the flour and nutmeg over the mixture and stir.

2. In a separate saucepan heat the combined milk and broth to the boiling point and stir into the watercress mixture. Simmer for 15 minutes.

3. Purée 2 cups of the mixture at a time in a blender or food processor. Return the purée to a clean saucepan and heat thoroughly. Remove from the heat.

4. In a small bowl beat the egg yolks lightly with the cream. Add ¼ cup of the soup to the yolk mixture and stir. Whisk this mixture into the soup. Cook the soup over very low heat for 2 minutes, stirring constantly, until the soup thickens. Season with salt and pepper to taste. Garnish each serving with a sprig of watercress.

# Cold Soups

## Cold Fresh Lemon Soup

*Serves 4*

You can easily double the recipe to make 8 delicious servings.

2½   cups homemade chicken
      stock or canned broth
1    cup heavy cream
2    tablespoons cornstarch
3    large egg yolks, lightly
      beaten

¼    cup fresh lemon juice
8    small fresh mint leaves,
      or 4 small parsley
      flowerets

1. Bring the combined chicken stock and cream to a boil in a saucepan. Cook over medium-high heat for 5 minutes, whisking often.

2. Dissolve the cornstarch in 3 tablespoons of water and whisk into the mixture. Cook for 3 minutes, stirring constantly. Remove the pan from the heat.

3. Add ¼ cup of the hot mixture to the lightly beaten egg yolks and combine well. Add another ¼ cup of the hot mixture and combine. Stir the egg mixture into the soup. Add the lemon juice and combine well. Cool, cover, and refrigerate until very cold. Stir before serving in chilled soup bowls and garnish each of the 4 servings with 2 mint leaves or 1 parsley floweret.

*Variation:* One cup of cold cooked rice can be added to the soup before serving. Combine well.

# Orange–Buttermilk Borscht

*Serves 6*

1 8-ounce can sliced beets
  with liquid
1 quart buttermilk
¼ cup chopped onion
2 tablespoons tomato paste
1 teaspoon fresh lemon
  juice
1 cup fresh orange juice

Salt and freshly ground
  black pepper
1 cup sour cream
1 chilled navel orange,
  peeled (white pith, too)
  and cut into individual
  sections, removing any
  membranes

1. Put the beets and liquid, 1 cup of the buttermilk, the onion, tomato paste, and lemon juice into a blender and run until smooth. Pour the mixture into a large bowl.

2. Add the remaining 3 cups of buttermilk and the orange juice. Combine well. Season with salt and pepper to taste, cover, and refrigerate until thoroughly chilled. Garnish each serving with a dollop of sour cream and top with an orange section.

# Creamy Pimiento–Dill Soup

*Serves 6*

2 cups drained pimientos
2 cups tomato juice
1 cup canned chicken broth
1 tablespoon chopped fresh
  dill, or 1 teaspoon dried
  dill, plus 6 sprigs of dill
  for garnish

2 tablespoons fresh lemon
  juice
1 teaspoon Worcestershire
  sauce
1 cup heavy cream
  Salt and freshly ground
  black pepper

1. Put the pimientos, 1 cup of the tomato juice, the stock, chopped dill, lemon juice, and Worcestershire sauce in a blender. Purée until smooth.

2. Pour the mixture into a large bowl and add the remaining cup of tomato juice and the heavy cream. Combine well. Season with salt and pepper to taste. Cover and chill thoroughly. Garnish each serving with a sprig of dill.

# Creamy Avocado with Hearts of Palm

*Serves 4*

1 large ripe avocado,
  peeled, pitted, and cubed
1 garlic clove, chopped
1 small onion, chopped
2 tablespoons fresh lemon
  juice
2 cups milk
1 cup heavy cream
  Salt and freshly ground
  black pepper

1 cup thinly sliced canned
  hearts of palm
  (refrigerate can until
  hearts of palm are used
  in the recipe)
  Chopped fresh parsley
  leaves (optional)

1. Put the avocado, garlic, onion, lemon juice, and milk in a blender and purée until very smooth. Pour into a large bowl and stir in the cream. If the mixture is too thick add a little water. Season with salt and pepper to taste. (Go light on the salt because the hearts of palm that are added to finish the soup are packed in brine.)

2. Cover the soup and chill thoroughly. Just before serving stir the soup and add the hearts of palm. Combine well. If desired, garnish with parsley.

# Perfect Vichyssoise

*Serves 6*

Consider serving this potato and leek soup hot.

2 tablespoons butter
2 tablespoons olive oil
6 large leeks, white parts
  only, washed and sliced
5 cups homemade chicken
  stock or canned broth
3 cups cubed peeled
  potatoes

  Salt and freshly
  ground white pepper
1 cup heavy cream
⅓ cup well-drained diced
  cooked beets
1 tablespoon snipped fresh
  chives

1. Heat the butter and oil in a large heavy saucepan. Add the leeks and cook over medium-low heat for 5 minutes, stirring often. Add the broth and potatoes and bring to a boil. Lower the heat to medium and cook for 30 minutes, or until the potatoes are very tender.

2. Purée the mixture in a blender, 2 cups at a time, until very smooth. If a finer texture is desired, pass the purée through a fine mesh strainer. Season the soup well with salt and pepper to taste.

3. Return the mixture to a clean saucepan and add the cream. Season with salt and pepper to taste. If serving hot, heat thoroughly; if serving cold pour the mixture into a bowl, cover, and chill thoroughly. Garnish the soup (hot or cold) with diced beets and chives.

# Okroshka
# (Russian Cold Mixed Meat, Fish, and Vegetable Soup)

### Serves 6

2½ cups homemade beef stock or canned broth
1 cup dry white wine
1 cup sour cream
1 teaspoon Dijon mustard
1 teaspoon sugar
1 cup cooked chopped shrimp, crab, or lobster
1 cup cooked chopped ham, turkey, chicken, tongue, or beef
1 cup cubed, peeled, and seeded cucumber
¼ cup diced dill pickle

1 celery stalk, diced
2 scallions, sliced
1 tablespoon snipped fresh chives
1 tablespoon chopped fresh dill, or 1 teaspoon dried dill
1 tablespoon chopped fresh parsley leaves
Salt and freshly ground black pepper
1 cup cold club soda
2 hard-boiled large eggs, finely chopped

1. In a large bowl combine the broth, wine, sour cream, mustard, and sugar well. Add the remaining ingredients, except for the club soda and eggs. Cover and chill for several hours.

2. Just before serving stir in the club soda and garnish with the chopped eggs.

# Cold Shrimp–Tomato Gazpacho

*Serves 6*

1½ cups coarsely chopped
chilled boiled shrimp
4 medium-sized ripe
tomatoes
½ large green pepper,
seeded and chopped
2 scallions, sliced
1 large garlic clove,
chopped

2 tablespoons red wine
vinegar
3 slices day-old white
bread, crusts trimmed
and bread coarsely
chopped
1 teaspoon salt, or to taste
2 dashes of Tabasco sauce
3½ cups cold water

## GARNISHES

½ large green pepper,
seeded and diced
½ medium-sized
cucumber, peeled,
seeded, and diced

3 scallions, thinly sliced
1½ cups toasted croutons

1. In a blender or food processor combine all the Gazpacho ingredients, except for the shrimp, with 1 cup of the water.

2. Pour the mixture into a large bowl and stir in the remaining 2½ cups of water and the shrimp. Cover and chill for 2 hours. Stir the ingredients again before serving. Pass small bowls of the garnishes.

# Cold Zucchini Soup with Pickled Tomato Garnish

*Serves 6*

### PICKLED TOMATOES

| | |
|---|---|
| ¾ cup diced seeded tomatoes | 3 tablespoons white wine vinegar |
| 2 tablespoons minced cocktail onions | 2 tablespoons olive oil |
| 1 tablespoon jarred cocktail onion vinegar | ½ teaspoon dried thyme |

### ZUCCHINI SOUP

| | |
|---|---|
| 3 tablespoons olive or vegetable oil | 3 dashes of Tabasco sauce |
| 1 large garlic clove, minced | 1 tablespoon fresh lemon juice |
| 1 medium-sized onion, chopped | 1 tablespoon chopped fresh parsley leaves |
| 5 medium-size zucchini, scrubbed, ends trimmed, and zucchini shredded | Salt and freshly ground black pepper to taste |
| 4 cups homemade chicken stock or canned broth | ½ cup heavy cream |

1. Combine the ingredients for the Pickled Tomatoes in a small bowl, cover, and refrigerate.

2. Heat the oil in a large heavy saucepan and cook the garlic and onion over medium-low heat for 5 minutes, stirring often. Add the remaining ingredients, except for the cream, and bring to a boil. Lower the heat and simmer for 20 minutes.

3. Purée the soup in a blender or food processor, a few cups at a time, until smooth. Pour into a bowl, stir in the cream, and season with salt and pepper to taste. Cover and chill thoroughly.

4. When ready to serve the soup, drain the pickled tomatoes well and garnish each serving with a generous tablespoon of the Pickled Tomatoes.

# Egg Dishes and Crêpes

Eggs are nature's naturally portioned and packaged food: plentiful, versatile, nutritious, and inexpensive. As a child growing up in Kansas and Texas, I remember my grandmother pan-frying several dozen eggs each morning for her large family and farm hands. Gathered only minutes earlier from the hen house, the eggs had yolks that stood high, pouring a circle of gold onto the plate when they were pierced. Grandmother's hot fresh biscuits were the perfect *pushers* to scoop up the last drop.

Crêpes are great company fare. They suggest that the cook intends for the meal to be a special one, for making a batch of crêpes does take time and attention.

Because they are extremely versatile, crêpes can be cut into strips to add substance to hot broth or stuffed with practically anything. Imagine them rolled around cooked Italian sausage and gratinéed with a Fontina cheese sauce and bread crumbs or mixed with herbs covering a cheese omelet or scrambled eggs.

# Eggs

Most of us know how to fry an egg, or scramble one, or even boil one. But there are many more interesting ways to use this delicious, naturally prepackaged food. Graduating from fried eggs to omelets and souffleés is not nearly so traumatic as graduating from grandmother's wood-burning stove to the kitchens and restaurants of today. All it takes is following cooking directions and timing closely.

## Omelets

In many fine restaurants, the test a prospective chef must pass often includes the preparation of an omelet. Omelets may require a few simple ingredients and seconds to cook, but only skill and technique can produce a superior one. In my judgment, an omelet is second only to a soufflé in the hierarchy of egg dishes.

While omelets never ought to be well done or stiff, there are different consistencies. The French have a word to describe their perfect omelet's doneness: *baveuese.* There is no comparable word in the English language. Baveuese means very moist, or just this side of runny. Since this consistency may not appeal to most Americans, it's a good idea to ask your guests how they would like their omelet cooked.

The omelet pan ideally is a 7- to 8- inch nonstick or well-seasoned pan with curved sides. Before cooking the omelet it is essential that everything is ready—the ingredients prepared, plates warmed, and all within easy reach of the stove. An omelet takes about 45 seconds to cook.

After the following master omelet recipe there are several suggestions for unusual omelet fillings. Quickly place your preferred filling across the top of the eggs immediately after spreading the partially set eggs over the bottom of the pan.

3   large eggs (the fresher the better)
    Salt and freshly ground black pepper

1   teaspoon finely chopped fresh parsley leaves
1   tablespoon butter

1. Put the eggs in a bowl and mix thoroughly with a fork. Season the eggs lightly with salt and pepper and add the parsley. Combine.

2. Melt the butter in the omelet pan and turn the pan to coat the bottom evenly.

3. When the foaming subsides, add the egg mixture but don't allow the butter to brown. Cook over medium heat, stirring the eggs with a fork and folding them until they are still quite moist but have begun to set. Spread the eggs evenly over the bottom of the pan. (If using a filling, add it at this point—spreading it across the center of the eggs with a tablespoon.) Elevate one end of the pan and begin turning the eggs over and turn out onto a warmed plate.

*Serving Suggestions:* Tossed green salad and croissants or brioches or toasted French bread.

## Omelet Fillings

Mixed herbs, cheese, sautéed mushrooms, onions, tomatoes and peppers, ham, sausage, bacon and sour cream, and red salmon caviar are the most common omelets. While they are all excellent fillings for omelets, here is a list of more uncommon fillings.

The amount of the filling can range from a total of ¼ to ½ cup for each omelet, never more.

Do not forget to consider leftover meat, seafood, fish, pasta, rice, or vegetables as omelet fillings. Whatever the filling, cut it into bite-sized pieces or cubes or thin slices, and warm the filling, if necessary.

1. Butter-fried Croutons and Grilled Onion Slices: Melt 4 tablespoons of butter in a saucepan and fry ½-inch cubes of bread until golden brown all over. Cook 1 small sliced onion in the butter until golden brown. Place the croutons and onions over the surface of the eggs spread over the bottom of the pan. Tilt the pan and fold the omelet over the filling. Turn it onto a warmed plate. A plain herb omelet with butter-fried croutons is also excellent.

2. Chopped Duck or Chicken Livers with Mustard: Sauté 2 duck or chicken livers in 3 tablespoons of butter until done. Chop finely and toss in ½ teaspoon Dijon mustard. Sprinkle with 2 teaspoons chopped fresh parsley leaves and toss again. Fill the omelet with the mixture at the appropriate moment.

3. Parmesan Cheese and Caponata: Combine 1 tablespoon of freshly grated Parmesan cheese with the basic omelet mixture. At the appropriate moment, spoon ⅓ cup of Caponata over the partially cooked eggs.

4. Sautéed Zucchini Julienne and Salami: Sauté ¼ cup julienne strips of zucchini in 2 tablespoons of butter for 5 minutes. Toss with 2 thin slices of Genoa salami cut into julienne strips. Fill the omelet at the appropriate moment.

5. Curried Chicken and Chutney: Combine and warm ¼ cup diced cooked chicken, 1 teaspoon curry powder, and ¼ cup finely chopped chutney in a saucepan. Fill the omelet at the appropriate moment.

6. Smoked Salmon Strips with Dill and Crème Fraîche: Place ⅓ cup smoked salmon strips, a sprinkling of snipped fresh dill, and 2 tablespoons of Crème Fraîche (page 277) over the partially cooked eggs at the appropriate moment.

7. Sautéed Potatoes and Bacon: Fill the omelet with ⅓ cup sautéed cubed potatoes and 2 strips of crumbled crisp-cooked bacon at the appropriate moment.

8. Chopped Watercress and Chèvre: Fill the omelet with ¼ cup chopped watercress and ¼ cup diced Chèvre at the appropriate moment.

9. Sautéed Leek and Kielbasa: Sauté ¼ cup thinly sliced leek and ¼ cup diced kielbasa sausage in 2 tablespoons of butter over medium heat for about 5 minutes. Fill the omelet with the mixture at the appropriate moment.

10. Black Beans and Rice: Fill the omelet with ¼ cup hot cooked black beans and ¼ cup warmed rice at the appropriate moment. Chili beans or pinto beans can also be used.

Other filling suggestions:

Fried clams
Sliced turkey and whole cranberry sauce
Hot German potato salad
Sliced Avocado, chicken, and sour cream
Sautéed apple wedges
Sautéed thin bratwurst slices and roasted red pepper strips
Chopped boiled shrimp and pimiento
Hot cooked chopped broccoli
Hot cooked corn and lima beans
Ratatouille
Sliced mortadella and mozzarella strips

# French Onion Tart
## with Pepper-flecked Pastry

*Serves 6*

### PASTRY

1½  cups sifted all-purpose
    flour
½  teaspoon salt
½  teaspoon freshly ground
    black pepper

1  large egg yolk
6  tablespoons butter
3  tablespoons ice water

### ONION TART FILLING

3  tablespoons butter
3  medium-to-large onions
    (about 3 inches in
    diameter), thinly sliced
    and separated into rings
1  cup milk
1  cup heavy cream
3  large eggs
¼  cup freshly grated
    Parmesan cheese

1  tablespoon all-purpose
    flour
½  teaspoon salt
    Freshly ground black
    pepper to taste
1  tablespoon Dijon
    mustard

1. To make the pastry, combine the flour, salt, pepper, egg yolk, and butter with a pastry blender or combine in a food processor until a coarse crumb consistency. Add the water and combine until smooth. Shape into a ball, wrap in plastic, and refrigerate for 30 minutes.

2. Meanwhile, make the tart filling: Melt the butter in a large frying pan and cook the onions over medium-low heat for 10 minutes, stirring occasionally. Do not let the onions brown. Remove from the heat and set aside.

3. Preheat the oven to 425 degrees.

4. Roll out the pastry to a ⅛-inch thickness and fit it into a 10-inch tart pan. Prick the crust in several places with a knife point. Place a circle of foil over the pastry and fill the foil with 2 cups of dried beans or rice. Bake for 10 minutes, remove the foil and beans, and bake for 5 minutes longer.

5. Meanwhile, heat the milk and cream, but do not bring to a boil. Set aside.

6. In a large bowl beat together the eggs, Parmesan cheese, flour, salt, and pepper. Slowly beat in the milk and cream mixture.

7. Remove the tart shell from the oven and brush the bottom of the shell with the mustard. Distribute the onions evenly over the shell.

Pour in the custard mixture and return the tart to the oven. Bake for about 30 minutes, or until the top of the tart is golden brown.

*Variation:* To make a Western Tart, cut 1 medium-sized green pepper into thin strips and cook with the onions. Proceed with the recipe following the directions above.

## Four Individual Spicy Cheese Soufflés

### Serves 4

| | |
|---|---|
| 4 tablespoons butter, plus extra for greasing the soufflé dishes | 2 tablespoons grated onion |
| ¼ cup freshly grated Parmesan cheese, plus extra for coating the soufflé dishes | ¼ teaspoon salt |
| | Freshly ground black pepper to taste |
| 4 tablespoons all-purpose flour | 2 dashes of Tabasco sauce |
| | 1 teaspoon Worcestershire sauce |
| 1½ cups milk | 5 large eggs, separated |
| 1½ cups grated Cheddar cheese | |

1. Grease 4 1½-cup soufflé dishes with butter and sprinkle each with a little Parmesan cheese. Turn the dishes to coat them evenly. Refrigerate until needed.

2. Melt the butter in an enamel or heavy stainless steel saucepan and whisk in the flour. Stir and whisk over medium heat for 1 minute. Add the milk, whisking constantly until the sauce boils, has thickened, and is smooth. Stir in the Cheddar and Parmesan cheeses, combining well. Remove from the heat and stir in the grated onion, salt, pepper, Tabasco sauce, and Worcestershire sauce. Turn into a large bowl and cool for 5 minutes, stirring occasionally. Beat the egg yolks into the mixture.

3. Preheat the oven to 375 degrees.

4. Remove the prepared soufflé dishes from the refrigerator and place them near your work area.

5. Beat the egg whites until stiff but not dry and fold into the cheese mixture. Turn equal amounts of the mixture into the soufflé dishes. Bake for 30 minutes and serve immediately.

*Serving Suggestions:* Mixed green salad with vinaigrette dressing, crusty French bread, and dry white wine.

# Crêpes

---

When Yellowfingers, a New York restaurant on Third Avenue across the street from Bloomingdales, first opened, about a decade ago, it had a crêpe counter. Although the restaurant still exists, the crêpe counter is long gone. I recall stopping there either after shopping or a movie for a large hot plain crêpe slathered with butter and lightly sprinkled with sugar. In anticipation of a savory crêpe, I often used to cut my shopping short or wished that a perfectly good movie would end.

Recently in Avallon, France, the first stop on a Burgundy wine tour, on a cool and rainy day, I spotted a crêpe stand on the sidewalk outside a small market. A rosy-cheeked young boy was preparing the steaming crêpes, and, of course, I sampled one. His crêpe was delicious and soothing, as are all well-made crêpes. For me they fall into the category of security food, next to potatoes.

It is comforting to note that crêpes can be made the day before using them. They can be arranged in layers with a piece of plastic wrap between every other crêpe, covered tightly, and stored in the refrigerator.

## Basic Crêpes

### Makes 12 to 16 crêpes

¾ cup water
⅔ cup milk
⅔ cup all-purpose flour

3 large eggs
½ teaspoon salt
2 tablespoons butter

1. Combine the water, milk, flour, eggs, and salt in a blender, or beat until smooth with a whisk.

2. Melt 1 teaspoon of the butter in a crêpe pan. Pour enough crêpe batter into the pan to just cover the bottom of the pan when the pan is tilted in a circular motion. Brown the crêpe on both sides. Make additional crêpes in the same manner.

# Herb Crêpes with a Cheese Omelet Filling

To the basic crêpe recipe add 1 tablespoon chopped fresh parsley leaves, ½ teaspoon dried tarragon, and ½ teaspoon dried chervil. Cook the crêpes as directed. Serve plain with butter or make 2-egg cheese omelets and roll up in the Herb Crêpes. Scrambled eggs can also serve as a filling for the Herb Crêpes. Serve 1 per person.

# Sausage-stuffed Crêpes with Fontina Cheese Sauce

### Serves 6

| | |
|---|---|
| 6 **Italian sweet sausages** | 3 **tablespoons freshly grated** |
| 6 **crêpes** | **Parmesan cheese** |
| 3 **tablespoons unseasoned** | |
| **bread crumbs** | |

### FONTINA CHEESE SAUCE

| | |
|---|---|
| 2 **tablespoons butter, plus** | 1 **cup warmed milk** |
| **extra butter for greasing** | ½ **cup diced Fontina cheese** |
| **the baking dish** | **Salt and freshly ground** |
| 2 **tablespoons all-purpose** | **black pepper** |
| **flour** | |

1. Prick each sausage in several places with the sharp point of a knife and simmer in water to cover for 15 minutes, turning often.
2. Meanwhile, prepare the sauce: Melt the butter in a heavy saucepan and whisk in the flour. Cook over medium heat for 1 minute, stirring. Add the milk, whisking constantly, until the sauce boils and is smooth and thickens. Stir in the cheese and season with salt and pepper to taste. Cover and set aside.
3. Preheat the broiler.
4. Drain the sausages and pat them dry.
5. Lightly grease an au gratin or shallow baking dish with butter.
6. Roll each sausage up in a crêpe and place them seam side down in the au gratin dish. Whisk the sauce and spoon it over the stuffed crêpes. Combine the bread crumbs and Parmesan cheese and sprinkle

the mixture over the top. Run under the broiler until the top sizzles and is golden brown.

*Serving Suggestion:* Haitian-style Braised Cabbage.

# Roti

## Serves 4

Roti, Trinidad's flat bread, is traditionally filled with a curried mutton, goat, or chicken stew-like mixture. It is often rolled up and eaten in the hand, sandwich or eggroll style.

My version is a spicy chicken curry wrapped in a giant crêpe served on a dinner plate with mango chutney.

| | |
|---|---|
| 2 cups ½-inch peeled and cubed potatoes | 2 cups cubed cooked chicken |
| 4 tablespoons butter, plus extra for cooking the crêpes | 1 cup homemade chicken stock or canned broth, or as needed |
| 1 medium-sized onion, thinly sliced and separated into rings | 1 tablespoon chopped fresh parsley leaves |
| 1 garlic clove, minced | Salt and freshly ground black pepper |
| ½ cup diced celery | 4 crêpes made in a 14-inch nonstick frying pan |
| 1 tablespoon curry powder | 1 cup mango chutney |
| 2 dashes of Tabasco sauce, or to taste | |

1. Turn the oven to low.

2. Cook the potatoes in boiling water until just tender, about 12 minutes.

3. Meanwhile, melt the butter in a large saucepan. Add the onion, garlic, and celery and cook over medium heat for 5 minutes, stirring often. Stir in the curry and Tabasco and cook for 1 minute. Add the chicken, broth, and parsley. Stir and bring to a boil. Immediately lower the heat to a simmer. Add the drained potatoes. Combine gently and season with salt and pepper to taste. Cook over very low heat until the crêpes are done. (It may be necessary to add a little more broth to the mixture. The consistency should be thick but not dry.)

4. Place the cooked crêpe on a dinner plate and spoon one quarter of the curry mixture across the center of the crêpe, then roll it up. Keep the crêpe warm in the oven. Prepare the remaining crêpes

in the same manner, keeping each warm in the oven as they are made. Spoon one-quarter cup of the mango chutney over the center of each Roti and serve immediately.

*Serving Suggestions:* Mixed green salad with Vinaigrette Dressing and Grandmother's Evans' Devil's Food Cake.

# Fruit of the Sea

On the Adriatic coast of Yugoslavia I once sampled fresh-caught fish, grilled over a wood fire with only olive oil brushed on as seasoning. For all its simplicity, it remains the most memorable fish I've ever eaten.

Fish and shellfish must be fresh. A fish is fresh when there is no fishy smell; the eyes of fresh whole fish are bright, clear, and bulging; the gills are bright red and clean; and the skin shines and the flesh is firm to the touch. Fish fillets, the cut of fish we buy most often, must not appear dry; they should glisten, and the color should not look dull or faded.

When selecting live shellfish, lobster, and crabs make certain that the legs move actively. Live oysters, hard-shelled clams, and mussels will close their shells when lightly tapped.

However, a preoccupation with freshness should not be allowed to inhibit the selections or preparation of fish for company. Most reputable supermarkets and fish markets are as concerned as their customers about the quality of the fish they sell and it takes just a minimum of alert shopping to find the best.

# Sautéed Soft-shelled Crabs Parmesan

*Serves 4*

| | |
|---|---|
| 12 small soft-shelled crabs, cleaned | 2 tablespoons butter |
| Salt and freshly ground black pepper | 3 tablespoons freshly grated Parmesan cheese |
| All-purpose flour | 1 lemon, cut into wedges and seeded |
| 4 tablespoons clarified butter (see recipe page 105) | |

1. Preheat the broiler.
2. Season the crabs lightly with salt and pepper and coat them with flour; shake off any excess.
3. Heat the 4 tablespoons of clarified butter in a large frying pan and sauté the crabs over medium-high heat until they are golden brown on each side. Put the cooked crabs in a broiling pan.
4. Melt the 2 tablespoons of butter and brush over the crabs. Sprinkle the crabs with the Parmesan cheese.
5. Run under the broiler for a few minutes until the cheese sizzles. Serve with the lemon wedges.

*Variation:* Of course, the crabs can be simply sautéed and served without the extra butter and Parmesan cheese.

*Serving Suggestions:* Hot Cooked Asparagus with Butter, Emily McCormack's Tomatoes, and Crêpes with Cream Filling Flamed in Cointreau.

# Boiled Lobster

Serves 4

4  1½-pound live lobsters

1. Bring 4 quarts of water to a boil in a large pot (10 to 12 quarts). Add the lobsters, heads down, cover the pot, and return to a boil. Cook for 18 minutes.

2. Drain the lobsters in a colander, turning them several times to release as much liquid as possible before serving. Nutcrackers or lobster crackers are necessary.

*Variation:* The lobsters can also be cooked in 2 bottles of dry white table wine mixed with 2 quarts of water.

*Serving Suggestions:* Baked Italian-style Mushrooms in Scallop Shells, hot corn on the cob, and Cold Lemon Mousse with Raspberry Purée.

# Oven-barbecued Shrimp

Serves 4

| | |
|---|---|
| 2  pounds large shrimp, shelled and deveined<br>Freshly ground black pepper<br>Paprika | 8  tablespoons (1 stick) very cold butter<br>2  lemons, halved and seeded<br>French bread |

1. Preheat the oven to 450 degrees.

2. Place equal amounts of the shrimp in 4 individual au gratin dishes. Sprinkle liberally with pepper and paprika.

3. Slice the butter thin and cover the shrimp with equal amounts. Squeeze 1 lemon half over the butter in each dish. Bake for 12 minutes. Remove and place the hot dishes on individual dinner plates. Serve with sliced French bread for dunking in the butter sauce.

*Serving Suggestions:* Caesar Salad and Frozen Piña Colada Ice Cream Cake.

# Shrimp Savannah

Serves 6

| | |
|---|---|
| 8 tablespoons (1 stick) butter | 1 cup milk |
| ½ pound fresh mushrooms, sliced | ¾ cup heavy cream |
| ¾ cup diced sweet green pepper | 2¼ pounds large shrimp, shelled and deveined |
| 1 tablespoon paprika | ¾ cup freshly grated Parmesan cheese |
| ¼ cup diced pimientos | Salt and freshly ground black pepper |
| 4 tablespoons all-purpose flour | 1½ tablespoons unseasoned dry bread crumbs |

1. Preheat the broiler.

2. Melt 4 tablespoons of the butter in a frying pan. Add the mushrooms and green pepper and cook over medium heat for 5 minutes, stirring often. Sprinkle with the paprika and pimientos and set aside.

3. Melt the remaining 4 tablespoons of butter in a heavy saucepan and add the flour. Whisk constantly over medium-high heat for 1 minute. Add the milk and cream and bring to a boil, whisking constantly, until the sauce thickens and is smooth. Add the mushroom mixture, shrimp, and half the Parmesan cheese to the sauce and stir. Simmer for 5 minutes and season with salt and pepper to taste.

4. Spoon the mixture into an au gratin dish and sprinkle with the remaining Parmesan cheese combined with the bread crumbs. Run under the broiler until the top sizzles and turns golden brown. Serve immediately.

*Serving Suggestions:* Buttered green peas and hot cooked rice.

# Chinese Hot Pepper Shrimp

*Serves 4*

| | | | |
|---|---|---|---|
| 1 | tablespoon cornstarch | 2 | scallions, thinly sliced |
| ½ | cup water | ¼ | cup tomato paste |
| 1 | tablespoon soy sauce | 1 | tablespoon dry sherry |
| 4 | large egg whites | 1 | tablespoon sugar |
| 24 | jumbo shrimp, shelled and deveined | 1 | tablespoon chopped Chinese hot peppers, or as desired (more or less) |
| ½ | cup peanut oil | | |
| 1 | large garlic clove, minced | 1 | tablespoon Oriental sesame oil |
| 1 | teaspoon grated fresh ginger | | Salt to taste |

1. In a large bowl dissolve the cornstarch in the water. Add the soy sauce and egg whites and combine thoroughly. Add the shrimp to the mixture and toss to coat evenly. Cover and refrigerate for 30 minutes.

2. Heat the oil in a wok or large frying pan over high heat. When the oil is hot but not smoking, add the shrimp one at a time, removing them from the bowl with tongs. Shake any excess egg white mixture back into the bowl. Stir-fry the shrimp over high heat for about 2 minutes, or just until pink. Drain the shrimp on paper towels.

3. Pour off all but 1 tablespoon of oil from the pan. Add the garlic, ginger, scallions, tomato paste, sherry, sugar, and peppers. Stir-fry for 30 seconds. Add the sesame oil and egg white mixture and stir constantly over high heat for 30 seconds. Return the shrimp to the pan and cook for 30 seconds, or until the shrimp are hot. Season with salt, if desired.

*Serving Suggestions:* Stir-fried Snow Pea Pods and Polynesian Rice.

# Jumbo Shrimp Meunière

### Serves 4

20  jumbo shrimp, shelled
    and deveined, with tails
    left intact
    Salt and freshly ground
    black pepper
    All-purpose flour

8  tablespoons (1 stick)
   sweet butter
1  lemon, halved and
   seeded
1  tablespoon chopped fresh
   parsley leaves

1. Rinse the shrimp under cool running water and shake off any excess water. Season the shrimp with salt and pepper and coat with the flour.

2. Melt 4 tablespoons of the butter in a large frying pan and cook the shrimp for 3 minutes on each side over medium-high heat until lightly browned and tender. Transfer the cooked shrimp to a warmed serving dish.

3. Add the remaining 4 tablespoons of butter to the pan and heat until light brown in color. Immediately squeeze the juice of the lemon halves into the pan. Stir and add the parsley. Stir and immediately pour the mixture over the shrimp.

*Serving Suggestion:* Lima Beans with Roast Red Peppers.

# Coconut Shrimp

### Serves 4

1  cup all-purpose flour
1  large egg
1  cup beer
1  3½-ounce can shredded
   coconut
2  pounds jumbo shrimp,
   shelled and deveined,
   with tails left intact

   Peanut or vegetable
   oil for deep-frying
1  lemon, cut into wedges
   and seeded

1. In a bowl beat together the flour, egg, and beer.

2. Spread the coconut on a plate. Holding each shrimp by the tail, dip them into the batter, coating them evenly. Roll the batter-coated shrimp in the coconut.

3. In a large heavy saucepan heat 2 inches of oil to 375 degrees. Gently lower the shrimp into the hot oil, 4 or 5 at a time. Fry for only 4 or 5 minutes, turning often, or until the shrimp are golden brown all over. As the shrimp are cooked, drain them on paper towels. Serve with the lemon wedges.

*Variations:* If desired, instead of the lemon wedges, serve the shrimp with Norman Hodgson's Mustard Sauce (recipe page 156).
*Serving Suggestions:* Creamy Pimiento–Dill Soup, Creole Rice, and Lime Pie with Gingersnap Crust.

## Scallops Provençale

### Serves 4

¼ cup olive oil, plus oil for greasing the baking dish

1½ pounds bay scallops

¼ cup minced onion

1 large garlic clove, minced

4 anchovy fillets, drained and coarsely chopped

¼ cup quartered black olives

1¼ cups diced peeled tomatoes (fresh or canned)

½ teaspoon dried thyme
Pinch of dried rosemary leaves

1 tablespoon chopped fresh parsley leaves
Salt and freshly ground black pepper to taste

2 tablespoons drained capers

1. Preheat the oven to 375 degrees.
2. Brush oil over the bottom and sides of a shallow au gratin or baking dish. Put the scallops in a single layer in the dish.
3. Heat ¼ cup oil in a saucepan and cook the onion and garlic over medium-low heat for 5 minutes. Add the remaining ingredients, except for the capers. Bring the mixture to a boil and spoon the sauce over the scallops. Cover and bake for 15 minutes. Sprinkle with the capers and serve immediately.

*Serving Suggestions:* Zucchini and Carrots Julienne and Rice Pilaf.

# Sautéed Sea Scallops with Butter Sauce

### Serves 4

| | |
|---|---|
| 1 cup all-purpose flour | 2 tablespoons butter, or |
| 1 teaspoon salt | as needed |
| 1/4 teaspoon freshly ground white pepper | 2 tablespoons vegetable oil, or as needed |
| 1¾ pounds sea scallops, drained | 1 tablespoon chopped fresh parsley leaves |

## BUTTER SAUCE (BEURRE BLANC)

| | |
|---|---|
| 3 tablespoons white wine vinegar | Freshly ground white pepper to taste |
| 3 tablespoons white wine | Salt |
| 1 tablespoon minced shallots | ½ pound (2 sticks) butter |

1. Preheat the oven to 275 degrees.

2. Combine the flour, salt, and pepper in a plastic bag. Shake 4 or 5 scallops at a time in the seasoned flour. Shake off any excess flour and transfer the scallops to a plate.

3. When all the scallops are coated, heat the butter and oil in a large frying pan and sauté the scallops, a dozen or so at a time, until they are golden brown all over. Transfer the cooked scallops to an ovenproof serving dish. Continue cooking the scallops adding equal amounts of butter and oil as needed. Keep the cooked scallops warm in the oven while preparing the sauce.

4. Combine the vinegar, wine, and shallots in a medium-sized enamel-coated or nonstick heavy saucepan. Boil the mixture until it reduces to about 1½ tablespoons. Remove the pan from the heat and whisk in 1 tablespoon of the butter. Over very low heat, continue whisking in the butter a tablespoon at a time, until all of it is used. The sauce will be thick and creamy. Immediately remove the sauce from the heat and taste for seasoning. Pour the sauce into a sauceboat. Sprinkle the scallops with the parsley and serve with the Butter Sauce.

*Serving Suggestions:* Hot cooked string beans and Arugola and Endive Salad with Herb Dressing.

# Fried Scored Cod Fillets with Sweet and Sour Cherry Sauce

*Serves 4*

## SWEET AND SOUR CHERRY SAUCE

½ cup red wine vinegar
½ cup dark brown sugar
½ cup cherry preserves
¼ cup ketchup
¼ cup crushed pineapple
(optional)

1 minced scallion
1 tablespoon cornstarch
dissolved in 3
tablespoons water

1¼ cups peanut or
vegetable oil
4 6-ounce 1-inch-thick cod
fillets, scored ¼ inch
deep in a ½-inch
crisscross pattern

Salt and freshly ground
black pepper
All-purpose flour

1. First make the sauce: Combine the ingredients, except for the cornstarch and water, in a saucepan and bring to a boil. Lower the heat and simmer for 10 minutes, stirring often.

2. Meanwhile, heat the oil in a large frying pan.

3. Season the fish fillets with salt and pepper and coat with flour, shaking off any excess. Fry the fish for about 4 minutes per side, or until golden brown and tender. Drain on paper towels.

4. Stir the dissolved cornstarch into the sauce and stir until the sauce thickens. Serve the sauce with the cooked cod fillets.

*Serving Suggestions:* Lemon Rice and buttered broccoli.

# Oven-fried Cod Fillets with Ground Almond Crust

*Serves 4*

1   cup milk
1   teaspoon salt
    Freshly ground black
    pepper
4   6-ounce cod fillets
½   cup ground almonds
½   cup unseasoned dry
    bread crumbs

3   tablespoons butter,
    melted, plus 1 tablespoon
    butter for greasing the
    baking dish
1   lemon, cut into 4 wedges
    and seeded

1. Preheat the oven to 450 degrees.

2. In a shallow bowl combine the milk, salt, and pepper to taste. Dip the fillets in the milk and coat with the combined almonds and bread crumbs.

3. Rub 1 tablespoon of butter over the inside of a shallow baking pan and place the fish in the pan. Drizzle the melted butter over the fish and bake for 12 to 15 minutes, or until the fish flakes easily. Serve each fillet with a lemon wedge.

*Serving Suggestions:* Avocado and Prosciutto, Sautéed Tomato Fillets, and Orange Slices with Strawberry Purée.

# Stuffed Flounder Rolls

*Serves 4*

Here's one of my favorites, which is inexpensive, too.

4 *flounder fillets (about 6 ounces each)*
*Salt and freshly ground black pepper*
2 *tablespoons butter*
½ *cup minced celery*
¼ *cup minced onion*
¼ *cup finely chopped fresh parsley leaves*

½ *cup unseasoned dry bread crumbs*
3 *tablespoons dry white wine*
2 *tablespoons melted butter*
*Paprika*
½ *cup homemade chicken stock or canned broth*

1. Preheat the oven to 400 degrees.

2. Season the fish on the boned side with salt and pepper. Set aside.

3. Melt 2 tablespoons of butter in a frying pan and add the celery and onion. Cook over medium heat for 5 minutes, stirring often. Remove from the heat and stir in the parsley, bread crumbs, and wine.

4. Spread equal portions of the mixture over each fillet and roll up. Place the fish rolls in a shallow baking dish seam side down. Brush the top of each with the melted butter and sprinkle lightly with salt, pepper, and paprika. Pour in the chicken stock and bake for 25 minutes, or until the fish flakes easily.

*Serving Suggestions:* Buttered Carrots with Grand Marnier and Individual Roesti Potatoes.

# Baked Snapper with Mustard–Butter and Wine Sauce

*Serves 4*

| | |
|---|---|
| 2 tablespoons butter | 1 tablespoon fresh lemon juice |
| 4 snapper fillets (about 6 ounces each) | Salt and freshly ground white pepper |
| 3 tablespoons butter, melted | 1 tablespoon chopped fresh parsley leaves |
| 1 tablespoon Dijon mustard | |
| 1 cup dry white wine | |
| 1 tablespoon minced shallots | |

1. Preheat the oven to 350 degrees.

2. Spread 1 tablespoon of the butter over the inside of a shallow baking dish large enough to just hold the fillets. Place the fillets in the dish.

3. In a bowl combine the mustard, wine, shallots, and melted butter with a whisk. Pour the mixture over the fish.

4. Bake for 15 minutes.

5. Carefully drain the liquid in the baking dish into a saucepan. Cover the fish and set it aside.

6. Cook the liquid over high heat until it is reduced to ½ cup. Whisk in the lemon juice and the remaining 1 tablespoon of butter. Season with salt and pepper to taste. Spoon the sauce over the fish and sprinkle with the parsley. Serve immediately.

*Serving Suggestions:* Rice Pilaf and hot cooked Italian green beans.

# Red Snapper with Garlic and Herbs and Wine Sauce

*Serves 4*

1   3½ pound whole red snapper, cleaned
1   large garlic clove, crushed
¼   cup olive oil
     Salt and freshly ground black pepper

½   teaspoon dried tarragon leaves
½   teaspoon dried thyme
1   pimiento, cut into thin strips
1   lemon, cut into wedges and seeded

### WINE SAUCE

4   tablespoons butter
3   tablespoons all-purpose flour
1   cup milk
     Salt and freshly ground white pepper

¼   cup dry white wine
½   teaspoon dried tarragon leaves
1   tablespoon chopped fresh parsley leaves

1. Preheat the oven to 450 degrees.

2. Score the fish ⅓ inch deep on the diagonal in 3 places on each side. Put the fish in a roasting pan and brush it with the combined garlic and oil. Reserve the remaining mixture.

3. Season the fish well with salt and pepper and sprinkle it with the tarragon and thyme. Bake for about 40 minutes, or until the fish flakes easily.

4. Meanwhile, prepare the sauce: Melt 3 tablespoons of the butter in an enamel or nonstick saucepan. Whisk in the flour and cook over medium heat for 1 minute. Add the milk and whisk over high heat until the sauce has thickened and is smooth. Season well with salt and pepper and stir in the wine, the remaining tablespoon of butter, and the herbs. Cook over medium heat, stirring constantly, for 5 minutes. Cover and set aside.

5. Remove the cooked fish to a serving platter. Brush with the remaining garlic oil. Sprinkle the fish with the parsley and garnish it with the pimiento strips and lemon wedges.

6. Reheat the sauce and serve in a sauceboat with the fish.

*Serving Suggestions:* Mixed Vegetables with Fine Egg Noodles and Prune and Orange Whip.

# Sea Bass à la Reid's Hotel

## Serves 4

The Grill Restaurant at luxurious Reid's Hotel on Madeira prepares this succulent dish totally at tableside, a rapidly dwindling art. The entire cooking time is about 20 minutes. This recipe was adapted from memory after ordering it on two separate evenings.

4   1-inch-thick sea bass
    fillets (about 6 ounces
    each)
    Salt and freshly ground
    black pepper
4   tablespoons butter
1   medium-to-large onion,
    very thinly sliced and
    separated into rings

1   cup homemade fish stock
    or bottled clam juice
2   tablespoons Pernod
1   tablespoon chopped fresh
    parsley leaves

1. Season the fish with salt and pepper.
2. Melt the butter in a large frying pan and add the onion. Cook for 4 minutes, stirring occasionally. Stir in the stock and Pernod.
3. Lay the fish fillets on top of the onions. Sprinkle with the parsley, cover, and simmer for 15 minutes. Serve immediately.

*Variations:* Halibut, cod, scrod, or swordfish can be substituted for the sea bass.
*Serving Suggestions:* Boiled potatoes, green peas, and Zabaglione Coupes.

# Broiled Salmon Steaks with Parsley Butter and Bacon

*Serves 6*

## PARSLEY BUTTER

| | |
|---|---|
| 8 tablespoons (1 stick) butter, softened | ½ cup finely chopped fresh parsley leaves |
| 6 ½-inch-thick strips slab bacon, cut crosswise into ¼-inch strips | 3 tablespoons butter, melted |
| | 1 tablespoon fresh lemon juice |
| 6 1-inch-thick salmon steaks | 2 tablespoons dry sherry |

1. At least 1 hour before cooking the salmon, prepare the Parsley Butter by combining the butter and parsley well in a bowl. Turn the mixture onto a double sheet of plastic wrap and roll it up into a sausage shape about 1½ inches thick. Twist the ends of the plastic wrap to secure the shape, and fold the ends under. Refrigerate the butter until needed.

2. Preheat the broiler.

3. Bring 3 cups of water to a boil in a saucepan. Add the bacon, remove the pan from the heat, and blanch the bacon for 3 minutes. Drain well and pat the bacon dry. Set the bacon aside.

4. Put the salmon steaks in a broiling pan. Combine the melted butter, lemon juice, and sherry. Brush both sides of the salmon with the mixture.

5. Broil the salmon 6 inches away from the flames for about 12 minutes, or until the fish flakes easily.

6. Five minutes before the end of cooking time for the salmon, sauté the bacon until it is golden brown. Garnish each cooked salmon steak with equal-sized slices of the Parsley Butter and equal amounts of the bacon.

*Serving Suggestions:* Creamed Zucchini and Creole Rice.

# Salmon and Sole Fillets on Braised Cabbage with Creamy Buerre Blanc Sauce

*Serves 4*

This recipe is adapted from a dish served at Toit de Passy, a Michelin one star restaurant in Paris' 16th arrondissement. The flavors and textures of the dish make a perfect marriage. It was one of the most memorable dishes sampled on a recent food and wine tour of France.

Toit de Passy also serves an unusual apéritif of combined champagne, blue Curaçao, and William's pear brandy. Once back home, I tried a combination of a glass of champagne and a splash of William's pear brandy, which turned out to be the best of all possible champagne kirs. The blue Curaçao, while good in flavor on its own, made the drink far too strong, not to mention odd in color.

| | |
|---|---|
| 4 tablespoons sweet butter, or as needed | Salt and freshly ground black pepper |
| 3½ cups shredded cabbage | 4 salmon steaks |
| ¼ cup dry white wine | 4 small sole fillets |

## BUERRE BLANC SAUCE

| | |
|---|---|
| 1 tablespoon minced shallots | 3 tablespoons heavy cream |
| 3 tablespoons white wine vinegar | 6 tablespoons butter, cut into 8 pieces |

1. Melt 2 tablespoons of the butter in a saucepan. Add the cabbage and wine and season lightly with salt and pepper. Cover and simmer for 15 minutes.

2. Meanwhile, cut 2 fillet slices from each side of the bone from each salmon steak lengthwise, discarding the bones and skins. Cut each sole fillet in half lengthwise, removing the center cartilage. Pat the fish dry.

3. Melt the remaining 2 tablespoons of butter in a large frying pan and quickly brown the salmon and sole fillets on each side. It will be necessary to cook the fish in 2 batches. Add a little extra butter to the second batch, if necessary. Transfer the cooked fish to a warmed dish and cover it lightly. Keep warm in a low oven.

4. Stir the cabbage and recover the pan.

5. Prepare the sauce: Put the shallots and vinegar in a small saucepan and cook over high heat until the liquid is reduced to about

1 tablespoon. Whisk in the cream. Then whisk in the butter, piece by piece, until all of it is used and the sauce thickens.

6. Put equal portions of the drained cabbage on each of 4 warmed dinner plates. Top each with 2 salmon and 2 sole fillets. Spoon the sauce over the fish and serve immediately.

*Serving Suggestions:* Toit de Passy Apéritif (see recipe in introduction of this recipe), Carrots Vichy, Three-Green Salad with Hazelnut Dressing, and Chocolate Tart.

# Poached Scrod in Crêpes with Red Wine Sauce

### Serves 4

Red wine with fish? Yes. I sampled it in Switzerland last spring at Fredy Giradet's superb restaurant, but the red wine sauce was served with a shellfish. Tested here, with scrod over crêpes, the result was delicious, too.

| | |
|---|---|
| 1 cup bottled clam juice | 4 scrod fillets (about 6 ounces each) |
| 2 medium-sized onions, thinly sliced | 4 crêpes (see recipe page 81) |
| 1 tablespoon chopped fresh parsley leaves | |

## RED WINE SAUCE

| | |
|---|---|
| 1½ tablespoons finely chopped shallots | ½ cup heavy cream |
| ½ cup dry red wine | 4 tablespoons butter, cut into 4 or 5 pieces |

1. Bring the clam juice, onions, and parsley to a boil in a frying pan. Add the fillets, cover, and simmer for 15 minutes. Drain the fillets well, cover, and keep them warm.

2. Meanwhile, put the shallots and red wine in a heavy saucepan. Boil until the mixture is reduced to 2 tablespoons. Whisk in the heavy cream and cook over high heat until the sauce thickens, only a few minutes. Whisk the butter into the sauce, piece by piece.

3. Fold up each scrod fillet in a crêpe and spoon equal amounts of the sauce over the tops. Serve immediately.

*Serving Suggestions:* Risi e Bisi and assorted sorbets with Tuiles.

# Turban of Sole with Salmon Mousse and Hollandaise Sauce

Serves 6

This marvelous and elegant classic dish is one that I have never seen on a restaurant menu or been served in anyone's home. It is certainly not an overcomplicated dish, and it can be prepared an hour in advance of cooking. Whenever I serve it requests for the recipe are followed by "Is it hard to make?" The answer is no, but it will certainly take a little time and care.

## SALMON MOUSSE FILLING

| | | | |
|---|---|---|---|
| ½ | cup homemade fish stock or bottled clam juice | 2 | whole large eggs |
| ½ | cup water | 2 | large egg whites |
| 4 | tablespoons butter, plus extra for butter greasing the mold | 1 | pound fresh salmon, skinned and boned |
| | Salt | | Freshly ground white pepper |
| 1 | cup all-purpose flour | 2 | gratings of nutmeg |
| | | ½ | cup heavy cream |
| 8 | sole fillets | | Butter |

1. Put the stock, water, butter, and ½ teaspoon salt into a saucepan. Bring to a boil and remove from the heat. Immediately add the flour all at once and beat with a wooden spoon until well blended. Beat in 1 whole egg at a time, and then the egg whites, one at a time. This mixture is called a panade.

2. Grind the salmon in a food processor or grinder. Measure the salmon; it should yield about 1½ cups.

3. Measure the same amount of the panade and combine with the salmon in a bowl. Season with salt, white pepper, and nutmeg to taste. Gradually beat in the heavy cream.

4. Preheat the oven to 350 degrees.

5. Grease a 6-cup ring mold well with butter.

6. Season the sole with salt and pepper. Lightly score the skin side of the fillets, and place the fillets at right angles, scored side up, centered, in slightly overlapping layers in the ring mold.

7. Spoon the salmon mousse into the center of the mold and fold the ends of the fillets over the top of the mousse.

8. Butter a piece of foil to fit the top of the mold and cover the mold with it. (At this point the Turban of Sole can be refrigerated for

1 hour before baking, if desired. In which case, don't preheat the oven until 10 minutes before cooking time.)

9. Place the mold in a large pan into which you have poured 1 inch of boiling water. Bake the mold in the pan for 1 hour. Let the mold stand for 5 minutes before unmolding.

10. During the last 5 minutes of baking time for the mold, prepare the Hollandaise Sauce. (Either make the classic or blender sauce. Both are included. If making the blender sauce, prepare it when the mold is removed from the oven.)

11. To unmold the turban, tip it to the side and drain out the accumulated liquid, then invert it onto a round serving dish.

12. Spoon a little of the sauce over the turban and serve the rest in a warmed sauceboat. If desired, fill the center of the turban with washed and dried watercress.

*Serving Suggestions:* Hearts of Palm Salad, sautéed mushrooms, Creole Rice, and Frozen Grand Marnier Soufflé.

# Hollandaise Sauce

### Makes about 1 cup

3 large egg yolks
2 tablespoons cold water
8 tablespoons (1 stick) cold butter, cut into 8 pieces
Pinch of cayenne pepper

1 tablespoon fresh lemon juice
Salt and freshly ground white pepper

Put the eggs in the top of a double boiler over simmering water and whisk until the eggs are lemon-yellow in color. Add the cayenne pepper and lemon juice and heat for 1 minute, whisking constantly. When the mixture begins to thicken, whisk in the butter, piece by piece, until all of it is used and the mixture is thick and creamy. Season with salt and pepper to taste.

*Variation:* To make Curried Hollandaise Sauce, add 2 teaspoons of curry powder with the lemon juice as directed.

# Quick Blender Hollandaise Sauce

*Makes about 1 cup*

| | |
|---|---|
| 3 large egg yolks | ¼ teaspoon salt |
| 1 tablespoon fresh lemon juice | 8 tablespoons (1 stick) hot melted butter |
| Pinch of cayenne pepper | Freshly ground white pepper |

Put the egg yolks, lemon juice, cayenne pepper, and salt in a blender. Cover and turn on low speed. Remove the lid and pour in the hot butter in a slow steady stream. As soon as the butter is added, the sauce is ready. Add white pepper to taste.

# Sautéed Sole and Julienne of Vegetables with Beurre Blanc Sauce

*Serves 6*

| | |
|---|---|
| Salt | 2 tablespoons butter |
| 2 carrots, peeled and cut into julienne strips | 6 sole fillets (about 6 ounces each) |
| 2 medium-sized zucchini, cut into julienne strips | Freshly ground black pepper |
| ½ pound string beans, ends trimmed and cut in half lengthwise | 4 tablespoons clarified butter (see Note) |

## BEURRE BLANC SAUCE

| | |
|---|---|
| ¼ cup dry white wine | 8 tablespoons (1 stick) butter |
| ¼ cup white wine vinegar | |
| 2 tablespoons minced shallots | |

1. Preheat the oven to low.

2. Bring 2 quarts of water to a boil in a large saucepan and add 2 teaspoons of salt. Add the vegetables, return the water to a boil, and cook for 4 minutes. Remove the vegetables with a slotted spoon and set them aside. Leave the water in the saucepan, cover, and simmer.

3. Cut the sole fillets crosswise into 1-inch slices. Season the sole with salt and pepper.

4. Heat the clarified butter in a large frying pan and lightly brown the sole over medium-high heat, cooking half of the fish at a time. Transfer the first batch to a serving platter and keep it warm in the oven. Cook the remaining sole pieces. Transfer the cooked sole to the platter and return it to the oven.

5. Prepare the Beurre Blanc by combining the wine and vinegar with the shallots in a nonstick or enamel saucepan. Reduce the liquid to half over high heat. Lower the heat and whisk in the butter a tablespoon at a time. Set aside.

6. Return the vegetables to the simmering water and cook for 1 minute. Drain the vegetables in a colander and spoon them over the fish in the platter. Spoon the Beurre Blanc over the vegetables and fish. Serve immediately.

NOTE: To make clarified butter melt at least ½ pound of butter in a saucepan over very low heat. Remove the pan from the heat and let it stand. Spoon off the white particles that rise to the top and pour the clear butter into a jar or dish. Leave the white sediment in the bottom of the pan. Clarified butter can be kept for up to 2 weeks in a covered container in the refrigerator.

*Serving Suggestions:* Potato Croquettes and mixed green salad.

## Poached Sole Strips with Orange Sauce

### Serves 4

| | |
|---|---|
| 2 navel oranges | 8 tablespoons (1 stick) |
| 4 sole fillets, cut crosswise | butter, cut into 8 pieces |
| into ½-inch strips | Salt and freshly ground |
| ¼ cup dry white wine | black pepper |
| ½ cup fresh orange juice | |

1. Finely grate the rind from both oranges and blanch it in 1 cup of boiling water for 2 minutes. Drain in a fine mesh strainer and set aside.

2. Bring the wine and 1 cup of water to a boil in a frying pan. Add the sole strips, turn gently, cover, and simmer for 5 minutes. Drain the sole strips and lay them on a warmed serving dish. Cover loosely to keep warm.

3. Pour the orange juice into a heavy saucepan and boil until it

is reduced to about 2 tablespoons. Piece by piece, whisk in the butter, until all is used and the sauce is thickened. Add the reserved orange rind and combine. Spoon the sauce over the sole. Serve immediately.

*Serving Suggestions:* Gruyère, Mushroom, and Celery Salad with Walnut Oil Dressing, Lemon Rice, and buttered green peas.

# Broiled Swordfish Steaks with Lime and Fried Onion Garnish

*Serves 6*

| | |
|---|---|
| 6 1-inch-thick swordfish steaks, (about 6 ounces each) | 2 tablespoons fresh lime juice |
| ⅓ cup olive oil | Freshly ground black pepper |
| 2 tablespoons soy sauce | 6 lime wedges |

### FRIED ONION GARNISH

| | |
|---|---|
| 4 medium-sized onions, very thinly sliced and separated into rings | 2 cups peanut or vegetable oil |

1. Put the swordfish steaks in a shallow dish.
2. Combine the olive oil, soy sauce, and lime juice and pour the mixture over the fish. Sprinkle liberally with freshly ground pepper. Turn the fish to coat each piece evenly. Let it stand at room temperature for 15 minutes. Turn and let stand for 15 minutes longer.
3. Preheat the broiler.
4. Transfer the steaks to a broiling pan and broil 5 to 6 inches below the flame for 12 to 15 minutes, or until the fish flakes easily.
5. After the fish has cooked for 4 minutes, heat the peanut oil to 375 degrees in a large heavy saucepan. Add the onions, stir, and cook until they are golden brown, stirring often. Drain the onions and garnish each swordfish steak with a little mound of the onions and a lime wedge on the side.

*Serving Suggestions:* Melon and prosciutto, herbed rice, Crostini, and Strawberries in Cream.

# Golden Tuna and Macaroni Casserole

### Serves 8

This humble dish falls into the category of simple American home-style cooking: our own peasant food that is delicious, and, therefore, often craved. I adapted this recipe many times during my days in the theater, when I entertained many on a tight budget. In those days buying the fresh mushrooms and almonds were a great extravagance. It remains a favorite and treasured recipe.

| | | | |
|---|---|---|---|
| 1 | pound elbow macaroni | ½ | pound fresh mushrooms, thinly sliced |
| 5 | tablespoons butter | | |
| 1 | medium-to-large onion, chopped | 1 | cup black pitted olives, cut into slivers |
| 2 | celery stalks, chopped | 2 | 7-ounce cans white meat tuna packed in oil, drained |
| 1 | 10-ounce can cream of mushroom soup | | |
| 1 | 10-ounce can golden mushroom soup | ¾ | cup slivered almonds |

1. Cook the macaroni in 3½ quarts of boiling water with 1 tablespoon of salt, stirring occasionally, until *al dente*, or just until tender.

2. Meanwhile, melt 3 tablespoons of the butter in a frying pan and cook the onion and celery for 5 minutes, stirring often.

3. Preheat the oven to 350 degrees.

4. Drain the cooked macaroni and put it in a large bowl with the remaining ingredients, except the almonds, and the onion and celery mixture. Combine well and turn into a 3- or 4-quart casserole.

5. Sprinkle the top of the casserole with the almonds. Dot the remaining 2 tablespoons of the butter over the top. Cover and bake for 15 minutes. Remove the cover and cook for 20 to 25 minutes, or until the top is golden and the casserole bubbles. To further brown the almonds, run the casserole briefly under the broiler.

*Serving Suggestions:* Mixed green salad and a double recipe of Banana Batter Banana Fritters.

# Poultry

Until I was thirteen years old I thought that chicken only came one way—fried. When my family moved from Kansas to Albany, New York, and then to the Chicago suburbs, I had the opportunity to sample many new delicious varieties of chicken dishes. I developed an early passion for all poultry. Today whenever I read a new poultry recipe in the newspaper, a magazine, or a cookbook, or see an interesting poultry dish listed on a restaurant menu, I immediately want to cook the recipe, or order the dish to see what wonderful new things are happening to chicken, Cornish game hens, duck, or turkey. For me, poultry is the most versatile and irresistible entrée.

Universally, chicken has become the basic black dress of meat. It lends itself to all methods of cooking and is enhanced by other flavors such as herbs, spices, vegetables, fruit, and sauces. Chicken is readily available and every portion of the bird can be bought separately and savored. Chicken, inexpensive and nutritious, is also low in calories and fat, and has a unique subtle flavor and texture. The versatility of chicken and poultry also rests in the second chances it gives to the cook, the chance to transform leftovers of yesterday's dinner party into the soups, sandwiches, salads, and stews of today's lunch or dinner.

Serving poultry to company offers a safety that is sometimes not available from other meat or seafood dishes, since most people would put some form of poultry on any list of favorite foods or diets.

# Chicken

## Perfect Butter-roast Chicken

### Serves 4

1  3½-pound roasting
   chicken
   Salt and freshly ground
   black pepper

3  tablespoons butter, softened
   Juice of 1 lemon, at
   room temperature

1. Preheat the oven to 350 degrees.

2. Remove the giblets and save for stuffing or gravy.

3. Season the chicken well with salt and pepper inside and out.
Tie the legs together and fold the wings back. Rub the butter evenly
over the entire surface of the chicken.

4. Put the chicken in a roasting pan and roast for 1½ hours. Don't
open the oven door during the roasting time. Remove the chicken
from the oven and squeeze the lemon juice over the chicken. Let rest
for 10 minutes before quartering or carving.

SPECIAL NOTE: This chicken will have crispy skin and fork-
tender meat. It will be well done, so if a less well done chicken is
desired, simply cook it for only 18 to 20 minutes per pound.

*Variations:* For an aromatic garlic-scented chicken, place 6 halved
garlic cloves in the body cavity before tying the legs together. For
tarragon- or thyme-flavored chicken, stuff the cavity with 6 to 8 fresh
sprigs of either herb before tying the legs together.

*Serving Suggestions:* Sweet Potato Soup and Sautéed Stuffed Zucchini Medallions.

# Roast Chicken Stuffed Under the Skin with Shallots and Herbs

*Serves 6*

## STUFFING

3 tablespoons chopped shallots

¼ cup chopped fresh parsley leaves

1 tablespoon fresh tarragon, or 1 teaspoon dried tarragon

½ cup unseasoned dry bread crumbs (fresh are best)

3 tablespoons butter, melted

Salt and freshly ground black pepper

1 5½-pound roasting chicken

Juice of ½ lemon

Salt and freshly ground black pepper

2 tablespoons butter, softened

1. Preheat the oven to 375 degrees.

2. In a large bowl, combine the stuffing ingredients. Rub the inside of the chicken with the lemon juice and sprinkle it with salt and pepper.

3. Break the membrane at the vent opening at one side of the breast and work your forefinger between the skin and the meat. Work your finger carefully over the breast area, thigh, and leg. Take care not to tear the skin at the vent opening or over the center of the breastbone. Repeat the procedure on the opposite side.

4. A little at a time, spread half the stuffing evenly under the skin over the leg, thigh, and breast on one side of the chicken. Repeat on the other side.

5. Fold the wings back and tie the legs and tail together with kitchen string.

6. Rub the chicken all over with the softened butter and put it in a roasting pan. Roast for 1½ to 1¾ hours, or until the chicken golden all over. To test for doneness, prick the thickest area of the thigh with a fork—if the juices run clear the chicken is done.

*Serving Suggestions:* Hot Cooked Asparagus and Potato Croquettes with Almond Crust.

## Roast Chicken Antibes

*Serves 4*

| | | | |
|---|---|---|---|
| 1 | 3½-pound roasting chicken, quartered with backbone removed | ¼ | cup extra virgin olive oil Juice of 1 lemon, at room temperature |
| ¼ | cup butter, melted | 4 | teaspoons chopped fresh parsley leaves |
| 1 | large garlic clove, crushed Salt and freshly ground black pepper | | |

1. Preheat the oven to 425 degrees.

2. Combine the butter and garlic in a small bowl and let stand for 5 minutes. Strain the butter and brush it liberally over each side of the chicken pieces. Sprinkle the chicken pieces lightly with salt and pepper and put them skin side up in a roasting pan. Roast for 40 minutes, or until the chicken is tender and golden brown.

3. Remove the chicken from the oven and immediately brush with the combined olive oil and lemon juice. Sprinkle each chicken quarter with 1 teaspoon of the parsley and serve immediately.

*Serving Suggestions:* Bobbe Hart's Fresh Mushroom and Three-Cheese Soup, steamed spinach, and baked potatoes.

## Chicken Normandy Style

*Serves 4*

| | | | |
|---|---|---|---|
| 8 | serving pieces chicken (combination of legs, thighs, and breast halves are best) Salt and freshly ground black pepper | 1 | cup apple juice |
| | | ½ | pound fresh mushrooms, sliced |
| | | 2 | cooking apples, peeled, cored, and cut into ¼-inch-thick slices |
| 5 | tablespoons butter | ¼ | cup Calvados |
| 1 | medium-to-large onion, chopped | 2 | tablespoons all-purpose flour |
| 1 | large garlic clove, minced | | |

1. Pat the chicken pieces dry with paper towels. Season them well with salt and pepper.

2. Melt 3 tablespoons of the butter in a large frying pan and brown the chicken on each side over medium heat. Add the onions and garlic and turn the chicken. Pour in the apple juice and bring to a boil, lower the heat, cover, and simmer for 15 minutes.

3. Turn the chicken and add the mushrooms, apples, and Calvados. Cover the pan and simmer for 10 minutes.

4. Transfer the chicken, mushrooms, and apples to a warmed serving dish.

5. Mash together the remaining 2 tablespoons of butter with the flour and whisk it into the sauce over high heat, stirring until the sauce thickens. Season the sauce with salt and pepper to taste and pour it over the chicken, mushrooms, and apples. Serve immediately.

*Serving Suggestions:* Rice Pilaf and Arugola and Endive Salad with Herb Dressing.

# Lemon and Garlic Chicken with Onions

### Serves 4

8 serving pieces chicken (combination of legs, thighs, and breast halves are best)

4 tablespoons butter, softened

1 large garlic clove, crushed

3 medium-sized onions, thinly sliced and separated into rings

1 6-ounce can frozen lemonade concentrate, thawed

¾ cup homemade chicken stock or canned broth

1. In a small bowl, mash together the butter and garlic with a fork. Rub the butter over the chicken pieces.

2. Preheat the oven to 350 degrees.

3. Arrange half the onion rings on the bottom of a 9- by 13-inch baking pan. Put the chicken skin side up over the onions and top with the remaining onions. Combine the lemonade and chicken broth and pour it over the top. Bake for 1 hour, basting with the liquid in the pan twice during the cooking time. If desired, run the cooked chicken in the pan under the broiler for a few minutes for further browning.

*Variation:* This dish can also be made by substituting frozen limeade for the lemonade.

*Serving Suggestions:* Lima Beans with Roast Red Peppers and Skillet Corn Bread.

# Scarpariello Chicken

### Serves 4

8 serving pieces chicken (combination of legs, thighs, and breast halves are best), each cut into 1½-inch pieces with the bones
   Salt and freshly ground black pepper
¼ cup olive oil
2 tablespoons butter
1 teaspoon minced garlic

1 tablespoon fresh lemon juice
1 teaspoon grated lemon rind
½ cup dry white wine
1 tablespoon chopped fresh parsley leaves
½ teaspoon dried rosemary leaves
¼ teaspoon hot red pepper flakes

1. Pat the chicken pieces dry with paper towels and season them well with salt and pepper.

2. Heat the oil and butter in a large frying pan. Add the chicken and cook over medium heat until it is golden on each side and tender.

3. Remove from the heat, add the remaining ingredients, and toss. Return to the heat, and cook over medium heat until the liquid is reduced slightly. Season with salt and pepper to taste.

*Serving Suggestions:* Broccoli and Broken Spaghetti Soup and Grilled Stuffed Tomatoes with Fried Bread Crumbs and Herb Butter.

# Garlic Butter-fried Chicken

### Serves 4

1 teaspoon crushed garlic
8 serving pieces chicken (combination of legs, thighs, and breast halves are best)
   Salt and freshly ground black pepper

   All-purpose flour
¼ cup peanut or vegetable oil
¼ pound (1 stick) unsalted butter

1. Rub the garlic over the chicken pieces and season them with the salt and pepper. Coat the chicken with flour, shaking off any excess.

2. Heat the oil and butter in a large frying pan. Add the chicken and cook over medium heat for 10 minutes. Turn the chicken and cook for 10 minutes longer. Turn the chicken and cook until golden brown and tender, about 10 minutes. Season with salt and pepper to taste.

*Serving Suggestions:* Tomatoes Provençale and Skillet Corn Bread.

# Chicken with Orange and Raisin Sauce

## Serves 4

8   serving pieces chicken
    (combination of legs,
    thighs, and breast
    halves are best)
4   tablespoons butter
1   tablespoon vegetable oil
½   cup fresh orange juice
1   cup homemade chicken
    stock or canned broth
1½  teaspoons fresh lemon
    juice

1   tablespoon grated
    orange rind
    Few gratings of nutmeg
½   cup raisins
2   tablespoons Grand
    Mariner
    Salt and freshly ground
    black pepper

1. Pat the chicken pieces dry with paper towels.

2. Heat 2 tablespoons of the butter and the oil in a large skillet. Brown the chicken on both sides over medium-high heat.

3. Stir the orange juice, stock, lemon juice, orange rind, and nutmeg into the skillet. Bring to a boil, immediately lower the heat, and simmer for 15 minutes. Turn the chicken pieces and sprinkle with the raisins, partially cover, and continue simmering for about 15 minutes, or until the chicken is tender.

4. Transfer the chicken to a heated serving dish and cover to keep it warm. Remove the raisins with a slotted spoon and sprinkle them over the chicken.

5. Add the Grand Marnier to the pan and cook over high heat for 2 minutes. Whisk the remaining 2 tablespoons of butter into the sauce and cook, stirring constantly, over high heat for 2 minutes. Season with salt and pepper to taste. Pour the sauce over the chicken and serve immediately.

*Serving Suggestions:* Minnesota-style Wild Rice and buttered Brussels sprouts.

# Delicious Marinated Barbecued Chicken

*Serves 8*
*(Preparation begins the night before)*

## MARINADE

| | |
|---|---|
| ½ cup fresh lemon juice, warmed | 1 bay leaf, crumbled |
| 2 tablespoons sugar | 1 teaspoon dried basil |
| 1 cup olive oil | 1 teaspoon dried oregano |
| ½ cup dry white wine | 1 teaspoon salt |
| 2 large garlic cloves, crushed | 1 teaspoon paprika |
| 1 medium-sized onion, grated | ½ teaspoon freshly ground black pepper |

| | |
|---|---|
| 5 chicken legs | 3 chicken breasts, split |
| 5 chicken thighs | |

1. The night before serving the meal, pour the warm lemon juice into a large bowl. Add the sugar and stir until it dissolves. Add the remaining marinade ingredients and mix well. Add the chicken, turning to coat it evenly. Cover and refrigerate overnight.

2. Light the fire in your outdoor barbecue.

3. One hour before cooking, remove the chicken from the refrigerator and let it stand at room temperature.

4. Remove the chicken from the marinade and put it on a platter. Strain the marinade and reserve it.

5. Broil the chicken on the grill about 6 inches over the hot coals. Turn and baste the pieces with the marinade occasionally, until the chicken is tender and golden, about 25 to 30 minutes. The breast halves will be done about 5 minutes before the legs and thighs, so remove them when they are cooked. Baste the cooked chicken with the marinade just before serving.

NOTE: Be sure to turn the chicken with tongs and not a fork, because piercing the chicken's skin releases the flavorful delicious juices and also dries out the meat. This chicken dish can also be cooked 6 inches under an oven broiler. Remove the chicken from the marinade and pat dry with paper towels. Turn the chicken every 5 minutes for 25 minutes or until it is tender. Heat marinade and brush it over the chicken before serving.

*Variations:* Instead of white wine use rum in the marinade. It is also possible to substitute equal amounts of a variety of other herbs, such as rosemary, thyme, tarragon, dill, etc., for the basil and oregano.

*Serving Suggestions:* Potato Salad with Dill Dressing, a double recipe of Corn on the Cob with Chili Butter, and Prize-winning Carrot Cake.

# Chicken à l'Orange

### Serves 4

Sometimes the simplest recipes with the fewest ingredients become the most requested recipes by our families. Here is just such a recipe.

| | |
|---|---|
| 2 *tablespoons butter* | 1 *tablespoon grated orange rind* |
| 1 *tablespoon peanut or vegetable oil* | ½ *cup fresh orange juice* |
| 8 *serving pieces chicken (combination of legs, thighs, and breast halves are best)* | 1 *teaspoon fresh lemon juice* |
| | 1 *tablespoon arrowroot or cornstarch* |
| 1 *cup rich homemade chicken stock or canned broth* | *Salt and freshly ground black pepper* |

1. In a large frying pan, heat the butter and oil.

2. Pat the chicken pieces dry with paper towels and brown them well on each side. Transfer the chicken to a plate.

3. Add the stock, orange rind, orange juice, and lemon juice to the pan. Bring the mixture to a boil, stirring to release any food particles on the bottom of the pan. Return the chicken to the pan, lower the heat, and simmer for 15 minutes. Turn the chicken pieces and simmer about 10 minutes longer, or until the chicken is fork-tender.

4. Transfer the chicken to a warmed serving dish and cover to keep it warm.

5. Dissolve the cornstarch in a little water and add the mixture to the pan. Cook over high heat, stirring, until the sauce thickens. Season with salt and pepper to taste. Pour the sauce over the chicken and serve immediately.

*Serving Suggestions:* Buttered beets and Individual Roesti Potatoes.

# Oven-baked Ginger Chicken

*Serves 4*

8  serving pieces chicken
   (combination of legs,
   thighs, breast halves,
   and wings)
3  tablespoons soy sauce
⅓  cup honey
¼  cup light rum
1  tablespoon fresh lime
   juice

½  cup homemade chicken
   stock or canned broth
2  tablespoons chopped
   onion
2  garlic cloves, chopped
1½ teaspoons grated fresh
   ginger
   Freshly ground black
   pepper to taste

1. Preheat the oven to 350 degrees.
2. Put the chicken in a shallow baking dish skin side up.
3. Combine the remaining ingredients in a blender and pour the mixture over the chicken. Bake for 1 hour, or until chicken is tender. Baste twice during cooking time. Baste again liberally with liquid in the pan just before serving.

*Serving Suggestions:* Zucchini and Carrots Julienne and Frozen Piña Colada Ice Cream Cake.

# Crisp-fried Pepper Chicken

*Serves 4*

1  3-pound frying chicken,
   cut into serving pieces
1  cup all-purpose flour
1½ teaspoons seasoned salt
1  teaspoon paprika

1  teaspoon freshly ground
   black pepper
1½ cups vegetable oil
4  tablespoons butter

1. Rinse the chicken pieces. Put the flour, seasoned salt, paprika, and pepper in a plastic bag and shake to mix well.
2. Heat the oil and butter in a large skillet.
3. Drop a piece of chicken into the flour mixture, hold the top of the bag closed, and shake, coating the chicken well. Shake off any excess flour and lay the chicken in the hot oil and butter skin side down. Repeat this procedure until all the chicken is coated and in the skillet.

4. Cook over medium-high heat for 12 minutes, or until the chicken is lightly golden. Turn the chicken and lower the heat to medium. Cook for 10 minutes, turn again, and cook until the chicken is golden brown and tender, about 8 to 10 minutes.

*Variation:* The flour mixture with pepper is also a fine breading for fish fillets, such as flounder or cod. Fry the fish, turning it twice, for about 12 minutes total cooking time.

*Serving Suggestions:* Phyllis' Potato Salad and Cold Marinated Zucchini.

## Creamy Chicken Cacciatore

### Serves 4

| | |
|---|---|
| 3 tablespoons olive oil | 1½ cups homemade chicken stock or canned broth |
| 4 chicken breasts, quartered | ¼ cup dry white wine |
| 4 chicken thighs, each cut in half crosswise | ½ teaspoon dried thyme |
| | 1 teaspoon dried basil |
| 1 large onion, thinly sliced | 1 bay leaf |
| | 1 cup heavy cream |
| 2 large garlic cloves, minced | Salt and freshly ground black pepper |
| 2 sweet green peppers, seeded and cut into thin strips | 3 tablespoons butter, softened |
| 1 cup chopped canned tomatoes with liquid | 2 tablespoons all-purpose flour |

1. Heat the oil in a large frying pan. Add the chicken pieces and turn them in the oil in the pan. Brown the chicken on each side over medium-high heat.

2. Add the onion, garlic, and peppers. Stir and cook for 10 minutes over medium heat. Add the tomatoes, stock, wine, herbs, and bay leaf. Bring to a boil, lower the heat, and simmer for 20 minutes, partially covered, or until the chicken is tender.

3. Bring the cream to a boil in a saucepan and add it to the chicken mixture. Stir and season with salt and pepper to taste.

4. Mash the butter and flour together with a fork and stir it into the cacciatore. Cook over medium-high heat for 2 or 3 minutes, stirring often, until slightly thickened. Discard the bay leaf before serving.

*Serving Suggestions:* Hot cooked spaghetti with butter, Parmesan cheese, and parsley, mixed green salad with Italian vinaigrette dressing, and Cheesecake.

# Paella

### Serves 8

| | |
|---|---|
| 4 sweet Italian sausages | ½ teaspoon ground saffron |
| 3 large chicken breasts, halved and cut crosswise into 3 pieces each | 1 teaspoon paprika |
| | ⅛ teaspoon hot red pepper flakes |
| | Salt and freshly ground black pepper |
| ½ cup olive oil | |
| 3 loin pork chops, boned and cut into 1-inch cubes | 4½ cups homemade chicken stock or canned broth |
| 2 large garlic cloves | 2½ cups long-grain rice |
| 1 cup chopped onion | 1 10-ounce package green peas, thawed |
| 1 medium-sized sweet green pepper, seeded and diced | 1 pound large shrimp, shelled and deveined |
| 1 cup drained chopped canned tomatoes | 1 large pimiento, cut into strips |

1. Prick the sausages on all sides with a fork. Put the sausages in a saucepan with 2 inches of boiling water and simmer for 10 minutes.

2. Meanwhile, pat the chicken pieces dry with paper towels.

3. Heat ¼ cup of the olive oil in a large frying pan and brown the chicken pieces on both sides over medium-high heat.

4. Remove the sausages, drain, and cool on a large plate.

5. Transfer the browned chicken to the plate with the sausages.

6. Add the remaining ¼ cup of olive oil to the frying pan and add the pork cubes, garlic, onion, and green pepper. Cook for 5 minutes over medium heat, stirring often.

7. Add the tomatoes, saffron, paprika, red pepper flakes and season lightly with salt and pepper. Simmer for 10 minutes.

8. Preheat the oven to 400 degrees.

9. Bring the stock to a boil in a saucepan.

10. Put the onion and pork mixture into a paella pan or 4-quart shallow ovenproof casserole or baking dish.

11. Cut the sausages into ¼-inch-thick slices and add them to the pan with the rice, chicken, and green peas.

12. Pour the boiling stock over the mixture and combine gently.

13. Press the shrimp down into the mixture around the edge of the pan. Bake for 30 minutes, or until the rice is tender.

14. Remove from the oven and garnish the top with the strips of pimiento. Allow the paella to stand for 10 minutes before serving.

*Serving Suggestions:* A double recipe of Cold Fresh Lemon Soup, mixed green salad with Sherry Vinegar Dressing, and vanilla ice cream with Kahlua and toasted almonds.

# *Broiled Chicken Sates*

## *Serves 4*

| | |
|---|---|
| *3 large chicken breasts, skinned, boned, and halved* | *1 tablespoon grated onion* |
| | *1 large garlic clove, crushed* |
| *½ cup olive oil* | *Freshly ground black pepper to taste* |
| *¼ cup honey* | |
| *¼ cup soy sauce* | *1 tablespoon sesame seeds, toasted* |
| *3 tablespoons dry sherry* | |

1. Cut the chicken breast halves crosswise into 4 equal-sized pieces.

2. In a large bowl, combine the oil, honey, soy sauce, sherry, onion, garlic, and pepper. Add the chicken pieces and turn to coat them well. Cover and refrigerate overnight.

3. When ready to cook, preheat the broiler.

4. Thread 6 pieces of the chicken on each of 6 10-inch wooden skewers and broil 5 or 6 inches from the heat for about 5 minutes per side.

5. Meanwhile, heat the marinade in a saucepan. Brush the cooked sates with the hot marinade and sprinkle with the toasted sesame seeds. Serve immediately.

*Serving Suggestions:* Lemon Rice, Zucchini and Carrots Julienne and, Coconut–Buttermilk Tart.

# Curried Lime Chicken Breasts

*Serves 4*

## CURRIED LIME SAUCE

2    teaspoons Dijon mustard
     Juice of 2 limes
     Grated rind of 1 lime
½    cup honey
1    tablespoon curry powder
2    dashes of Tabasco sauce
¼    teaspoon salt, if desired
     Freshly ground black
     pepper to taste

2    scallions, very thinly
     sliced
1    garlic clove, minced
1    medium-sized apple,
     peeled, cored, and finely
     chopped

4    medium-sized chicken
     breasts, boned and
     halved

**Butter for greasing the
baking dish**

1. Mix together the sauce ingredients in a large bowl. Add the chicken pieces and turn them to coat them evenly. Cover and marinate at room temperature for 15 minutes.

2. Preheat the oven to 350 degrees.

3. Grease a shallow baking dish large enough to hold the chicken pieces in a single layer. Put the chicken in the dish skin side down.

4. Spoon half of the sauce over the chicken, cover the dish, and bake for 30 minutes. Turn the chicken and spoon the remaining sauce over the pieces. Bake, uncovered, for 25 to 30 minutes longer, or until the chicken is fork-tender.

*Serving Suggestions:* Rice with Vegetables and Cream and Coconut–Buttermilk Tart.

# Sautéed Chicken Rosemary

## Serves 4

3 large chicken breasts, skinned, boned, and halved
Salt and freshly ground black pepper
All-purpose flour
¼ cup olive oil
1 cup thinly sliced onion
2 large garlic cloves

¾ cup dry white wine
1 cup homemade chicken stock or canned broth
2 teaspoons fresh rosemary, or 1 teaspoon dried rosemary
3 tablespoons butter, cut into 5 or 6 pieces

1. Cut the chicken breast halves crosswise into 3 equal-sized pieces. Season the chicken well with salt and pepper and dust it with flour.

2. Heat the oil in a large frying pan and brown the chicken, half at a time, on each side. Remove the chicken to a plate.

3. Add the onion and garlic to the pan and cook over medium heat for 5 minutes, stirring often. Return the chicken to the pan and add the wine, stock, and rosemary. Bring to a boil, lower the heat to medium, and cook for about 15 minutes.

4. Transfer the chicken to a warmed serving dish and stir the butter into the sauce. Continue stirring until the butter is thoroughly combined with the sauce. Spoon the sauce over the chicken. Serve immediately.

*Serving Suggestions:* Risi e Bisi and tomato and red onion salad.

# Sautéed Chicken Breast Scallops with Honey Butter

*Serves 4*

## HONEY BUTTER

6 tablespoons butter, softened

2 tablespoons honey

## CHICKEN SCALLOPS

4 medium-sized chicken breasts, skinned, boned, and halved
Salt and freshly ground black pepper
All-purpose flour

2 tablespoons butter, or as needed
2 tablespoons peanut oil, or as needed
1 tablespoon chopped fresh parsley leaves

1. Combine the butter and honey well, cover, and refrigerate until needed.

2. Put each breast half between 2 pieces of wax paper and flatten it to a ¼-inch thickness. Season the flattened chicken lightly with salt and pepper. Coat the scallops with flour and shake off any excess.

3. Heat the butter and oil in a large frying pan and cook the chicken 2 or 3 pieces at a time until it is golden brown on each side. Transfer the cooked chicken to an ovenproof platter and keep it warm in a 250-degree oven. Finish cooking the remaining chicken, adding 1 or 2 tablespoons of equal amounts of butter and oil as needed.

4. Spread 1 tablespoon of Honey Butter over each piece of cooked chicken and arrange them on a platter. Sprinkle with parsley and serve immediately

*Serving Suggestions:* Black Bean Soup with Sherry, Sour Cream, and Avocado, Carrots Vichy, and Buñeulos.

# Chicken Torcello

*Serves 4*

2 large chicken breasts, skinned, boned, and halved
Salt and freshly ground black pepper
2 tablespoons vegetable oil
2 tablespoons butter
1 large garlic clove, minced
½ pound fresh mushrooms, cut into ¼-inch-thick slices
2 tablespoons minced shallots
½ cup dry white wine
¾ cup heavy cream
½ cup coarsely chopped sun-dried tomatoes (see Note)

1. Put each chicken breast half between 2 pieces of wax paper and flatten it to a ⅛-inch thickness. Cut each piece in half. Pat the chicken pieces dry with paper towels and sprinkle them lightly with salt and pepper.

2. Heat the oil and butter in a large frying pan and brown the chicken on each side. (You may have to do this in 2 batches.) Transfer the cooked chicken to a plate.

3. Add the garlic and mushrooms to the frying pan and cook over medium-high heat for 5 minutes, stirring often. Transfer the mushrooms and garlic to the plate with the chicken.

4. Add the shallots to the frying pan and cook, stirring, for 1 minute. Add the wine and bring it to a boil. Reduce it to half and stir in the cream. Cook over high heat, stirring constantly, until the sauce thickens, about 4 minutes.

5. Stir the sun-dried tomatoes into the sauce and return the mushrooms and garlic to the pan. Turn the chicken pieces and stir the sauce to combine it. Simmer for 5 minutes.

NOTE: Sun-dried tomatoes are available in specialty food stores or Italian markets.

*Serving Suggestions:* Buttered fine egg noodles, sautéed baby zucchini, and Zabaglione Coupes.

# Chicken Club Sandwiches

## Serves 4

After a six-hour grueling, fascinating drive from Fez to Marrakesh, four tired and hungry people arrived at the Mamounia hotel. It was mid-afternoon, and the hotel's restaurant had just closed. Famished, but looking forward to a Moroccan dinner, we ordered club sandwiches from room service.

The sandwiches arrived on a huge oval silverplate platter around a mountain of tiny fresh fried potato chips, still warm. The sandwiches and chips were superb in their simplicity and quality. Although we gazed from our balcony out over the date palms, the sandwiches reminded us all of the club sandwiches served in the dining room cars on the trains of yesteryear back at home. The combination of the sandwiches and the chips provides a lovely simple luncheon any time of the year, especially if a more elaborate dinner is planned. Club Sandwiches are easy to prepare, of course. They are included here as a reminder of the correct formula, and because they are frequently requested by weekend guests.

| | |
|---|---|
| 12 slices firm white bread | 12 slices crisp-cooked bacon, |
| 3 tablespoons unsalted | well drained |
| butter, softened | 8 slices firm ripe tomato |
| Mayonnaise | Freshly ground black |
| 4 Boston lettuce leaves | pepper |
| 8 slices cooked chicken | |
| breast | |

1. Spread 4 slices of the bread on both sides with the butter and set aside.

2. Spread mayonnaise on one side of the remaining 8 slices of bread.

3. Top 4 slices of bread spread with mayonnaise with a lettuce leaf and 2 slices of the chicken. Top the chicken with 1 slice of the buttered bread for each sandwich.

4. Lay 3 bacon strips over the top of the bread for each sandwich and then top with 2 tomato slices each. Sprinkle with pepper and cover with the remaining bread slices.

5. Cut each sandwich in half crosswise twice, making 4 triangles. Secure each triangle with a toothpick placed in the center of each. Place on a platter cut side up.

*Serving Suggestions:* Fresh Potato Chips, iced tea, and fruit in season.

# Turkey

## Roast Turkey Breast Cooked with Wine and Aromatic Vegetables

*Serves 8*

1   7-pound turkey breast
    Salt and freshly ground
    black pepper
3   tablespoons butter,
    softened
2   cups homemade chicken
    stock or canned broth
2   cups dry white wine
2   medium-sized onions,
    quartered

2   carrots, sliced
2   celery stalks, sliced
1   turnip, peeled and sliced
1/4 teaspoon dried thyme
1   bay leaf
1   teaspoon whole black
    peppercorns

1. Preheat the oven to 350 degrees.

2. Season the turkey all over with salt and pepper and rub with the butter.

3. Put the stock, wine, vegetables, thyme, bay leaf, and peppercorns in a medium-sized roasting pan. Lay the turkey breast on top. Bake for about 2 hours, basting twice with the pan juices during the cooking time.

4. Remove the cooked turkey to a carving platter, cover it loosely with foil, and let it rest for 30 minutes before slicing.

*Serving Suggestions:* Gougère Puffs, Norman Hodgson's Mustard Sauce, Pasta Primavera with Crisp Bacon Strips, Emily McCormack's Tomatoes, and Nancy Dussault's Deluxe Monkey Bread.

# Roast Turkey with Pilgrim Stuffing and Homemade Giblet Gravy

### Serves 8 to 10

1 14- to 15-pound turkey
Salt and freshly ground
black pepper
8 tablespoons (1 stick)
butter
1 cup chopped onion
2 celery stalks, chopped
1 16-ounce package
cornbread stuffing mix

1 10-ounce package frozen
corn kernels, thawed
1 cup hot homemade
chicken stock or canned
broth, or as needed
3 tablespoons vegetable oil

### HOMEMADE GIBLET GRAVY

Turkey giblets, chopped
6 chicken wings
1 medium-to-large onion,
chopped
2 carrots, chopped
2 celery stalks, chopped
2 turnips, peeled and
quartered
6 sprigs fresh parsley
½ teaspoon dried thyme
½ cup dry white wine

1 quart homemade chicken
stock or canned broth
1 quart water
1 tablespoon salt
Freshly ground black
pepper to taste
2 tablespoons all-purpose
flour
3 tablespoons butter,
softened

1. Preheat the oven to 325 degrees.

2. Remove the giblets from the turkey and reserve for the gravy. Season the turkey inside and out, including the neck cavity, with salt and pepper.

3. Melt the butter in a large frying pan. Add the onion and celery and cook for 5 minutes, stirring often.

4. Put the stuffing mix in a large bowl and add the onion and celery mixture, corn, and stock. Combine well, adding a little more stock, if necessary, so that the stuffing is moist, but not soggy.

5. Stuff the body and neck cavities of the turkey. Tie the legs together. Fold the neck skin over the stuffing onto the back of the turkey and secure it with a small metal skewer or 2 toothpicks.

6. Put the bird in a large roasting pan and rub it all over with the oil. Roast for about 4 to 5 hours, or until tender, basting twice during the cooking time. Test for doneness by piercing the thickets area of the thigh; if the juice runs clear, the turkey is done. The legs should also move freely if the bird is cooked.

7. When the turkey is sufficiently browned, cover it loosely with buttered foil.

8. Meanwhile, make the gravy: Put all the ingredients, except the flour and butter, into a Dutch oven or large pot. Bring to a boil, lower the heat, and simmer for 2 hours. (This should yield about 3½ cups of liquid.) Strain the liquid into a bowl and set it aside until the turkey is cooked.

9. When the turkey is cooked, remove it to a serving platter, cover it loosely with foil, and let it rest for 30 minutes before carving. This is imperative. If the turkey is carved right after it is taken from the oven, the meat will crumble.

10. Meanwhile, pour off the fat from the roasting pan. Pour in the gravy liquid and cook over high heat, stirring to release the browned particles in the bottom of the pan.

11. Mash the flour and butter together with a fork and whisk it into the gravy. Whisk until the gravy thickens. Season it with salt and pepper to taste. Serve the hot gravy in a warmed sauceboat with the turkey and stuffing.

*Serving Suggestions:* Diane Terman's Shrimp in Dill Sauce, mashed potatoes, a double recipe of Buttered Brussels Sprouts with Bacon, Double Cranberry Mold, Sweet Potato Biscuits, and Vanilla Cake with Butter Pecan Frosting.

# Cornish Game Hens

## High-temperature Roast Cornish Game Hens

### Serves 6

This dish requires only 30 minutes of cooking time at 500 degrees. The meat of the Cornish hens is succulent and the skin crisp. It's a good dish for a first-rate quick dinner.

6   Cornish game hens (fresh if possible), without giblets
    Salt and freshly ground black pepper
1   tablespoon dried tarragon
12  shallots, peeled and left whole
3   tablespoons vegetable oil
4   tablespoons butter, melted
    Chopped fresh parsley leaves

1. Preheat the oven to 500 degrees.
2. Season the hens well in the body cavities and add equal amounts of the tarragon. Put 2 shallots in each cavity. Tie the legs together and fold the wings back.
3. Put the hens in a roasting pan and brush each with oil. Roast in the oven for 30 minutes.
4. Remove the hens from the oven and brush with the butter and sprinkle with parsley. Serve immediately.

*Serving Suggestions:* String Beans with Walnuts and Zabaglione Coupes.

# Roast Cornish Hens with Sauerkraut Stuffing

*Serves 6*

6  Cornish game hens
   (fresh if possible),
   without giblets
   Salt and freshly ground
   black pepper
4  tablespoons butter
1  medium-sized onion,
   thinly sliced and
   separated into rings

1½  cups drained
    sauerkraut
1   teaspoon caraway seeds
    Paprika

1. Preheat the oven to 400 degrees.

2. Season the hens inside and out with salt and pepper.

3. Melt 2 tablespoons of the butter in a large frying pan. Add the onions and cook over medium heat for 5 minutes, stirring often.

4. Meanwhile, rinse the sauerkraut under running water in a strainer and drain it well. Add the sauerkraut and caraway seeds to the onions and combine. Stuff the hens with equal amounts of the mixture.

5. Tie each hen's legs together and fold the wings back.

6. Put the hens in a roasting pan. Rub the remaining 2 tablespoons of butter over the hens and sprinkle them lightly with paprika. Cook for 1 hour, or until the hens are golden brown and tender.

*Serving Suggestions:* Cream of Carrot Soup, buttered string beans, and Chocolate Mousse.

# Tandoori Roast Cornish Game Hens with Fried Onion Rings

*Serves 4*
*(Preparation begins the night before)*

4 Cornish game hens (fresh if possible), without giblets
2 large garlic cloves, minced
1½ teaspoons ground cumin
1½ teaspoons ground turmeric
1½ teaspoons ground cinnamon
1½ teaspoons ground ginger
2 teaspoons ground coriander
Pinch of cayenne pepper
¼ cup fresh lime juice
1½ cups plain yogurt

Salt and freshly ground black pepper
4 tablespoons sweet butter, melted
Peanut or vegetable oil for deep frying, plus extra for greasing the roasting pan
2 medium-sized onions, thinly sliced and separated into rings
4 slices white bread, toasted and crusts trimmed
1 lime, cut into 4 slices and seeded

1. Tie each hen's legs together and fold the wings back.

2. In a large bowl, combine the garlic, spices, lime juice, and yogurt well. Season the mixture with salt and pepper to taste. Roll the hens in the mixture, completely covering them. Put the hens in a shallow dish. Pour any leftover marinade over the hens, cover, and refrigerate overnight.

3. Turn the hens in the morning, cover, and refrigerate.

4. Preheat the oven to 375 degrees.

5. Lightly grease a roasting pan with oil. Place the hens in the roasting pan breast side up without allowing the hens to touch. Sprinkle 1 tablespoon of the melted butter over each hen. Roast for 1 hour and 10 minutes.

6. Ten minutes before the hens are cooked, heat 1½ inches of oil to 375 degrees in a large heavy saucepan. Fry the onion rings all at once, stirring often, until they are golden brown, about 5 minutes. Remove the onions and drain on paper towels. Separate the onions into 4 equal portions.

7. Serve each cooked hen on a slice of the toast and place 1 portion of the onions alongside each hen. Top the hens with a lime slice and serve immediately.

*Serving Suggestions:* Individual Composed Salads, Rice Pilaf, and Cantaloupe, Raspberries, and Oranges with Framboise.

# Braised Cornish Game Hens with Lemon–Cream Sauce

*Serves 4*

| | |
|---|---|
| 4 Cornish game hens (fresh if possible), without giblets Salt and freshly ground black pepper | ½ teaspoon dried thyme 1½ cups homemade chicken stock or canned broth |
| 3 tablespoons unsalted butter | ½ cup dry white wine 1 cup heavy cream |
| 1 medium-to-large onion, quartered | 3 large egg yolks 1 tablespoon fresh lemon juice |
| 2 garlic cloves, halved | Chopped fresh parsley leaves |
| 1 bay leaf | |

1. Season the hens inside and out with salt and pepper and truss them.

2. Melt the butter in a large heavy flameproof casserole and brown the hens lightly on the breast sides.

3. Turn the hens over on their backs and add the onion, garlic, bay leaf, and thyme to the casserole. Add the chicken stock and wine and bring to a boil. Cover and simmer for about 40 minutes, or until the hens are tender.

4. Remove the hens to a large warmed serving dish. Remove the trussing strings and cover the hens loosely with foil to keep them warm.

5. Strain the liquid from the casserole into a large saucepan. Discard the solids. Over high heat reduce the liquid to half, about 1 cup.

6. Combine the cream with the egg yolks. Spoon several tablespoons of the hot liquid from the pan into the cream mixture and combine well. Lower the heat under the pan to low, and whisk in the cream mixture. Do not allow the sauce to boil. Add the lemon juice and season with salt and pepper to taste. Whisk constantly until the sauce thickens and is smooth.

7. Spoon a few tablespoons of the sauce over the hens and sprinkle them with parsley. Serve the remaining sauce in a warmed sauceboat.

*Serving Suggestions:* Hot Cooked Asparagus and Potato Croquettes.

# Roast Cornish Game Hens with Leek and Rosemary Stuffing

### Serves 4

4   Cornish game hens (fresh
    if possible), without
    giblets
    Salt and freshly ground
    black pepper
1   cup thinly sliced leeks,
    white parts only (about 2
    leeks)

1   teaspoon dried rosemary
1   tablespoon chopped fresh
    parsley leaves
4   tablespoons butter, melted

1. Preheat the oven to 400 degrees.
2. Season the hens inside and out with salt and pepper.
3. In a bowl, combine the leeks, rosemary, parsley, and 3 tablespoons of the butter. Stuff the hens with equal amounts of the mixture.
4. Tie each hen's legs together and fold the wings back. Put the hens in a roasting pan and brush with the remaining tablespoon of butter. Roast for 1 hour, or until the hens are golden brown and tender.

*Serving Suggestions:* Rice with Vegetables and Cream and Cold Lemon Mousse with Raspberry Sauce.

# Duck

## Roast and Braised Duck Quarters with Sausages

### Serves 4

| | |
|---|---|
| 1 4½- to 4-pound duck | 1 tablespoon all-purpose |
| Salt and freshly ground | flour |
| black pepper | 1½ cups homemade chicken |
| 2 tablespoons butter | stock or canned broth |
| 1 tablespoon minced | ¼ cup Madeira |
| shallots | 4 Italian sweet sausages |

1. Preheat the oven to 450 degrees.

2. Cut off the duck's cavity fat and wing tips. Season the body cavity with salt and pepper.

3. Put the duck in a roasting pan and roast for 30 minutes.

4. Meanwhile, melt the butter in a heavy saucepan. Add the shallots and cook over medium heat for 5 minutes. Whisk in the flour and cook for 1 minute. Add the stock and Madeira and bring to a boil. Lower the heat and simmer for 15 minutes. Season with salt and pepper to taste.

5. After the duck has roasted for 30 minutes, remove it and cut it into quarters. Place the quarters in a heavy casserole. Pour the sauce over the duck, cover, and place in the oven. Lower the oven temperature to 350 degrees and roast for 45 minutes.

6. Fifteen minutes before the duck is done sauté the sausages until they are golden brown. Quarter the sausages and serve them with the duck.

*Serving Suggestions:* Zucchini Robinson and Watercress and Orange Salad with Puréed Scallion Dressing.

# Peking Duck
## Serves 4

1  5-pound duck
2  quarts water
½  cup honey
1  cup hoisin sauce
   (available in Oriental
   grocery stores)

8  scallions

### PANCAKES

2  cups sifted all-purpose
   flour
⅔  cup hot water, or as
   needed

Peanut oil

1. Cut off the fat from the duck's body cavity opening.
2. Bring the water to a boil in a large pot. Stir in the honey. Put the duck in the water and roll it over to coat it completely. Immediately remove the duck, drain, and cool slightly.
3. Tie a piece of kitchen string around the neck fat or under the wings and hang the duck up. The easiest place is from a kitchen cabinet knob. Place a bowl under the duck to collect any drippings. Let the duck hang for 4 hours, or put a fan on the duck for 2 hours to dry out the skin. This procedure is essential for a successful Peking Duck.
4. Preheat the oven to 400 degrees.
5. Put the duck on a rack in the oven with a roasting pan containing 1 inch of boiling water resting on the floor of the oven directly below the duck. Roast the duck for 1 hour and 15 minutes, or until it is tender and the skin is very crisp and golden brown.
6. Meanwhile, pour the hoisin sauce into a serving bowl, cover, and set aside.
7. Prepare the scallion brushes by cutting off each root end and all but 1 inch of the greens. The scallion should be about 3½ inches long. Cut through 1 inch of both ends of each scallion; turn and cut through the same length at the opposite angle. Separate the layers with your fingers and put the scallions in a bowl of ice water. Cover and refrigerate. (The ends will curl up.)
8. Then make the pancakes: Combine the flour and water in a large bowl to form a soft pliable dough. Knead the dough on a lightly floured surface for 5 minutes, cover and let rest for 15 minutes.
9. Roll the dough into a circle ¼ inch thick and cut with a 2-inch

cutter. Reshape the dough and make more 2-inch rounds. The dough should make 10 to 12 pancakes.

10. Brush oil lightly on top of half of the circles. Place the unoiled circles on top of the oiled ones and roll out to about 6 inches a pair.

11. Heat a wok or skillet and lightly cook the double pancakes quickly, about 15 seconds per side, until they are light brown. Separate the pancakes, cover, and wrap in aluminum foil.

12. When the duck is cooked, remove it from the oven to a carving board. Put the pancakes, still in the foil, in the turned-off hot oven. Drain the scallions and pat them dry with paper towels.

13. To carve the duck, first cut off the legs using a circular motion to separate them from the body and set them aside. With kitchen scissors, cut off the crisp skin from the breast area, sides, and back. Cut the skin into even rectangular pieces. Scrape off and discard any fat. Set the skin aside. Cut the breast halves off the duck and cut into ½- by 1-inch pieces.

14. Put the meat on a warmed serving platter with the drumsticks. Decorate the platter with the crisp skin pieces and scallion brushes. Serve with the hoisin sauce and pancakes.

15. To serve, let each guest take a pancake and a scallion brush. The brush is used to spread hoisin sauce over the pancake. Then the scallion brush is put in the center of the pancake with a piece of crisp skin and a piece of meat. One end of the pancake is turned up over the ingredients and the pancake is then rolled up or folded envelope-style.

*Serving Suggestions:* Chinese Velvet Corn Soup, Mixed Vegetables with Fine Egg Noodles, Bibb lettuce salad, and Fresh French Apple–Hazelnut Tart with Frangelico Whipped Cream.

# Duck à l'Orange

*Serves 4*

## DUCK STOCK

Giblets from a 5-pound
duck
4 chicken wings
1 bay leaf
2 celery stalks, sliced
1 carrot, sliced
1 medium-sized onion,
coarsely chopped

1 large turnip, peeled and
coarsely chopped
1 garlic clove, chopped
6 sprigs fresh parsley
½ teaspoon dried thyme
10 whole black peppercorns
2 teaspoons salt
1 quart water

## DUCK

1 5-pound duck, cavity fat
removed
Salt and freshly ground
black pepper
Peel of 1 orange
6 navel oranges
1 lemon
¼ cup sugar
¼ cup red wine vinegar

2 cups duck stock (recipe
above)
1 tablespoon cornstarch
3 tablespoons Grand
Marnier or Cointreau
¾ cup dry white wine
2 tablespoons butter, cut
into small pieces

1. Preheat the oven to 375 degrees.

2. Prepare the Duck Stock: Put all the ingredients in a heavy saucepan. Bring the mixture to a boil, lower the heat, and simmer for 1¼ hours.

3. Cut the wing tips off the duck and add them to the stock. Season the body cavity well with salt and pepper. Put the whole orange peel in the cavity. Prick the duck all over, except for the breast area, with the sharp point of a knife.

4. Put the duck in a roasting pan and roast for 30 minutes. Lower the oven temperature to 350 degrees and roast for 1 hour, or until the juice from the thigh area runs clear when pricked and the skin is golden brown.

5. Meanwhile, peel the outer orange skin from 2 of the oranges and the lemon. Squeeze the juice from the fruit into a bowl. Also squeeze the juice from the peeled rind in the duck's cavity into the bowl.

6. Cut the zest into fine julienne strips. Put the strips into 2 cups of boiling water in a saucepan and cook over medium-low heat for 5 minutes. Drain and pat dry. Set aside.

7. Peel the skin and white membrane from the remaining 4 oranges and cut each into sections. Set aside.

8. Melt the sugar in a saucepan over medium heat. When it begins to turn light brown, whisk in the vinegar. Remove the pan from the heat and add the combined orange and lemon juice. Strain the stock and add it to the orange mixture.

9. Dissolve the cornstarch in the Grand Marnier and stir into the liquid. Boil and whisk until the sauce thickens slightly. Season with salt and pepper to taste. Cover and remove from the heat.

10. Transfer the cooked duck to a carving platter.

11. Pour out the fat from the pan. Add the wine to the pan and bring to a boil, scraping up any particles in the bottom of the pan. Immediately strain the liquid into the sauce and bring to a boil. Whisk the butter into the sauce.

12. Carve the duck and arrange it on a heated serving platter. Garnish the duck with the orange strips and orange sections. Spoon a few tablespoons of the sauce over the duck and serve the remainder in a sauceboat.

*Serving Suggestions:* Minnesota-style Wild Rice, Red Cabbage and Cranberry Sauce, and buttered green peas.

# Meat

The key to cooking meat fearlessly is having a dependable butcher, or a reliable supermarket where quality meat can be found. The second most important element in meat cookery is selecting the proper cut for the dish you are going to prepare. There is an infinite variety of beef, veal, pork, and lamb steaks and roasts, chops and racks, plus boneless meat whole and rolled or stuffed, cut into scallops, ground, butterflied, or cut into small pieces.

Selecting the right meat dish to serve should be determined by who and how many you are entertaining, the preparation time, serving circumstances, and the other dishes in the meal. It's a good idea to order the cut of meat required from the butcher in advance, or be flexible when shopping in the supermarket. If you plan a menu including lamb chops and there are no lamb chops available (or none of good quality), consider a menu change, and select the fine looking leg of lamb that is available, or another cut, or even a different meat.

Meat will always remain a favorite and dependable choice as the centerpiece of any meal.

# Beef

## Roast Fillet of Beef

*Serves 8*

| | |
|---|---|
| 1 whole beef tenderloin, trimmed and tied (about 3½ to 4 pounds) Salt and freshly ground black pepper | 3 tablespoons sweet butter ½ cup halved and peeled shallots |

1. Preheat the oven to 425 degrees.

2. Season the fillet well with salt and pepper.

3. Melt the butter in a large roasting pan and quickly sear the beef on all sides over high heat, about 8 minutes total cooking time.

4. Surround the beef with the shallots and roast for 10 minutes. Turn the fillet with spatulas and roast for 10 minutes for rare. Roast a few minutes longer for medium-rare. Let the fillet rest for 10 minutes before slicing.

*Serving Suggestions:* Quick Béarnaise or Norman Hodgson's Mustard Sauce, a double recipe of Sizzling Mushrooms Stuffed with Snails and Basil–Garlic Butter, platter of hot cooked buttered potatoes, carrots, broccoli, and string beans, and Chocolate Mousse Cake with Chocolate Glaze.

# Emilie Bartok's Ragout
## (with thanks to Vicki Sopkin)

### Serves 8

1  4-pound lean cross-rib roast
1  tablespoon salt
   Freshly ground black pepper to taste
3  tablespoons all-purpose flour
1  large onion, thinly sliced
½  cup diced sweet green pepper
6  young carrots, peeled and diced
1  teaspoon dried oregano

1  cup fresh or canned tomato sauce
1  cup dry red wine
1  pound fresh mushrooms, sliced
2  medium-sized potatoes, peeled and cut into ¼-inch-thick slices (If the potatoes are over 1 inch in diameter, cut them in half lengthwise before slicing.)

1. Preheat the oven to 450 degrees.

2. Cut the meat into ¼-inch-thick slices. Then cut the slices into strips about 2 inches long and 1 inch wide.

3. Put the meat into a 4- to 5-quart ovenproof casserole and sprinkle it with the salt and pepper. Toss well. Bake, uncovered, for 35 minutes. Stir in the flour and bake for 5 minutes.

4. Remove the casserole from the oven and lower the oven temperature to 275 degrees.

5. Add the remaining ingredients to the casserole, except for the mushrooms and potatoes. Combine well. *Cover* and bake for 1 hour.

6. Add the mushrooms and potatoes and combine gently with the other ingredients. Recover and bake for 45 minutes, or until the potatoes are fork-tender. Serve with hot cooked buttered egg noodles sprinkled with chopped fresh parsley leaves.

*Serving Suggestions:* This hearty dish requires only crusty French bread, hot cooked noodles, mixed green salad, and dry red wine. For dessert, try sliced fresh seasonal fruit with a scoop of the sorbet of your choice.

# Brisket with Cranberry Sauce

*Serves 4 to 6*

| | |
|---|---|
| 1   4- to 4½-pound brisket | ½   pound fresh mushrooms, |
| 1   cup chopped onion |       sliced |
| 2   celery stalks, chopped | 1   cup homemade beef stock |
| 1   garlic clove, minced |       or canned broth |
| 2   cups canned whole | |
|       cranberry sauce | |

1. Preheat the oven to 350 degrees.

2. Put the brisket in an ovenproof 3- or 4-quart casserole. Combine the onion, celery, garlic, and cranberry sauce and spoon the mixture over the meat. Surround the brisket with the mushrooms and pour in the stock.

3. Cover the casserole and bake for 1 hour. Lower the oven temperature to 325 degrees and bake for about 1½ hours longer, or until the brisket is fork-tender.

*Serving Suggestions:* Boiled potatoes, hot cooked broccoli, and Cheesecake.

# Sherry-braised Chuck Steak

*Serves 6*

1 4-pound chuck steak, 1½ inches thick
Freshly ground black pepper
3 tablespoons olive oil
2 large onions, thinly sliced
1 teaspoon minced garlic
2 tablespoons all-purpose flour

1 cup dry sherry
1 cup homemade beef stock or canned broth
½ teaspoon dried thyme
1 bay leaf, crumbled
1 tablespoon chopped fresh parsley leaves

1. Preheat the oven to 400 degrees.

2. Grate pepper liberally over each side of the steak.

3. Heat the oil in a heavy ovenproof casserole large enough to comfortably hold the steak.

4. Brown the steak quickly on both sides over medium-high heat and transfer it to a platter.

5. Add the onions and garlic to the pan, stir, and turn the heat to low. Cook for 5 minutes. Sprinkle the flour over the onion mixture, stir, and cook for 1 minute.

6. Remove the onions from the casserole and add the steak. Spoon the onion mixture on top of the steak and add the remaining ingredients, except for the parsley. Cover and transfer the casserole to the oven. Bake for 30 minutes.

7. Lower the oven temperature to 300 degrees and bake for 1 ½ hours, basting twice during the cooking time. Uncover, and bake for 15 minutes longer, or until the meat is fork-tender.

8. Carefully remove the steak to a serving platter using 2 spatulas. Pour off the accumulated fat and discard the bay leaf. Stir the onion mixture in the casserole and spoon it over the steak. Sprinkle with the parsley and serve at once.

*Serving Suggestions:* Puréed Cauliflower, mixed green salad, and Lemon Cake.

# Beef Carbonnade

## Serves 6

3½ pounds boneless beef
chuck, cut into 1½-inch
cubes
Salt and freshly ground
black pepper
3 tablespoons vegetable
oil, or as needed
6 tablespoons butter
4 large yellow onions, cut
into ⅛-inch-thick slices
6 tablespoons all-purpose
flour
1 cup homemade beef
stock or canned broth
2 cups beer

2 large garlic cloves,
minced
1 teaspoon dried thyme
½ teaspoon dried
marjoram
1 tablespoon red wine
vinegar
2 carrots, peeled and
quartered
2 celery stalks, quartered
1 bay leaf
6 sprigs fresh parsley

1. Season the meat cubes with salt and pepper.

2. Heat the oil in a large heavy skillet. Brown the beef cubes, about 10 pieces at a time, adding a small amount of oil if needed, depending on the amount of fat in the meat.

3. Meanwhile, melt 4 tablespoons of the butter in a Dutch oven. Add the onions and cook over low heat for about 20 minutes, stirring often. Don't let the onions brown. As the beef cubes are browned, transfer them to a heavy 4- to 5-quart casserole.

4. When all the meat is cooked, stir 2 tablespoons of the remaining butter into the skillet with the fat in the pan and add the flour. Stir and cook over low heat for about 10 minutes, stirring constantly, until the roux turns brown.

5. Meanwhile, preheat the oven to 325 degrees.

6. Add the stock and beer to the roux and whisk until the liquid boils and thickens. Add the garlic, thyme, marjoram, and vinegar. Put the onions, carrots, celery, bay leaf, and parsley sprigs in the casserole with the meat. Pour the sauce over the mixture and stir to combine well.

7. Cover the casserole and bake for about 2 hours, or until the meat is fork-tender.

8. Remove the carrots, celery, bay leaf, and parsley and discard. Season with salt and pepper to taste.

9. Serve immediately or remove from the casserole and cool throughly. Cover and refrigerate overnight. To reheat the Beef Car-

bonnade, warm it in a covered casserole in a preheated 325-degree oven for 30 minutes, or heat it in a covered Dutch oven or large saucepan on top of the stove.

*Serving Suggestions:* French fries, Red Cabbage and Cranberry Sauce, and Ellie Ashworth's Rum–Pecan Pie.

# Ground Sirloin Steaks with Provençale Tomato Sauce

*Serves 4*

## PROVENÇALE TOMATO SAUCE

| | | | |
|---|---|---|---|
| 4 | strips bacon | 1 | bay leaf |
| 1 | tablespoon olive oil | ¼ | teaspoon dried thyme |
| ¼ | cup minced onion | ½ | teaspoon dried basil |
| ¼ | cup minced celery | ½ | teaspoon sugar |
| 1 | large garlic clove, minced | | Salt and freshly ground black pepper to taste |
| 1 | tablespoon all-purpose flour | | Chopped fresh parsley leaves |
| ¾ | cup homemade chicken stock or canned broth | | |
| 1¾ | cups peeled, seeded, and diced fresh or canned tomatoes | | |

## GROUND SIRLOIN STEAKS

| | | | |
|---|---|---|---|
| 1¾ | pounds ground sirloin | | Salt and freshly ground black pepper to taste |
| 1 | tablespoon Worcestershire sauce | | |
| 2 | tablespoons minced shallots | | |

1. In a heavy saucepan, fry the bacon until it is crisp. Remove the bacon and drain on paper towels.

2. Add the olive oil to the pan and cook the onion, celery, and garlic over medium-low heat for 5 minutes, stirring often. Sprinkle with the flour and stir. Cook for 1 minute. Add the remaining ingredients, except for the salt, pepper, and parsley. Bring the sauce to a boil, lower the heat, and simmer for 30 minutes. Discard the bay leaf and purée the mixture in a blender or food processor.

3. Return the mixture to a clean saucepan and taste for seasoning. Stir in the parsley.

4. During the last 10 minutes of cooking time for the sauce, prepare the ground steaks: Combine the beef well with all the ingredients. Divide the mixture into 4 equal parts and shape into oval shapes, making the center about 1½ inches thick.

5. Preheat the broiler.

6. Put the steaks on a boiling pan and broil about 6 inches from the heat for 6 minutes for rare or 8 minutes for medium-rare. Serve the steaks with the Provençale Tomato Sauce spooned over them.

*Serving Suggestions:* Parsleyed potatoes and Arugola and Endive Salad with Herb Dressing.

# Grilled Knockwursts with Honey Mustard

## Serves 6

| | |
|---|---|
| 12   *all-beef knockwursts* | ⅓   *cup honey* |
| 1¼  *cups whole-grain mustard* | |

1. Score each knockwurst ¼ inch deep in 6 places on each side.

2. Grill the knockwursts over hot coals on the grill or in a heavy iron ridged skillet until crisp and browned.

3. Meanwhile, thoroughly combine the mustard and honey in a bowl. When the knockwursts are cooked, pile them on a platter and pass the Honey Mustard.

*Serving Suggestions:* Mashed Potatoes with Sauerkraut and Nancy Dussault's Deluxe Monkey Bread.

# Veal

## Ossobuco

*Serves 6*

6  veal shanks, cut into
    2-inch-thick pieces
    All-purpose flour
3  tablespoons olive oil
1  cup dry white wine
2  tablespoons butter
1  medium-sized onion,
    chopped
1  large garlic clove,
    chopped
1  carrot, peeled and
    chopped
1  celery stalk, sliced

2  cups drained and
    chopped canned Italian
    plum tomatoes
2  tablespoons tomato paste
1/4  cup homemade chicken
    stock or canned broth
1/2  teaspoon dried thyme
    Salt and freshly ground
    black pepper
1  tablespoon chopped fresh
    parsley leaves
1  teaspoon grated lemon
    rind

1. Coat each side of the veal pieces with flour.

2. Heat the oil in a heavy ovenproof casserole and brown the veal on each side. Add the wine and simmer for 10 minutes.

3. Meanwhile, melt the butter in a skillet. Add the onion, garlic, carrot, and celery and cook for 10 minutes, stirring often. Add the tomatoes and tomato paste and stir.

4. Put the vegetable mixture in a food processor and run the machine for 5 seconds, or pass the mixture through a food mill. Add the broth and thyme, stir, and spoon the mixture over the veal in the casserole. Season with salt and pepper to taste.

5. Cover and simmer for 1 hour, or until the meat is fork-tender. Sprinkle the dish with parsley and grated lemon rind just before serving. If desired, cook rice for Ossobuco 30 minutes before the Ossobuco is done.

*Serving Suggestions:* Antipasto Salad, Ossobuco Rice, and Zabaglione Coupes.

# Ossobuco Rice

### Serves 6

| | |
|---|---|
| 1½ cups Italian Arborio rice | Freshly ground black pepper to taste |
| ½ teaspoon ground saffron | 2 tablespoons butter |
| ½ teaspoon salt | |

Cook the rice in a saucepan with 4 cups of boiling water flavored with the saffron, salt, and pepper for 5 minutes. Lower the heat, cover, and simmer for 20 minutes, or until the rice is tender. Drain well and stir in the butter.

# Veal Chops with Fresh Sorrel Sauce

### Serves 4

| | |
|---|---|
| 4 1-inch-thick veal chops | ¼ cup minced shallots |
| Salt and freshly ground black pepper | 1 cup washed and dried sorrel cut into thin strips |
| 4 tablespoons sweet butter | 1 cup Crème Fraîche (See |
| 2 tablespoons peanut or vegetable oil | recipe page 277. It must be prepared the day |
| All-purpose flour | before.) |
| ¼ cup dry white wine | |

1. Season the chops lightly with salt and pepper.
2. Heat 2 tablespoons of the butter and the oil in a large frying pan.
3. Lightly coat the chops with flour, shaking off any excess, and immediately put them in the frying pan. Brown the chops lightly over medium-high heat, about 3 minutes per side. Lower the heat to medium-low, cover the pan, and cook for about 18 minutes, or until the chops are tender.
4. Transfer the chops to a warm serving platter. Cover loosely with foil and place in low oven until served.
5. Add the wine and shallots to the pan and cook over medium-high heat for 4 minutes, stirring often. Add the remaining 2 table-

spoons of butter to the pan along with the sorrel. Stir and cook over medium heat for 3 minutes.

6. Add the Crème Fraîche and combine well. Season with salt and pepper to taste and cook over medium heat until slightly thickened. Serve the sauce in a warmed sauceboat with the veal chops.

*Serving Suggestions:* Baked Potato Slices with Bacon and Orange Slices with Strawberry Purée.

## Veal Birds Stuffed with Sausage and Mushrooms

*Serves 4*

| | | | |
|---|---|---|---|
| 8 | veal scallops | 1/4 | teaspoon dried thyme |
| | Salt and freshly ground black pepper | 3/4 | cup unseasoned fresh bread crumbs |
| 5 | tablespoons butter | 3 | tablespoons heavy cream |
| 1/4 | pound fresh mushrooms, finely chopped | 1 | medium-sized onion, halved |
| 2 | tablespoons minced shallots | 1/2 | cup dry white wine |
| 1/4 | pound bulk sausage | 1 | cup homemade chicken stock or canned broth |
| 2 | tablespoons chopped fresh parsley leaves | 1 | tablespoon arrowroot or cornstarch |
| 1/4 | teaspoon dried oregano | | |

1. Put each scallop between 2 pieces of wax paper and flatten to a 1/8-inch thickness without breaking the meat. Sprinkle with salt and pepper and set aside.

2. Melt 3 tablespoons of the butter in a large frying pan and sauté the mushrooms and shallots over medium heat for 8 minutes. Transfer to a bowl.

3. Cook the sausage in the skillet until it is no longer pink, but don't brown the sausage. Drain the sausage in a strainer and add it to the mushroom mixture.

4. Add the herbs, bread crumbs, and heavy cream to the bowl. Mix well and season with salt and pepper to taste.

5. Preheat the oven to 350 degrees.

6. Spread equal amounts of the mixture over each scallop and roll them up. Tie each scallop securely with kitchen string at the ends and in the middle.

7. Melt the remaining 2 tablespoons of butter in an ovenproof skillet and brown the veal birds on all sides. Add the onion, white wine, and chicken stock. Cover and bake for 45 minutes, basting twice during the cooking time.

8. Transfer the cooked veal birds to a warmed serving dish and discard the strings and the onion.

9. Dissolve the cornstarch in a little water and whisk into the boiling liquid in the skillet. Stir over high heat until the sauce thickens. Season with salt and pepper to taste and spoon the sauce over the veal. Serve immediately.

*Serving Suggestions:* Buttered Carrots with Grand Marnier and Romaine Strips Salad with Cucumber and Walnut Dressing.

# *Veal Scallops with Artichoke Hearts and Mushrooms*

### *Serves 4*

| | |
|---|---|
| 12 veal scallops | ½ pound fresh mushrooms, |
| Salt and freshly ground | sliced |
| black pepper | ¾ cup dry white wine |
| All-purpose flour | 2 tablespoons butter, cut |
| 3 tablespoons vegetable oil | in small pieces |
| 1 10-ounce package frozen | Chopped fresh parsley |
| artichoke hearts, thawed | leaves |
| and well drained | |

1. Season the veal scallops with salt and pepper and coat them lightly with flour. Shake off any excess flour.

2. Heat the oil in a large frying pan and brown the scallops over medium-high heat on each side. Add the artichoke hearts, mushrooms, and wine and bring to a boil. Lower the heat, cover, and simmer for 8 minutes.

3. Transfer the scallops and vegetables to a warmed serving platter.

4. Cook the sauce over high heat for 3 minutes, stirring often, then whisk in the butter. Pour the sauce over the scallops and sprinkle with the parsley. Serve immediately.

*Serving Suggestions:* Cream of Watercress Soup and Lemon Rice.

# Sautéed Breaded Calf's Liver with Sweetened Lemon Juice

*Serves 4*

1½ pounds calf's liver, cut
 into thin scallops
 All-purpose flour
2 tablespoons olive oil
2 tablespoons butter
¼ cup fresh lemon juice

2 teaspoons sugar
 Salt and freshly ground
 black pepper to taste
 Chopped fresh parsley
 leaves

1. Coat the liver scallops lightly with flour and shake off any excess.

2. Heat the oil and butter in a large frying pan over medium-high heat. Lightly brown the liver scallops.

3. Meanwhile, boil the lemon juice in a saucepan and reduce it to half. Add the sugar and stir to dissolve. Remove from the heat.

4. Season the cooked liver with salt and pepper and sprinkle with the sweetened lemon juice and parsley.

*Serving Suggestions:* Spinach Packets and parsleyed potatoes.

# Pork

## Fresh Roast Ham Shoulder

### Serves 6

Phyllis Hollands-Robinson, the talented artist and her irresistible husband, Dr. M. J. (Robbie) Robinson, now live in St. Thomas, U.S. Virgin Islands. Their combined cooking efforts produce memorable meals that enable them to be with their guests while entertaining. Phyl says, "Everything must be cooked in advance except for the vegetable."

Here is their most requested entrée, Roast Ham Shoulder; their favorite menu follows the recipe and all the dishes are included in this book.

| | | | |
|---|---|---|---|
| 1 | 5½- to 6-pound fresh ham shoulder | 1 | teaspoon dried thyme |
| 2 | teaspoons dry mustard | 1 | teaspoon cracked peppercorns |
| 2 | garlic cloves, crushed | | |

1. Preheat the oven to 325 degrees.
2. Cut away the rind from the roast. (If desired the rind can be cooked in the roasting pan with the roast and cut into squares for those who love crackling.) Leave the fat intact on the roast and score it. Rub the mustard, garlic, thyme, and peppercorns over the surface of the roast.
3. Put the ham shoulder in a roasting pan and roast for about 3 ½ hours, or until the juice runs clear. (The internal temperature should register 185 degrees on a meat thermometer.)
4. Pour off the fat from the pan and allow the ham to rest for 30 minutes before carving.

*Variations:* The Robinsons frequently cook 2 roast hams, serve one hot and with the other one they prepare Barbecued Sliced Pork. It is made by thinly slicing the roast and combining it in a large saucepan with 3 cups of OpenPit barbecue sauce. Bring the mixture to a boil, lower the heat, and simmer for 30 minutes, stirring frequently. Serve piping hot on butter-toasted French bread, Kaiser rolls, or hamburger buns. Phyl also grinds any leftover cooked pork (about 2 cups are required) and combines it with 1 egg and Italian seasonings —oregano, basil, rosemary—and forms patties or balls that are sautéed in oil until golden brown.

*Serving Suggestions:* Phyllis' Potato Salad, Zucchini Robinson, and Lime Pie with Gingersnap Crust.

# Cider-baked Ham with Norman Hodgson's Mustard Sauce

*Serves 10 to 12*

1   *12-pound smoked ham (with bone)*
3   *cups apple cider or juice*

2½  *cups Norman Hodgson's Mustard Sauce (see recipe page 156)*

1. Preheat the oven to 325 degrees.
2. Score the fat side of the ham at 1-inch intervals, on the diagonal, forming a diamond pattern. Cut about ½ inch deep.
3. Put the ham in a roasting pan and bake for 2 hours.
4. Pour 1½ cups of the cider over the ham and bake for 15 minutes.
5. Pour the remaining 1½ cups of the cider over the ham and bake for 15 minutes.
6. Baste the ham with the liquid in the pan every 15 minutes for 1 hour longer, or for a total cooking time of about 3½ hours.
7. Transfer the ham to a carving platter and let it rest for 30 minutes before carving. Serve the ham with Norman Hodgson's Mustard Sauce. (The ham can be served warm, lukewarm, or cold.)

*Serving Suggestions:* Double recipe of Rum–Raisin Whipped Sweet Potatoes, String Beans with Walnuts, and Rosettes served with the ice cream of your choice.

# Norman Hodgson's Mustard Sauce

*Makes about 2½ cups*

This tangy mustard sauce is an excellent sidekick to ham, roast beef, lamb, or chicken, or as a dip for cold poached shrimp.

| | | | |
|---|---|---|---|
| 8 | tablespoons dry mustard | 1 | cup white wine vinegar |
| 4 | medium-sized eggs | 2 | tablespoons butter |
| 1 | cup sugar | ¼ | teaspoon salt |
| 1 | cup heavy cream | | |

1. With a wire whisk, combine the mustard, eggs, sugar, and cream in the top of a double boiler over simmering water. Cook for about 15 minutes, stirring often, or until the sauce thickens enough to coat a spoon.

2. Stir in the vinegar, butter, and salt and continue cooking for about 30 minutes, stirring every 4 or 5 minutes.

3. Cool, cover, and refrigerate for several hours. (The sauce keeps well for 2 weeks in a tightly covered jar or container.)

# Pork Chops with Cranberry and Walnut Stuffing

*Serves 4*

| | | | |
|---|---|---|---|
| 4 | 1-inch-thick loin pork chops | ½ | cup canned whole cranberry sauce |
| | Salt and freshly ground black pepper | ¼ | cup chopped walnuts |
| 1 | cup herb-seasoned stuffing mix | 2 | tablespoons butter, melted |
| ½ | teaspoon dried sage | ¼ | cup boiling water |
| 2 | teaspoons grated orange rind | ¼ | cup homemade chicken stock or canned broth |

1. Preheat the oven to 350 degrees.

2. With a small sharp knife, make pockets in each chop by cutting from the outer side of the meat through the center to the bone. Season the chops inside and out with salt and pepper.

3. In a large bowl, combine the remaining ingredients, except for the stock, thoroughly. Stuff each pocket with equal amounts of the mixture.

4. Put the chops in a baking dish and pour in the stock. Cover and bake for 30 minutes. Uncover and bake for 30 minutes longer, or until the chops are tender.

*Serving Suggestions:* Individual Roesti Potatoes and applesauce.

# Butterflied Pork Chops with Vinegar

### Serves 4

4   2-inch-thick loin pork
   chops
   Salt and freshly ground
   black pepper

All-purpose flour
Peanut or vegetable oil
White wine vinegar

1. Leaving the bone intact, pound the meat of each chop between 2 pieces of plastic wrap to a ¼-inch thickness; near the bone, of course, the meat must be a little thicker. (The butcher can also flatten the meat.) Season the chops lightly on both sides with salt and pepper and coat them with flour, shaking off any excess.

2. Heat ½ inch of oil in 2 frying pans and cook one chop in each pan over medium heat until golden brown and tender. Keep the cooked chops warm on a dish in the oven while cooking the remaining chops.

3. Sprinkle the cooked chops lightly with the vinegar. Serve with extra vinegar.

*Serving Suggestion:* Escarole with Onion–Mozzarella Topping.

# Tender Oven-baked Spareribs

*Serves 4*

4½ pounds pork spareribs
    (about 2 sides of ribs)
¼ cup fresh lemon juice

Salt and freshly ground
black pepper

## BARBECUE SAUCE

3 tablespoons butter
1 cup ketchup
½ cup red wine vinegar
½ cup cold water
3 tablespoons
    Worcestershire sauce
¼ teaspoon Tabasco sauce

1 teaspoon Dijon mustard
1 large garlic clove,
    chopped
2 celery stalks, sliced
1 medium-sized onion,
    chopped

1. Preheat the oven to 425 degrees.

2. Put the rib sides in a large roasting pan. Brush them with the lemon juice and sprinkle them with salt and pepper. Bake the ribs for 30 minutes.

3. Meanwhile, put all the Barbecue Sauce ingredients in a large saucepan and combine well. Bring to a boil, lower the heat, and simmer for 20 minutes.

4. Purée the mixture in a blender.

5. Pour the sauce over the ribs and lower the oven temperature to 350 degrees. Bake for 1 hour, basting twice during the cooking time.

6. Cut the ribs into single rib pieces and pile onto a heated platter. Serve at once.

*Serving Suggestions:* **Corn on the Cob with Chili Butter and Sautéed Stuffed Zucchini Medallions.**

# Sausage and Black Bean Burritos with Cheese and Corn Purée

*Serves 4*

½ pound bulk sausage, crumbled

1 16-ounce can Goya black beans

2 scallions, thinly sliced

2 jalapeño chili peppers, seeded and chopped (optional)

1 10-ounce package frozen corn kernels

2 tablespoons butter

½ cup sour cream

¾ cup grated Monterey Jack cheese

4 large flour tortillas

1. Cook the sausage in a frying pan until it is lightly browned. Drain well.

2. Put the black beans with their liquid into a saucepan. Add the sausage, scallions, and peppers. Simmer for 10 minutes.

3. Preheat the oven to 425 degrees.

4. Cook the corn following the package directions and drain it well. Purée the corn with the butter in a food processor or blender. Transfer to a bowl and stir in the sour cream.

5. Fill the 4 tortillas with equal amounts of the strained bean and sausage mixture. Roll up each tortilla and tuck the ends underneath.

6. Put the burritos seam side down in individual au gratin dishes and spoon equal amounts of the corn purée over the burritos. Sprinkle each with equal amounts of the cheese and bake for 10 minutes. Run under the broiler briefly for a golden brown topping.

*Serving Suggestions:* Sautéed Tomato Fillets and Buñeulos.

# Chicago's Deep-dish Sausage Pizza

*Serves 4*

## PIZZA DOUGH

1   package dry yeast
1   cup warm water
1   tablespoon sugar
1   teaspoon salt
3   tablespoons olive oil, plus extra for greasing the bowl and pan

2¾   cups sifted all-purpose flour, plus extra for kneading
2   teaspoons coarse cornmeal

## PIZZA TOPPING

1   pound Italian sausages, casings removed, or bulk sausage
12   ounces mozzarella
1   28-ounce can imported Italian plum tomatoes, well drained and chopped

1   teaspoon dried oregano
1   teaspoon dried basil
    Freshly ground black pepper
½   cup freshly grated Parmesan cheese

1. First make the dough: Put the yeast and water in a large bowl and stir until the yeast dissolves. Add the sugar, salt, and oil and combine. Stir in the flour.

2. Turn the dough out onto a lightly floured board and knead until the dough is smooth and elastic, about 10 minutes. (Up to ½ cup of flour may be needed to knead into the dough until it is no longer sticky.) If using an electric mixer with a dough hook, knead the dough at medium speed for 5 minutes.

3. Lightly grease a large clean bowl with olive oil and place the dough in the bowl; turn the dough to coat it evenly with the oil. Cover the bowl and let the dough double in size, about 1 hour.

4. Just before shaping the dough, grease a 14-inch pizza pan with 2-inch sides with olive oil and sprinkle the bottom with the cornmeal.

5. Punch the dough down. Flatten it with the palms of your hands and gently pull it out from the edges in a circular motion making a large round shape. Press the dough evenly across the bottom of the pan and about 1 inch up the sides. Let the dough rise for 15 minutes.

6. Meanwhile, cook the crumbled sausage in a frying pan over medium-low heat for 10 minutes. Don't allow the sausage to brown. Drain the sausage well.

7. Preheat the oven to 450 degrees, with a pizza stone or quarry tiles on the lower shelf for crustier dough, if possible.

8. Sprinkle half of the mozzarella over the dough and top with the sausage and tomatoes. Sprinkle the oregano and basil over all and add pepper to taste. Top with the remaining half of the mozzarella and the Parmesan cheese.

9. Bake the pizza on the stone, if used, for 25 minutes, or until the cheese sizzles and the crust is golden brown.

*Variations:* Sprinkle any one or a combination of no more than 3 of the following ingredients over or in place of the sausage layer in making the pizza (follow directions after the sausage addition as given in the recipe): $\frac{1}{4}$ pound thinly sliced fresh mushrooms; 1 cup chopped sweet green pepper; 1 medium-to-large onion, thinly sliced; 8 chopped anchovy fillets; 1 cup thinly sliced pepperoni (if not using sausage); 8 thin slices boiled ham. Sprinkle the cooked pizza with hot red pepper flakes, if desired.

*Serving Suggestion:* Arugola and Endive Salad with Herb Dressing.

# Lamb

## Braised Lamb

*Serves 6*

| | | | |
|---|---|---|---|
| 1 | 6½-pound leg of lamb | 2 | sprigs fresh rosemary, |
| 3 | tablespoons peanut or | | or ½ teaspoon dried |
| | vegetable oil | | rosemary |
| 2 | carrots, sliced | 1 | fresh sage leaf, or ½ |
| 1 | large onion, coarsely | | teaspoon dried sage |
| | chopped | | leaves |
| 2 | celery stalks, sliced | 1½ | cups dry white wine |
| 2 | large garlic cloves, | 1 | cup homemade beef |
| | chopped | | stock or canned broth |
| 1 | bay leaf | | Salt and freshly ground |
| 4 | sprigs fresh parsley | | black pepper |
| 2 | sprigs fresh thyme, or | | |
| | ½ teaspoon dried thyme | | |

1. Preheat the oven to 325 degrees.

2. Heat the oil in a large heavy casserole and brown the lamb on all sides. Transfer the lamb to a plate and add the vegetables to the casserole. Stir and cook over medium heat for 5 minutes. Add the remaining ingredients and bring to a boil. Return the lamb to the casserole, cover, and bring to a boil.

3. Transfer the casserole to the oven and bake for 2¼ hours, or until the lamb is tender.

4. Transfer the lamb to a warmed serving platter.

5. Strain the ingredients in the casserole, collecting the liquid in a bowl. Discard the solids. Skim off as much fat as possible.

6. Pour the liquid into a saucepan and reduce it to about 2 cups. Season with salt and pepper to taste. Serve the sauce with the sliced lamb. If desired, thicken the sauce by adding *beurre manie* (a combined mixture of 2 tablespoons softened butter and 2 tablespoons all-purpose flour) and whisking, while boiling, until the sauce thickens.

*Serving Suggestions:* Mixed Vegetables with Fine Egg Noodles and Three-Green Salad with Hazelnut Dressing.

# Broiled Lamb Chops with Honey–Mint Sauce

*Serves 4*

8   1½-inch-thick loin
    lamb chops
    Salt and freshly ground
    black pepper
⅓   cup honey

⅓   cup water
1½  teaspoons red wine
    vinegar
1½  teaspoons dried mint

1. Preheat the broiler.
2. Season the lamb chops lightly with salt and pepper. Broil 5 to 6 inches from the heat for 5 minutes.
3. Meanwhile, combine the remaining ingredients in a saucepan and simmer for 3 or 4 minutes.
4. Turn the chops and brush with the mixture. Cook about 5 minutes, or until golden brown for "pink" or medium-cooked chops. Cook a few minutes longer for more well-done chops.

*Serving Suggestions:* Carrots Vichy and Individual Roesti Potatoes.


# Broiled Noisettes of Lamb with Herbs

*Serves 4*

8   1½-inch-thick loin lamb
    chops, boned, rolled up,
    and tied with kitchen
    string (Remove as much
    fat as possible.)
    Salt and freshly ground
    black pepper

1   teaspoon dried thyme
1   teaspoon dried dill
1   tablespoon chopped fresh
    parsley leaves
2   tablespoons butter, melted

1. Preheat the broiler.
2. Season the noisettes on each side with salt and pepper.
3. Combine the herbs and butter and brush over the noisettes on each side.
4. Broil the noisettes 6 inches from the heat for 5 minutes per side for pink; or to the desired doneness.

*Serving Suggestions:* Minted Fresh Peas and Lemon Rice.

# Lamb Tagine

*Serves 6*

| | |
|---|---|
| 3 tablespoons butter | 2 cups homemade chicken stock or canned broth |
| 1 tablespoon olive oil | |
| 2 teaspoons ground ginger | 1 large onion, thinly sliced |
| ½ teaspoon ground coriander | |
| | ¼ cup honey |
| 1 teaspoon ground cinnamon | 12 ounce package pitted prunes |
| 1 teaspoon ground turmeric | 2 tablespoons toasted sesame seeds (see Note) |
| ¼ teaspoon powdered saffron | |
| 3½ pounds shoulder of lamb, cut into 1½-inch pieces | |

1. In a heavy 2-quart pot, heat the butter and oil. Add the spices and stir. Immediately add the lamb pieces and toss to coat evenly with the spiced butter. Cook over low heat for 10 minutes.

2. Add the stock and bring to a boil. Simmer, covered, for 1 hour, stirring occasionally.

3. Add the onions and honey and continue simmering, uncovered, for 45 minutes, or until the meat is tender.

4. Stir in the prunes and sesame seeds and simmer for about 10 minutes, or until the prunes swell.

NOTE: To toast the sesame seeds, spread them on a baking sheet and place them under a hot broiler for about 3 minutes or until lightly browned. Stir once.

*Variations:* Substitute dried apricots for the prunes in the recipe. Chicken breasts cut into 1½-inch pieces can be substituted for the lamb. The only change in the recipe is to add the onions with the chicken and cook the dish for 45 minutes. Add the prunes or apricots and cook for 10 minutes as directed.

*Serving Suggestions:* Avocado vinaigrette, hot cooked rice, and toasted pita bread.

# Broiled Lamb Burgers with Chutney and Sour Cream–Curry Sauce

*Serves 4*

1¾ pounds ground lamb shoulder
1 small onion, minced
1 large garlic clove, minced
2 tablespoons unseasoned dry bread crumbs

1 tablespoon chopped fresh parsley leaves
½ teaspoon salt
Freshly ground black pepper to taste

## CHUTNEY AND SOUR CREAM–CURRY SAUCE

½ cup chutney, chopped
½ cup sour cream

2 teaspoons curry powder, or to taste

1. Preheat the broiler.
2. Put the lamb, onion, garlic, bread crumbs, parsley, salt, and pepper in a large bowl. Mix until just well combined. Shape into 4 equal-sized patties about 1 inch thick.
3. Broil the patties in a broiling pan about 6 inches from the heat for about 5 minutes per side.
4. Meanwhile, combine the sauce ingredients. Serve the sauce with the burgers.

*Serving Suggestions:* Stir-fried Snow Pea Pods and Lemon Rice.

# Individual Racks of Lamb

### Serves 4

2  racks of lamb, each cut
   in half and trimmed of
   fat
   Salt and freshly ground
   black pepper
3  tablespoons butter,
   melted

½  cup unseasoned fresh
   bread crumbs
3  tablespoons chopped fresh
   parsley leaves
1  large garlic clove, minced

1. Preheat the oven to 450 degrees.
2. Season the meat with salt and pepper.
3. In a bowl, combine the butter, bread crumbs, parsley, and garlic and season well with salt and pepper. Press the mixture, in equal amounts, onto the meat side of the racks of lamb.
4. Put the racks in a roasting pan, bone side down, and roast for 15 minutes for pink; or to the desired doneness.

*Serving Suggestions:* Creamed spinach and sautéed potatoes.

# Pasta, Rice, and Potatoes

It is no surprise that pasta has become increasingly popular in the last several years. Americans have "discovered" pasta because they are eating less meat, because pasta is inexpensive, and because pasta is a beautifully soothing and honest food. When cooked properly, pasta has a satisfying flavor. It comes in many varying shapes, sizes, and textures, and it is the shape and size of pasta that determines the sauce best suited for it. Vermicelli, fedelini, and the thinner, more fragile pastas require a lighter sauce. Rigatoni, ziti, or larger and more sturdy shapes call for a heartier sauce, which may contain meat and other more substantial ingredients.

The variety of ingredients that can go into a sauce for pasta is unlimited. Cheese, seafood, fish, meat, vegetables, and herbs combined with sauces of tomatoes, cream, olive oil, or butter, in correct proportions, make pasta one of the most versatile foods available. It is this combination of shapes, sauces, and other ingredients that make up the vast repertoire of pasta dishes. But this spectrum of tastes and textures should not exclude a simple plate of spaghetti with butter and cheese or oil and garlic, which can be delicious. Although all pasta is made of essentially the same dough, I prefer Italian imports.

Natural rice, in some form, is one of the few foods to have earned acceptance as a staple in both Eastern and Western cultures. World travelers can count on seeing rice on the menu in virtually every corner of the world, and it is remarkable that a single product can be transformed into so many different dishes, each reflecting the local character and taste preferences of the population. On the palate, the wonderful Risotto served at Harry's Bar in Venice has little in common with the extraordinary Paella of Valencia, the Arroz con Pollo at the Don Pepe in San Juan, Puerto Rico, or the creole specialties of New Orleans.

Most references to "meat and potatoes" meals suggest hearty but somewhat standard fare. While meat needs no defense, the potato deserves more applause than it normally receives, if for no other reason than because of its extraordinary versatility.

I can think of no other food in any category that arrives at the dinner table transformed into so many different forms and functions: boiled, baked, whipped, fried, sautéed, stuffed, in salads, casseroles, as a pancake, pudding, bread, stuffing, pie, or cake—even reaching the bar as vodka or accompanying chip. All this and it's a nutritionist's delight, with its high protein and vitamin content, and relatively low calories.

# Pasta

I vividly recall the first meal I ate in Italy, but unfortunately I've forgotten the name of the restaurant. It was a tiny trattoria in Porto Fino, and the meal consisted of a plate of paper-thin wide green noodles with an oil and butter sauce, tiny crisp lettuce greens with pungent sliced tomatoes, Italian bread with oil and vinegar, and a glass of red table wine. The simple silky pasta was superb. It was a spiritual moment, and my love of pasta has grown stronger ever since.

*Al dente,* or "firm to the tooth," is what is commonly accepted as the proper doneness for pasta. It is a definition that has remained vague. Cooking pasta to the correct point of doneness is simply to cook it in rapidly boiling, lightly salted water until it has a pleasing "cooked" taste and tenderness. Cooking time ranges from 6 to 12 minutes, depending on the pasta's shape and size. Properly cooked pasta swells slightly and has a pale creamy color, but the proof is in the taste.

All of the following pasta recipes make excellent first courses as well as main dishes for company. A recipe for 4 will serve 6 as a first course. A recipe for 6 serves 8 to 10 as a first course, and a recipe for 10 will make 16 to 18 first-course servings.

# Marinara Sauce

*Makes about 2½ cups, or enough for 1 pound of pasta*

Double the recipe for more servings. The sauce freezes well in tightly covered containers. In late summer, when there are lovely farmers' tomatoes available, make several double batches and freeze the sauce. Then you can enjoy fresh Marinara in the winter.

| | | | |
|---|---|---|---|
| 2½ | pounds fresh tomatoes, chopped, or 2 cups chopped canned tomatoes with juice | 2 | celery stalks, diced |
| | | 2 | carrots, scraped and diced |
| ⅓ | cup olive oil | ½ | teaspoon sugar |
| 1 | medium-to-large onion, finely chopped | | Salt and freshly ground black pepper |
| 1 | large garlic clove, minced | | |

1. Put the tomatoes in a saucepan, cover, and simmer for 10 minutes.

2. Force the mixture through a food mill into a bowl and set aside.

3. Heat the oil in a saucepan and add the onion, garlic, celery, and carrots. Cook over medium heat for 4 minutes. Add the tomato purée and sugar, stir, and simmer for 20 minutes. Season with salt and pepper to taste.

*Variations:* For a richer sauce, stir in 3 tablespoons of butter after 15 minutes cooking time and simmer for 5 minutes. Add 1 tablespoon chopped fresh parsley leaves, ½ teaspoon dried rosemary, and ½ teaspoon dried basil for an Herb Marinara. For Bolognese Sauce, cook the tomatoes as directed, then brown 1 pound of lean ground beef in the oil with the vegetables. Follow the remaining instructions.

# Bucatini all'Amatriciana

*Serves 4*

½ pound slab bacon, cut
   into ⅓-inch cubes
6 tablespoons olive oil
¾ cup chopped onion
1 teaspoon minced garlic
3 cups chopped fresh or
   canned peeled and
   seeded tomatoes
   (imported Italian plum
   tomatoes are best)
¼ cup homemade chicken
   stock or canned broth

1 tablespoon chopped fresh
   basil, or 1 teaspoon
   dried basil
1 tablespoon chopped fresh
   parsley leaves
   Salt and freshly ground
   black pepper
1 pound bucatini or
   spaghetti
   Freshly grated
   Parmesan cheese

1. Bring 3½ quarts of water to a rolling boil in a large pot.

2. Meanwhile, fry the bacon cubes in a frying pan until they are crisp. Drain on paper towels.

3. Pour off all but 1 tablespoon of the bacon fat from the skillet and add 3 tablespoons of the olive oil. Add the onion and garlic and cook over medium-low heat for 8 minutes, stirring often. Add the tomatoes, chicken stock, and herbs. Stir and simmer over very low heat until the pasta is cooked.

4. Add 1 tablespoon of salt to the boiling water, stir, and add the pasta. Stir again and cook, *al dente,* just this side of tender.

5. Just before the pasta is done, stir the remaining 3 tablespoons of olive oil and the bacon cubes into the sauce and season with salt and pepper to taste.

6. Drain the pasta well and transfer it to a large serving bowl. Pour the sauce over the pasta and toss. Serve with the Parmesan cheese.

*Serving Suggestions:* Herb-breaded Fried Sardines and watercress and endive salad.

# Fedelini with Olive Oil, Red Pepper, and Garlic Sauce

*Serves 4*

½   cup olive oil
1   cup julienne strips
    sweet red pepper
1½  teaspoons minced garlic
¼   teaspoon hot red pepper
    flakes (optional)

1   pound imported Italian
    fedelini (thin pasta)
    Salt and freshly ground
    black pepper
    Freshly grated
    Parmesan cheese

1. Bring 3½ quarts of water to a rolling boil in a large pot.
2. Meanwhile, heat the oil in a frying pan and add the red pepper strips and garlic. Cook over medium-low heat for 10 minutes.
3. When the water boils, add 1 tablespoon salt, stir, and add the pasta. Stir and cook until *al dente,* or until just tender. Drain well and transfer to a bowl.
4. Immediately add the oil and pepper mixture and pepper flakes. Toss and season well with salt and pepper. Sprinkle with the Parmesan cheese and toss again. Serve immediately.

*Variation:* Yellow peppers can be substituted for the sweet red peppers in the recipe. Green peppers aren't nearly as sweet.
*Serving Suggestions:* Escarole with Onion–Mozzarella Topping and/or Perfect Butter-roast Chicken.


# Fettuccine Gorgonzola

*Serves 4*

    Salt and freshly ground
    black pepper
1   pound fettuccine
    (imported if possible)
2   cups heavy cream
1   cup diced Gorgonzola
    cheese

2   tablespoons freshly
    grated Parmesan cheese
    Chopped fresh parsley
    leaves

1. Bring 3½ quarts of water to a rolling boil in a large pot. Add 1 tablespoon salt, stir, and add the fettuccine. Stir and cook until the pasta is *al dente.*
2. Meanwhile, bring the heavy cream to a boil in a large enamel-coated or stainless steel saucepan. Cook over high heat for 4 minutes,

stirring to prevent boiling over. Add the Gorgonzola and Parmesan cheeses to the cream and stir until the cheeses melt. Season with salt and pepper to taste.

3. Pour the sauce into a large bowl and drain the pasta well. Immediately transfer the pasta to the bowl with the sauce and toss. Sprinkle with parsley.

*Serving Suggestions:* Individual Composed Salads and Chocolate Tart.

# Fusilli with Uncooked Tomato–Basil Sauce with Mozzarella

*Serves 4*

1¾ pounds peeled fresh ripe
    or canned imported
    Italian plum tomatoes,
    halved, seeded, and
    cubed
¼ cup minced scallions
½ cup olive oil
1 tablespoon fresh lemon
    juice
12 large fresh basil leaves,
    chopped, or 1 teaspoon
    dried basil

1 tablespoon chopped
    fresh parsley leaves
    Salt and freshly ground
    black pepper
1 pound fusilli
6 ounces mozzarella, cut
    into ½-inch cubes

1. One hour before serving dinner, combine the cubed tomatoes, scallions, olive oil, lemon juice, basil, and parsley in a large bowl. Season well with salt and pepper. Cover and let stand at room temperature.

2. Twenty minutes before serving, bring 3½ quarts of water to a rolling boil in a large pot. Add 1 tablespoon salt, stir, and add the pasta. Cook until the pasta is *al dente,* just until tender.

3. Drain the pasta well and transfer it to the bowl with the tomato mixture. Toss and let the pasta cool for 5 minutes. Add the mozzarella and toss.

*Variations:* Spaghetti or linguine can be substituted for the fusilli, and 1 tablespoon of chopped drained anchovies can be added to the sauce when mixing it.

*Serving Suggestions:* Creamed Spinach with Pine Nuts and Fresh Cantaloupe and Cherries.

# Fedelini Puttanesca

Serves 4

¼ cup olive oil
2 large garlic cloves, minced
6 anchovy fillets, drained and finely chopped
2½ cups chopped fresh peeled and seeded tomatoes
3 tablespoons tomato paste
¼ cup cocktail onions, drained
2 tablespoons thinly sliced cornichon

1 tablespoon well-drained capers
½ cup black olive slivers
½ cup homemade chicken stock or canned broth
Pinch of dried hot red pepper flakes
¼ teaspoon dried oregano
¼ teaspoon dried basil
Salt and freshly ground black pepper to taste
1 pound fedellini
Chopped fresh parsley leaves

1. Bring 3½ quarts of water to a rolling boil in a large pot.

2. Meanwhile, heat the olive oil in a large frying pan. Add the garlic and cook over medium-low heat for 3 minutes, stirring often. Add the remaining ingredients, except the fedellini and parsley. Bring to a boil, immediately lower the heat, and simmer over very low heat for 10 minutes while the pasta is cooking.

3. Add 1 tablespoon of salt to the boiling water and cook the pasta *al dente,* or just this side of tender. Drain the pasta well and transfer it to a large serving dish.

4. Pour the sauce over the pasta and toss. Sprinkle with the parsley.

*Serving Suggestions:* Veal Scallops with Artichoke Hearts and Mushrooms and a mixed green salad.

# Rigatoni with Escarole and Broccoli

*Serves 4*

3 large stalks fresh broccoli
Salt
1 pound rigatoni
1 small head escarole, washed and chopped into 1½-inch pieces
⅔ cup olive oil, or as needed
2 large garlic cloves, finely chopped

¼ cup chopped fresh parsley leaves
½ cup freshly grated Parmesan cheese, or to taste (optional)
Freshly ground black pepper

1. Bring 3½ quarts of water to a rolling boil in a large pot.

2. Meanwhile, cook the broccoli in 2½ cups of simmering water for 6 to 8 minutes, or until it is just tender. Drain.

3. Add 1 tablespoon of salt to the boiling water, stir, and add the rigatoni. Stir the pasta and boil until it is *al dente,* just tender, stirring occasionally (about 10 to 12 minutes).

4. Meanwhile, blanch the escarole in 2 cups of boiling water for 2 minutes. Drain immediately and pat the pieces dry between paper towels. Set aside.

5. Chop the broccoli into bite-sized pieces.

6. Heat the olive oil in a large frying pan and add the garlic. Cook over low heat for 5 minutes, stirring occasionally.

7. One minute before the pasta is done, add the broccoli to the frying pan and stir-fry for 1 minute.

8. Drain the pasta and transfer it to a large bowl. Immediately add the broccoli mixture, the escarole, and parsley and toss. Add the Parmesan cheese and salt and pepper to taste. Toss. It may be necessary to add a little more olive oil. The oil should coat the pasta, but after tossing no oil should remain in the bottom of the bowl.

*Variation:* Half a cup of chopped roasted red, green, or yellow peppers can be added to the hot pasta when the broccoli and escarole are added.

*Serving Suggestion:* Oven-fried Cod Fillets with Ground Almond Crust.

# Linguine with Creamy Pesto Sauce

*Serves 4*

| | |
|---|---|
| 1 pound linguine | ½ cup plus |
| 1¾ cups packed fresh basil leaves, coarsely chopped | 2 tablespoons olive oil |
| | Salt and freshly ground black pepper to taste |
| ¼ cup coarsely chopped fresh parsley leaves | ¼ cup pine nuts |
| 1 8-ounce container soft cream cheese | Freshly grated Parmesan cheese |
| 1 minced garlic clove | |

1. Bring 3½ quarts of water to a rolling boil in a large pot.

2. Meanwhile, put the basil, parsley, cream cheese, garlic, ½ cup olive oil, and salt and pepper in a food processor or blender. Combine until very smooth, scraping down the sides of the container with a spatula once or twice. Turn the mixture into a bowl and set aside.

3. Add 1 tablespoon of salt to the boiling water, stir, and add the pasta. Cook until the pasta is *al dente,* just until tender.

4. Meanwhile, heat 2 tablespoons of the oil in a frying pan and lightly brown the pine nuts. Drain on paper towels.

5. Drain the pasta well and transfer it to a large bowl. Add the Pesto Sauce and pine nuts and toss well.

*Serving Suggestions:* Scarpariello Chicken and sliced tomato salad with Italian dressing.

# Pasta with Sun-dried Tomatoes, Pine Nuts, and Prosciutto

*Serves 4*

| | |
|---|---|
| ¼ cup pine nuts | 1 tablespoon salt |
| 3 tablespoons olive oil | 1 pound penne, ziti, or spaghetti |
| 6 tablespoons butter | |
| ½ cup finely chopped onion | ⅛ teaspoon hot red pepper flakes |
| 2 tablespoons finely chopped shallots | |
| 8 ounces sun-dried tomatoes, cut into ¼-inch-thick strips (see Note) | ¼ pound thinly sliced prosciutto, cut into thin strips |
| 2 cups heavy cream, or as needed | ¾ cup freshly grated Parmesan cheese |

1. Bring 3½ quarts of water to a rolling boil in a large pot.

2. Meanwhile, heat the oil in a medium-sized frying pan and cook the pine nuts over medium-high heat until lightly browned, tossing often. Drain on paper towels.

3. Melt the butter in a large frying pan. Add the onion and shallots and sauté over low heat for 10 minutes, stirring often. Add the tomatoes and cream. Stir and simmer the mixture for 10 minutes.

4. Add the salt to the boiling water and cook the pasta until it is *al dente,* or just until tender.

5. Meanwhile, stir the pepper flakes, prosciutto, and pine nuts into the sauce.

6. Drain the pasta well and transfer it to a large bowl. Pour the sauce over the pasta and toss well. Add the cheese and toss. Taste for seasoning. Pass the peppermill.

NOTE: Sun-dried tomatoes are available in specialty food stores or Italian markets.

The recipe can be made successfully without the pine nuts or prosciutto.

*Serving Suggestions:* Lemon and Garlic Chicken with Onions and Boston lettuce salad.

# Pasta Primavera with Crisp Bacon Strips

## Serves 10 to 12

The last-minute addition of crisp cooked bacon strips brings a new dimension to an already enormously appealing and delectable dish. Pasta Primavera can be served hot, lukewarm, or cold. Be sure to toss the ingredients thoroughly just before serving.

½   cup olive oil (virgin, if possible)
1   cup chopped onion
1   teaspoon finely chopped garlic
1   sweet red or green pepper, diced
1   medium-sized zucchini, quartered and cut into ¼-inch-thick slices
½   pound fresh mushrooms, thinly sliced
    Salt
1¼  cups fresh peas
2   cups chopped fresh broccoli stalks and flowerets

1   tablespoon chopped fresh basil, or 1 teaspoon dried basil
2   teaspoons finely chopped fresh oregano, or 1 teaspoon dried oregano
¼   cup finely chopped fresh parsley leaves
1   pound ziti or penne
    Freshly ground black pepper
1   cup freshly grated Parmesan cheese
1½  cups heavy cream
½   pound slab bacon, cut into strips ¼-inch thick by 1½ inches long, crisp-fried and drained

1. Bring 3½ quarts of water to a rolling boil in a large pot.

2. Meanwhile, in a large frying pan, heat ¼ cup of the olive oil and cook the onion, garlic, and pepper over medium heat for 5 minutes, stirring often. Add the zucchini and mushrooms to the pan, stir, and simmer for 8 minutes.

3. Meanwhile, cook the peas and broccoli in lightly salted boiling water in separate saucepans until they are just tender. Do not overcook them.

4. Add 1 tablespoon of salt to the boiling water in the large pot, stir, and add the pasta. Stir again and cook the pasta until it is *al dente,* or just tender.

5. Meanwhile, season the onion and vegetable mixture with salt and pepper to taste and add the basil, oregano, and parsley. Combine well and remove from the heat.

6. Drain the peas and broccoli well and put them in a large bowl. Add the onion mixture and toss gently.

7. Drain the pasta and add it to the vegetable mixture. Pour the remaining ¼ cup of olive oil over the top and add the cheese. Immediately toss. Add the heavy cream and bacon and toss. Season with salt and pepper to taste. Serve immediately.

NOTE: Substitute any of the following vegetables for one or more of the vegetables in the recipe, except for the onions: sautéed eggplant cubes, grated blanched carrots, cooked cauliflower flowerets, diced raw tomatoes, buttered sautéed shredded red cabbage, or 1-inch lengths of cooked asparagus.

*Serving Suggestions:* A double recipe of Antipasto Salad and Cheesecake.


# Ziti with Cherrystone Clams

*Serves 6*

| | |
|---|---|
| ¼ cup butter | Salt |
| 1 teaspoon minced garlic | 1 pound ziti |
| 1 cup finely chopped onion | ¼ cup olive oil |
| 1 cup dry white wine | 2 tablespoons chopped fresh |
| 1 8-ounce bottle clam juice | parsley leaves |
| 6 dozen cherrystone clams | Freshly grated |
| (the smallest possible) | Parmesan cheese |
| 1 teaspoon dried thyme | |

1. Bring 3½ quarts of water to a rolling boil in a large pot.

2. Meanwhile, melt the butter in a frying pan. Add the garlic and onion and cook over medium heat for 5 minutes, stirring often.

3. Put the wine, clam juice, and clams in a large flameproof casserole or Dutch oven. Cover and bring to a boil. Cook over medium-high heat until the clams open, about 5 minutes. Discard any clams that don't open.

4. Strain the liquid into a saucepan and cover the clams and vegetables to keep them warm. Return the clam liquid to a boil, add the thyme, and lower the heat to a simmer.

5. Meanwhile, add 1 tablespoon of salt to the boiling water and cook the pasta until it is *al dente,* or just tender.

6. Drain the pasta and transfer it to a large bowl. Toss with the oil and parsley. Add the clam liquid, clams, and vegetables. Toss gently. Serve with freshly grated Parmesan cheese.

*Serving Suggestions:* Miniature Puff Pastry Pizzas Niçoise, hot cooked broccoli, and Cheesecake.

# Linguine with Bouillabaisse Sauce

*Serves 6*

| | |
|---|---|
| 3 tablespoons olive oil | ½ teaspoon ground saffron |
| 1 medium-sized onion, chopped | 2 dashes of Tabasco sauce |
| 1 teaspoon minced garlic | ½ cup dry white wine |
| 1 leek (white part only), cleaned, washed, and thinly sliced | 1¼ cups bottled clam juice |
| | 1 pound boneless flounder fillets, cut into 1-inch pieces |
| 1 carrot, scraped and diced | 1 pound boneless sea bass fillets, cut into 1-inch pieces |
| 1½ cups chopped imported Italian plum tomatoes | Salt |
| 1 bay leaf | 1½ pounds linguine |
| ½ teaspoon dried thyme | ½ cup heavy cream |
| 1 tablespoon chopped fresh parsley leaves | Freshly ground black pepper |

1. Heat the olive oil in a large flameproof casserole. Add the onion, garlic, leek, and carrot, stir, and cook over medium low heat for 8 minutes. Add the remaining ingredients through the fish and stir. Bring to a boil, lower the heat, and simmer for 15 minutes.

2. Bring 4½ quarts of water to a rolling boil in a large pot. Add 1 tablespoon of salt, stir, and add the pasta. Stir and cook until the pasta is *al dente,* or just until tender.

3. Discard the bay leaf and stir the heavy cream into the sauce and season it with salt and pepper to taste.

4. Drain the pasta well and turn it into a large bowl. Pour the sauce over the pasta and toss. If desired, serve with freshly grated Parmesan cheese.

*Variation:* 1 pound shelled and deveined medium-sized shrimp can be substituted for the flounder.

*Serving Suggestions:* French Onion Tart with Pepper-flecked Pastry, Arugola and Endive Salad with Herb Dressing, and Broiled Fresh Peaches with Strawberry–Crunch Filling.

# Spaghetti with Creamy Mussel and Tomato Sauce

*Serves 4*

| | |
|---|---|
| 1 | bottle dry white table wine |
| 1 | medium-sized onion, quartered |
| 1 | bay leaf |
| 48 | mussels (the smallest possible), scrubbed and bearded |
| | Salt |
| 1 | pound spaghetti |
| 4 | tablespoons butter |
| 2 | tablespoons minced shallots |
| 6 | firm fresh mushrooms, thinly sliced |
| 1/4 | cup Marsala |
| 1 1/2 | cups heavy cream |
| 3/4 | cup diced, peeled, and seeded fresh tomatoes |
| 1 | tablespoon tomato paste |
| 1 | tablespoon chopped fresh parsley leaves |
| 1/4 | cup freshly grated Parmesan cheese, or to taste |

1. Bring 3½ quart of water to a rolling boil in a large pot.

2. In another large pot put the wine, onions, and bay leaf and bring to a boil. Add the mussels, cover, and cook over medium-high heat for about 6 minutes, or until the mussels open. Discard any mussels that don't open. Remove the mussels from the shells and set aside.

3. Add 1 tablespoon of salt to the boiling water, stir, and add the spaghetti. Stir and cook until the spaghetti is *al dente,* just until tender.

4. Meanwhile, melt the butter in a frying pan. Add the shallots, mushrooms, and Marsala and cook over medium heat for 4 minutes. Remove the shallots and mushrooms with a slotted spoon and put them on a plate. Add the heavy cream to the pan and bring to a boil. Cook over high heat for 3 minutes, or until thickened slightly. Add the mussels, mushroom mixture, tomatoes, tomato paste, and parsley. Stir and simmer until pasta is cooked.

5. Drain the pasta and transfer it to a large bowl. Top with the sauce and toss. Add the Parmesan cheese and toss.

*Serving Suggestions:* Scarpariello Chicken and cooked Italian green beans.

# Rice

Preparing superb rice dishes need not be complicated, but this natural wonder does require more than casual *heat and serve* treatment. For one thing, depending on which variety is to be prepared, rice requires precise cooking time and ingredient measurements. The nature of those ingredients may also call for cooking several items in advance of the final rice preparation. The results are worth the care and effort. Rice enhances the flavor of the added ingredients, provides the perfect texture to complement those ingredients, and supports the main dish without diluting its taste. It is no wonder that people the world over eat rice more than any other food.

## Creole Rice

*Serves 4 to 6*

2   tablespoons butter
2   tablespoons minced onion
2   cups homemade chicken stock or canned broth
1   cup long-grain rice
1   cup chopped fresh mushrooms

3   tablespoons diced pimiento
1   medium-sized tomato, peeled, seeded, and diced

1. Preheat the oven to 350 degrees.
2. Melt the butter in a 2-quart ovenproof saucepan. Add the onion and cook for 2 minutes, stirring often. Pour in the stock and stir. Bring to a boil. Add the remaining ingredients and stir. Cover and bake for 20 minutes, or until the rice is tender.

# Lemon Rice

*Serves 4*

| | |
|---|---|
| 1 tablespoon butter | 1 teaspoon grated lemon rind |
| 2 tablespoons minced shallots | 1 cup long-grain rice |
| 1¾ cups hot homemade chicken stock or canned broth | Chopped fresh parsley leaves |
| 1 tablespoon fresh lemon juice | |

1. Melt the butter in a heavy saucepan. Add the shallots and cook for 5 minutes over medium heat, stirring often. Add the stock, lemon juice, and rind and bring to a boil. Add the rice, stir, and lower the heat. Simmer, covered, for 20 minutes.

2. Remove the pan from the heat and let stand for 5 minutes. Toss with a fork and sprinkle with the parsley.

# Rice Pilaf

*Serves 4*

| | |
|---|---|
| 2 tablespoons butter | Chopped fresh parsley leaves |
| ¼ cup minced onion | |
| 1 cup long-grain rice | |
| 2 cups homemade chicken stock or canned broth | |

1. Preheat the oven to 350 degrees.

2. Melt the butter in an ovenproof 1½-quart saucepan. Stir in the onion and cook until transparent, stirring often, about 4 minutes. Stir in the rice and coat the rice with the butter. Pour in the chicken stock and bring to a boil.

3. Immediately cover and bake for about 20 minutes, or until tender. Sprinkle lightly with parsley before serving.

# Polynesian Rice

*Serves 4*

2   cups homemade chicken
    stock or canned broth
1   tablespoon butter
1   cup long-grain rice
1   tablespoon curry powder
½   cup drained crushed
    pineapple

¼   cup minced sweet green
    pepper
1   scallion, thinly sliced
1   cup seedless green grapes
¼   cup golden raisins
    Salt and freshly ground
    black pepper to taste

1. Bring the chicken stock to a boil in a small saucepan.

2. Melt the butter and add the rice in a heavy medium-sized saucepan. Stir and pour in the boiling chicken stock, stir, and lower the heat to a simmer. Cover and cook for 20 minutes.

3. Remove from the heat and let stand for 5 minutes. Add the remaining ingredients and toss gently. Recover and let stand 5 minutes longer.

# Risi e Bisi

*Serves 6*

1   tablespoon butter
1   tablespoon minced
    shallots
2   cups homemade chicken
    stock or canned broth

¾   cup fresh peas
1   cup long-grain rice
½   teaspoon salt

1. Melt the butter in a heavy saucepan. Add the shallots and cook for 1 minute. Add the chicken stock and peas and bring to a boil. Add the rice and salt, stir, cover, and simmer for 20 minutes.

2. Turn off the heat and let the mixture stand for 5 minutes. Toss gently and serve.

# Risotto Primavera

*Serves 6*

| | |
|---|---|
| ½ cup dry white wine | ½ cup green peas, cooked and drained |
| 6½ cups homemade chicken stock or canned broth | 2 cups Italian short-grain rice (Arborio) |
| 8 tablespoons (1 stick) butter | ⅛ teaspoon powdered saffron |
| 1 cup finely chopped onion | ½ cup freshly grated Parmesan cheese, or to taste |
| ¾ cup ½-inch lengths asparagus | Freshly ground black pepper |
| ¾ cup quartered ¼-inch-thick zucchini slices | |

1. Bring the wine and chicken broth to a boil in a saucepan. Lower the heat and simmer over very low heat.

2. Melt 6 tablespoons of the butter in a heavy enamel, stainless steel, or nonstick saucepan. Add the vegetables and cook over medium heat for 5 minutes, stirring often.

3. Add the rice and stir the mixture with a wooden spoon until the rice is evenly coated with the butter. Pour in 2 cups of the hot broth mixture, or enough to just cover the rice and vegetables. Bring to a boil, stir, and cook over medium heat, stirring often, until the broth is absorbed by the rice.

4. Add the saffron and 1 cup of the hot broth mixture and let it cook, stirring often, until more liquid is needed. Repeat this procedure until all the broth mixture is used. The cooking time is approximately 20 minutes. The rice should be tender and the mixture slightly creamy.

5. Remove the pan from the heat and stir in the Parmesan cheese and the remaining 2 tablespoons of butter. Season with pepper to taste.

*Variations:* 2 cups of diced fennel can be substituted for the asparagus, zucchini, and peas. For Risotto Milanese, just eliminate the green vegetables. For Shrimp Risotto, substitute 2 cups of small raw shrimp for the green vegetables in the recipe.

*Serving Suggestions:* Crusty Italian bread, mixed green salad, and dry white wine.

# Saffron Rice Ring with Sautéed Mushrooms

*Serves 8*

| | |
|---|---|
| 6 tablespoons butter | Vegetable oil for |
| 2 tablespoons minced shallots | greasing the ring mold |
| | 1 pound whole fresh mushrooms |
| 1 teaspoon powdered saffron | |
| ½ teaspoon salt | |
| 2 cups long-grain rice | |
| 3½ cups boiling homemade chicken stock or canned broth | |

1. Melt 2 tablespoons of the butter in a large heavy saucepan. Add the shallots and cook over low heat for 5 minutes, stirring often. Add the saffron, salt, and rice and stir. Cook for 1 minute, stirring constantly. Add the boiling stock, stir, and lower the heat to a simmer. Cover and simmer for 20 minutes. Remove from the heat and let stand, covered, for 5 minutes.

2. Spoon the rice into a well-greased 8-cup ring mold. Press the top of the rice down with the back of a large spoon.

3. Put the mold in a large pan filled with 1 inch of boiling water. Cover the rice and let it stand for 5 minutes.

4. Meanwhile, melt the remaining 4 tablespoons of butter in a large frying pan. Add the mushrooms and cook over medium-high heat for 5 minutes, shaking the pan often.

5. Remove the ring mold from the pan of water and dry the bottom. Place a round serving dish over the mold. Firmly holding the dish and mold, invert and shake once with vigor. The rice should release onto the dish. If it doesn't, repeat again.

6. Spoon the mushrooms into the center of the rice ring and serve immediately.

# Minnesota-style Wild Rice

*Serves 6*

| | |
|---|---|
| 1¼ cups wild rice (premium grade whole grain is best) | 1 small onion, minced |
| 1½ cups water | ¼ pound fresh mushrooms, chopped |
| 1½ cups homemade chicken stock or canned broth | ½ cup heavy cream |
| 5 tablespoons butter | Salt and freshly ground black pepper |

1. Rinse the rice in a strainer under cold running water and drain.

2. Combine the water and stock in a saucepan and bring to a boil. Add the rice, stir, and bring back to a boil. Immediately lower the heat, cover, and simmer for 45 minutes, or until the rice is tender, but not mushy.

3. Meanwhile, melt 3 tablespoons of the butter in a frying pan. Add the onion and sauté over medium heat for 5 minutes, stirring often. Add the mushrooms and cook for 5 minutes longer. Remove from the heat and set aside.

4. Preheat the oven to 375 degrees. Drain the cooked rice well in a strainer.

5. In a large bowl, combine the rice, onion, and mushroom mixture with the heavy cream. Season with salt and pepper to taste.

6. Transfer the mixture to a shallow baking dish and dot with the remaining 2 tablespoons of butter. Bake for 15 minutes.

*Variations:* Substitute beef stock for the chicken stock.

Add ½ cup toasted almonds, chopped walnuts, or pecans to the cooked rice with the onion and mushroom mixture and heavy cream.

One tablespoon of grated orange rind can also be added to the cooked rice before baking.

Two tablespoons minced shallots can be substituted for the onion in the recipe.

# Rice with Vegetables and Cream

*Serves 4*

| | |
|---|---|
| 2 tablespoons butter | ½ cup diced carrots |
| 2 tablespoons minced shallots | ½ cup seeded and diced zucchini |
| 2 cups boiling water | ½ cup heavy cream |
| 1 cup long-grain rice | Freshly ground black pepper |
| ½ teaspoon salt | |
| ½ cup frozen green peas | |

1. Melt the butter in a heavy saucepan. Add the shallots and cook over medium heat for 5 minutes, stirring often. Add the boiling water, rice, and salt. Stir, cover, and cook over low heat for 20 minutes.

2. Meanwhile, cook all the vegetables in 2½ cups of boiling water for 5 minutes, or just until they are tender. Drain and reserve.

3. Remove the cooked rice from the heat and let it stand, covered, for 5 minutes.

4. Meanwhile, bring the heavy cream to a boil in a saucepan and cook over medium-high heat for 3 minutes.

5. Uncover the rice and add the vegetables and cream. Gently combine and season with salt and pepper to taste.

# Potatoes

A generation of Americans has been raised to believe that potatoes grow fried in small paper sacks or cups, to be served with Big Macs and Whoppers. With an imagination and really very little effort, potatoes can be restored to their rightful position among the royal family of vegetables. When serving company a delicious potato dish, the cook can be almost certain that no leftovers will remain.

## Fresh Potato Chips

*Serves 8*

3 *pounds small Idaho
potatoes, peeled and sliced
very thin*

*Oil for deep frying
Salt*

1. As the potatoes are sliced, put them in a large bowl or container filled with cold water. Leave in the water for 30 minutes.

2. Drain and cover the potatoes with ice-cold water.

3. Drain and pat the potato slices dry. This is an essential step in making good potato chips.

4. Heat about 3 inches of oil to 375 degrees in a French potato fryer or a large heavy saucepan. Cook a fist full of the potatoes at a time, stirring often, until golden brown. This will only take 3 or 4 minutes.

5. Drain the cooked chips and continue cooking the rest in batches in the same manner. Keep the frying oil at 375 degrees.

6. Season the hot chips lightly with salt as they are cooked. To insure crispness, keep them separated until placing them in 1 or 2 serving dishes.

# Waffled Potato Chips

*Serves 6 to 8*

A mandoline is required to make waffled potato chips. It is an expensive piece of equipment, but masterful in slicing food in varying widths and lengths, cutting perfect julienne strips, and waffling.

| | |
|---|---|
| 4  *medium-sized potatoes (as uniform in shape as possible)* | *Peanut oil* *Salt and freshly ground black pepper* |

1. Pour 2 inches of oil into a French fryer or large heavy saucepan. Have the wire basket ready if using one.

2. Peel the potatoes and drop them into cold water. Pat one potato very dry.

3. Before heating the oil, practice waffling. Adjust the waffle plate to the desired thickness (very thin) from the top of the teeth to the fixed blade on the mandoline. By hand or with the carriage, make the first cut. Turn the potato a quarter turn and make the second cut. A lattice-patterned cut potato will drop down. Adjust the thickness if necessary. Turn and make another cut and, if uniform, heat the oil to 375 degrees while slicing the potatoes in the same manner.

4. Cook a batch of waffled potatoes in the basket or without after cutting each potato as quickly as possible, so that the potato won't discolor. Fry in the oil for only a few minutes, stirring to turn, until light golden brown.

5. Drain and season lightly with salt and pepper. Repeat until all the potatoes are cut and fried. These are best served warm.

# Baked Potato Slices with Bacon

*Serves 4*

4 medium-sized Idaho
   potatoes
3 tablespoons butter
1 cup homemade chicken
   stock or canned broth
¼ pound slab bacon, cut
   into ½-inch cubes, or 6
   strips of bacon,
   unseparated, cut into ½-
   inch squares

1 tablespoon chopped fresh
   parsley leaves
   Freshly ground black
   pepper

1. Preheat the oven to 425 degrees.
2. Peel the potatoes and cut them into ⅛-inch-thick slices. Rinse the slices under cold running water and pat them dry with paper towels. Put the slices in an au gratin or shallow baking dish.
3. Heat the butter and the broth in a saucepan and pour the mixture over the potatoes. Sprinkle the bacon over the top.
4. Bake for about 40 minutes, or until the potatoes are golden brown. Garnish with parsley and pass the peppermill.

# Individual Roesti Potatoes

*Serves 4*

2 tablespoons vegetable oil
1 tablespoon butter
4 small Idaho potatoes,
   peeled and grated

Salt and freshly ground
black pepper

1. Heat the oil and butter in a large nonstick frying pan.
2. Spoon 2 tablespoons of the grated potatoes onto 4 areas of the skillet and flatten. Fry over medium-high heat until golden brown on each side.
3. Transfer to a warmed serving plate and season with salt and pepper. Cook 4 more in the same manner.

# Open-faced Roast Potatoes with Rosemary Butter

*Serves 6*

12  small Idaho or baking potatoes (each about 3 inches long)
 4  tablespoons butter, melted
 ½  teaspoon paprika

 2  teaspoons fresh rosemary, or 1 teaspoon dried rosemary
    Salt and freshly ground black pepper

1. Preheat the oven to 400 degrees.
2. Prick each potato on each side with the sharp point of a knife.
3. Cook on a rack in the oven for about 35 minutes, or until the potatoes are tender.
4. Cut each cooked potato in half lengthwise and place in a shallow baking pan.
5. Combine the butter, paprika, and rosemary and spoon the mixture over the potatoes. Sprinkle lightly with salt and pepper.
6. Run under the broiler for 4 to 5 minutes, or until the tops are golden brown.

# Potato Croquettes

*Serves 6*

5  medium-sized potatoes, peeled and cut into 1½-inch pieces
   Salt and freshly ground black pepper
3  large eggs

2  large egg yolks
   All-purpose flour
   Unseasoned dry bread crumbs
   Peanut oil

1. Bring 1 quart of water to a boil. Add 1 teaspoon salt, stir, and add the potatoes. Cook in boiling water for about 15 minutes, or until the potatoes are tender. Drain well.
2. Rice the potatoes or force through a food mill. Season with salt and pepper to taste.
3. Beat 1 egg with the yolks and add to the potatoes. Combine well. Add another yolk if the mixture is too dry.

4. Shape the mixture into 1½-inch barrels or croquettes and roll them in flour. Dip the croquettes in the 2 lightly beaten eggs and coat with bread crumbs.

5. Heat 1 inch of oil in a French fryer or skillet and fry the croquettes for a few moments until they are golden brown. Drain immediately on paper towels.

*Variation:* The croquettes can be coated with finely chopped almonds instead of bread crumbs.

# Gratin Dauphinoise

## Serves 6

Butter for greasing the
dish
2½ pounds boiling potatoes,
peeled and thinly sliced
1½ cups milk
1½ cups heavy cream

1 teaspoon salt
Freshly ground black
pepper to taste
1 cup grated Gruyère or
Swiss cheese

1. Preheat the oven to 400 degrees.

2. Generously grease a 13- to 14-inch au gratin or shallow baking dish.

3. Put the potato slices in the dish.

4. Bring the milk and cream to a boil in a saucepan. Stir in the salt and pepper. Pour the liquid over the potatoes and sprinkle with the cheese.

5. Transfer the baking dish to a baking sheet and bake for about 55 minutes, or until the potatoes are tender and the top is golden brown.

# Potato Shells with Spinach and Duchess Potatoes

*Serves 6*

6   medium-to-large Idaho or baking potatoes
1   pound fresh spinach, washed, stemmed, and chopped
8   tablespoons (1 stick) butter
3   tablespoons heavy cream
    Salt and freshly ground black pepper
3   large egg yolks

1. Preheat the oven to 400 degrees.
2. Prick each potato once and bake in the oven for 45 minutes, or until tender.
3. Meanwhile, cook the spinach in a saucepan in 3 cups of boiling water for 3 minutes. Drain very well, pressing out as much moisture as possible.
4. Cut ⅓ inch off the tops of the flat side of the potatoes. Remove the potato pulp with a spoon to a large bowl.
5. Mash the potatoes well with the butter and cream. Season with salt and pepper to taste. Add the egg yolks and combine thoroughly.
6. Transfer the potato mixture to a pastry bag fitted with a rose tube.
7. Place equal amounts of the spinach in each potato shell. Pipe the puréed Duchess potatoes over the spinach in each potato shell.
8. Put the filled shells on a baking sheet and run under the broiler until the tops are golden brown, just 1 or 2 minutes.

# Broiled Potato Shells with Herb Butter and Cheddar Cheese

*Serves 4*

4 small Idaho potatoes (about 3½ to 4 inches long)
3 tablespoons butter, melted
1 teaspoon chopped fresh dill, or ½ teaspoon dried dill
2 teaspoons chopped fresh parsley leaves
Salt and freshly ground black pepper
½ cup shredded Cheddar cheese

1. Preheat the oven to 375 degrees.

2. Scrub and dry the potatoes. Prick each potato in 2 or 3 places with the sharp point of a small knife.

3. Place the potatoes on the lower oven rack and bake for about 45 minutes, or until they are tender.

4. Remove the potatoes and cool for 5 minutes. Cut each in half lengthwise and scoop out the potato pulp (use it to make croquettes or for another use), leaving about ⅓ inch of potato pulp attached to the skins. Take care not to break the skins.

5. Combine the melted butter with the dill and parsley and brush over the inside of each shell. Sprinkle the shells with salt and pepper. Then sprinkle 1 tablespoon of the cheese over each shell and put the shells on a baking sheet.

6. Run under the broiler until the cheese sizzles and the shells are golden brown.

*Variations:* One small crushed garlic clove can be added to the herb butter. Other herbs can also be used, such as rosemary or thyme.

# Potato Salad with Dill Dressing

*Serves 8*

3  pounds new potatoes,
   well-scrubbed and left
   whole

## DILL DRESSING

1  large egg yolk at room
   temperature
1  tablespoon Dijon
   mustard
2  tablespoons olive oil
1/3 cup vegetable oil
2  tablespoons white wine
   vinegar
2  tablespoons strained
   vinegar from a jar of
   cornichon pickles

1/4 cup minced shallots
1/4 cup minced cornichons
   (optional)
1  tablespoon chopped fresh
   dill, or 1 1/2 teaspoons
   dried dill
   Salt and freshly ground
   black pepper to taste

1. Cook the potatoes in a saucepan in rapidly boiling water for 15 to 18 minutes, or until they are just tender.

2. Meanwhile, prepare the dressing: In a shallow bowl, beat the egg yolk with a wire whisk for 15 seconds. Beat in the mustard and, drop by drop, beat in the olive and vegetable oils. Beat in the vinegars until well combined. Add the remaining ingredients and mix well. Set aside.

3. Drain the cooked potatoes well. When cool enough to handle, peel them and cut them into 1/4-inch-thick slices.

4. Put the potato slices in a large bowl and add the dressing. Toss gently. Taste for seasoning. Cover and chill in the refrigerator for at least 3 hours.

# Phyllis' Potato Salad

*Serves 6 to 8*

4½ pounds red or boiling
  potatoes, unpeeled
2 cups mayonnaise, or as
  needed
3 tablespoons sugar

1 tablespoon celery seeds
1 medium-sized onion,
  grated
  Salt to taste

1. Cook the potatoes covered with boiling water in a large saucepan or pot until they are just tender, about 15 to 18 minutes, depending on the thickness of the potatoes. Drain well.

2. In a large bowl, combine the mayonnaise, sugar, celery seeds, and onion.

3. Peel the potatoes and scoop into rounded oval pieces with a teaspoon. Add the potatoes to the mayonnaise mixture and combine gently. Season with salt. Serve throughly chilled.

# Mashed Potatoes with Sauerkraut

*Serves 6*

3½ pounds boiling potatoes,
  peeled and sliced
3 tablespoons butter
  Heavy cream as needed

  Salt and freshly ground
  black pepper
1 cup hot well-drained
  sauerkraut

Boil the potatoes, covered in lightly salted boiling water, for about 15 minutes. Drain and transfer to a large bowl. Mash the potatoes with the butter. Add just enough cream to make them fluffy and season with salt and pepper to taste. Stir in the hot sauerkraut.

# Rum–Raisin Whipped Sweet Potatoes

*Serves 6*

⅓ cup raisins
3 tablespoons light rum, warmed
4 medium-sized sweet potatoes, scrubbed and dried
3 tablespoons butter, softened, plus extra butter for greasing the dish

*Few gratings of nutmeg*
*Salt and freshly ground black pepper to taste*
¾ *cup heavy cream*

1. Preheat the oven to 375 degrees.
2. Put the raisins in a small bowl and add the rum. Set aside.
3. Bake the potatoes on a rack in the oven for about 40 minutes, or until they are tender. Remove and let cool for 5 minutes. Peel the potatoes and put the pulp into a large bowl.
4. Mash the potatoes with the butter until smooth. Add the rum–raisin mixture and nutmeg and combine. Season with salt and pepper to taste.
5. Whip the heavy cream and fold it into the potato mixture.
6. Transfer the potatoes to a lightly buttered shallow baking dish and smooth the top. Bake for 15 minutes. Serve immediately.

# Vegetables

Everyone should have a garden. It doesn't have to be a half acre of corn, radishes, lettuce, and zucchini in neat and labeled rows. Even a single tomato plant in a pot or a miniature herb garden can delight and educate us to the miracle of how things grow; and that understanding helps when it comes to selecting, preparing, and serving vegetables. Until you've snapped a string bean off the vine and bitten into it, you will never know what flavor, texture, and aroma a vegetable can have, and why overcooking robs green vegetables of both their nutritional value and taste. Watching vegetables ripen teaches invaluable lessons on what coloring, smells, sizes, and textures to look for when shopping for produce, and how to adjust the vegetable portions of the menu to the growing seasons of the year. Familiarity with the growing process opens your mind and your kitchen to the wonders and uses of vegetables that would otherwise remain hidden behind modern packaging and processing, and company always appreciates perfect fresh-cooked vegetable dishes.

All this effort to understand foods that are destined simply to round out the main course? On the contrary, the real contribution of *nouvelle cuisine* and Chinese cooking throughout the world has been the highlighting of vegetables as main courses in themselves, foods that compete on an equal footing with the meat and fish dishes that were once considered the only *real* food on the table.

# Hot Cooked Asparagus
## Serves 4

When firm, elegant asparagus are first sighted in the market it's a sure sign of spring. Asparagus, the king of vegetables, is best savored served in its simplest form: add only a little butter, Hollandaise sauce, or vinaigrette dressing. Cooking asparagus couldn't be easier, but there are some rules to follow.

First, the asparagus tough stalk ends should be cut off, not snapped off; the ragged ends are unattractive and unnecessary. Asparagus should be peeled for better color, texture, and even cooking. Peel the asparagus stalks from just below the tops to the stalk end. This is easily accomplished with a vegetable peeler. Peeling with a knife makes it too easy to cut off too much of the vegetable. (Very thin asparagus, those ⅛ to ⅓ inch in thickness, don't need to be peeled.)

Asparagus needn't be tied in bundles, for the center stalks don't cook to the same tenderness as the outer ones, when those outer ones are done. The only advantage of the bundles is that they are easier to remove from the boiling water. Remove cooked asparagus with two spatulas.

The right cooking time is most important of all. Depending on the thickness of the stalk, asparagus is cooked anywhere from 4 to 8 minutes. However 6 minutes seems to be the perfect timing, for peeling the stalk aids in shortening the cooking time. Unless the stalks are very small or very large, 6 minutes is best. Reducing the cooking time or increasing it by only 1 or 2 minutes is the rule for special-sized asparagus. To test for doneness the cooked stalk should bend slightly, but not be limp. The following recipe can be doubled easily.

| | |
|---|---|
| 1 *pound fresh firm asparagus* | *Salt* *Melted butter* |

1. Bring 2 inches of water to a boil in a large frying pan or pot. Add 1 teaspoon of salt, stir, and add the trimmed and peeled asparagus. Return the water to a full boil. Lower the heat only slightly, to a slow boil, and cook for 6 minutes.

2. Remove the asparagus with 2 spatulas and drain thoroughly. Brush with butter and serve immediately. Pass the peppermill.

*Variations:* Serve with 1 cup Hollandaise Sauce (see recipe page 103) or immediately plunge into ice-cold water. Drain and pat dry. Place in a dish and top with ½ cup Vinaigrette Dressing (see recipe page 237), cover, and chill thoroughly. The latter makes a fine first course or light meal.

# String Beans with Walnuts

### Serves 6

1½ pounds string beans, trimmed

3 tablespoons butter

1 tablespoon vegetable oil

½ cup chopped walnuts

1 tablespoon walnut oil

Salt and freshly ground black pepper

1. Bring 1½ quarts of water to a boil in a large saucepan. Add the beans and cook over medium heat for 8 minutes, or only until the beans are tender-crisp. Drain the beans well and pat them dry with a clean dish towel. `

2. Heat the butter and vegetable oil in a large frying pan. Add the walnuts and cook over medium-high heat for about 4 minutes, stirring often.

3. Add the beans and toss in the mixture. Sauté for 3 minutes and add the walnut oil. Toss well and season with salt and pepper to taste.

*Variations:* Chopped almonds, pecans, hazelnuts, or macadamia nuts can be substituted for the walnuts, but eliminate the walnut oil.

## Puréed White Beans

*Serves 8*
*(Preparation begins the night before)*

| | |
|---|---|
| 1 pound dry Great Northern beans | 1 tablespoon salt |
| | 3 tablespoons butter |
| 1 medium-to-large onion, chopped | ¼ cup heavy cream, heated, or homemade chicken stock or canned broth |
| 1 large garlic clove, chopped | Freshly ground white pepper |
| 1 bay leaf | |

1. In a large bowl, soak the beans overnight in 1 quart of cold water.

2. Drain the beans and put them in a large heavy pot or saucepan. Add the onion, garlic, bay leaf, and salt. Cover the ingredients with 1 inch of water and bring to a boil. Lower the heat and simmer for 2½ to 3½ hours. The beans should be very tender.

3. Drain the beans well and discard the bay leaf. Put the beans in a processor with the butter and cream. Purée until very smooth. Season with salt and white pepper to taste.

## Buttered Brussels Sprouts with Bacon

*Serves 4*

| | |
|---|---|
| 1 pint fresh Brussels sprouts | Freshly ground black pepper to taste |
| 1 teaspoon salt | |
| 3 tablespoons butter | |
| 6 strips crisp-cooked bacon, chopped | |

1. Wash the Brussels sprouts under cold running water and remove any damaged outer leaves. Trim off the stems.

2. Bring 2 inches of water to a boil in a large saucepan. Add the salt, stir, and add the Brussels sprouts. Cook, covered, for about 12 minutes, or until the Brussels sprouts are tender-crisp. Drain well.

3. Melt the butter in a frying pan and gently toss the Brussels sprouts in the butter and bacon. Season with pepper.

# Haitian-style Braised Cabbage

*Serves 6*

3  tablespoons butter
2  tablespoons vegetable oil
4  cups shredded cabbage
1  medium-sized onion,
    thinly sliced and
    separated into rings
½  cup homemade chicken
    stock or canned broth
½  teaspoon dried thyme

¼  pound fresh mushrooms,
    thinly sliced
1  cup chopped, peeled, and
    seeded tomato
    Salt and freshly ground
    black pepper
1  tablespoon chopped fresh
    parsley leaves

1. Heat 2 tablespoons of the butter with the oil in a flameproof heavy casserole or Dutch oven. Add the cabbage, onion, chicken stock, and thyme. Stir and cover. Simmer for 20 minutes, stirring occasionally.

2. Add the mushrooms and tomatoes and season with salt and pepper to taste. Stir, recover, and simmer for 10 to 15 minutes, or until tender-crisp.

3. Add the remaining tablespoon of butter and the parsley. Combine and taste for seasoning.

# Red Cabbage and Cranberry Sauce

*Serves 6*

Here's an instant recipe that I include because of repeated requests from friends.

2  cups jarred pickled red
    cabbage, drained
1½ cups whole cranberry
    sauce

1  Delicious apple, cored
    and diced

Combine the ingredients well, cover, and refrigerate until ready to be served.

# Braised Sweet and Sour Red Cabbage

*Serves 6*

3    tablespoons butter
½    cup chopped onion
1    medium-sized red
     cabbage, cored and
     thinly shredded
2    tablespoons dark brown
     sugar
¼    cup freshly squeezed
     orange juice
1    teaspoon grated orange
     rind

3    tablespoons red wine
     vinegar
¼    cup plus 2 tablespoons
     homemade chicken stock
     or canned broth
     Salt and freshly ground
     black pepper to taste
1    tablespoon cornstarch

1. Melt the butter in a Dutch oven and cook the onion for 5 minutes, stirring often over medium heat. Add the remaining ingredients, except the cornstarch and 2 tablespoons of chicken stock, stir, cover, and simmer for 45 minutes, stirring occasionally.

2. Dissolve the cornstarch in the 2 tablespoons of chicken stock and stir into the cabbage. Cook over medium-high heat until the liquid thickens. Check the seasoning.

# Buttered Carrots with Grand Marnier

*Serves 4*

1    pound carrots, scraped
     and cut into julienne
     strips
½    teaspoon salt
2    tablespoons Grand
     Marnier

3    tablespoons homemade
     chicken stock or canned
     broth
2    tablespoons butter
2    teaspoons chopped fresh
     parsley leaves

1. Bring 3 cups of water to a rolling boil in a saucepan. Add the salt and carrots, stir, and cook over medium heat for 6 minutes, or until the carrots are tender-crisp. Drain the carrots.

2. Pour the Grand Marnier and stock into the saucepan and cook over high heat for 30 seconds. Whisk in the butter a tablespoon at a time.

3. Return the carrots to the pan and toss with the parsley.

# Carrots Vichy

*Serves 4*

This inexpensive, simple, and quick carrot recipe focuses on the lovely fresh flavor of the carrots. Never use canned or frozen carrots, since fresh ones are available all year. Carrots Vichy can be easily doubled or tripled.

| | | | |
|---|---|---|---|
| 2 | *tablespoons butter* | 1 | *tablespoon chopped fresh* |
| ½ | *teaspoon sugar* | | *parsley leaves* |
| ½ | *cup homemade chicken* | 1 | *pound carrots, scraped,* |
| | *stock or canned broth* | | *ends trimmed, and* |
| | *Salt and freshly ground* | | *carrots sliced very thin* |
| | *black pepper* | | |

1. In a medium-sized saucepan, heat the butter with the sugar, broth, and salt and pepper to taste. Bring the mixture to a boil. Add the carrots and bring to a boil again, lower the heat, cover, and simmer for 8 minutes, shaking the pan occasionally to prevent sticking and for even cooking.

2. Transfer the carrots to a heated serving dish and sprinkle with the parsley.

# Cauliflower with Curried Mornay Sauce and Black Sesame Seeds

*Serves 6*

1 medium-to-large head cauliflower, cored and cut into small flowerets

½ teaspoon black sesame seeds (available in Oriental grocery stores)

## CURRIED MORNAY SAUCE

4 tablespoons butter
3 tablespoons all-purpose flour
1 tablespoon curry powder
1 cup milk

¼ cup shredded Cheddar cheese (about 1½ ounces)
Salt and freshly ground black pepper

1. Cook the cauliflower in 2 inches of slowly boiling water in a large saucepan for about 8 minutes, or until it is just tender.

2. Meanwhile, prepare the sauce: Melt 3 tablespoons of the butter in a saucepan. Whisk in the flour and stir constantly for 1 minute. Add the curry powder and stir. Add the milk and whisk until the sauce boils and has thickened and is smooth. Stir in the cheese and the remaining tablespoon of butter. Cook, whisking, for 1 minute.

3. Drain the cauliflower and put it in a serving dish. Spoon the sauce over the top and sprinkle with the sesame seeds.

*Variations:* Instead of the sesame seeds, brown ½ cup of sliced almonds in 3 tablespoons of butter, drain, and sprinkle over the cauliflower and sauce.

NOTE: The Curried Mornay Sauce makes an easy and delicious substitute for hollandaise sauce for eggs Benedict. The sauce can also be used effectively over other vegetables: broccoli, asparagus, or steamed cabbage wedges.

# Puréed Cauliflower

*Serves 6*

1 teaspoon salt
1 medium-sized cauliflower, cored and separated into flowerets
1 medium-sized potato, peeled and cubed

1 teaspoon salt
2 tablespoons butter
Freshly ground white pepper

1. Bring 1 quart of water to a boil in a large saucepan. Add the salt, stir, and add the cauliflower and potato. Cook for about 15 minutes, or until the vegetables are tender. Drain well.

2. Put the cauliflower and potato in a food processor with the butter and season with salt and pepper to taste. Purée until well combined, but don't over purée. Serve immediately.

# Corn on the Cob with Chili Butter

*Serves 4*

## CHILI BUTTER

1 stick (4 ounces) butter, softened

1 tablespoon chili powder

8 ears of corn, husked
Salt and freshly ground black pepper

1. At least 4 hours before serving the corn, beat the butter and chili powder together with a wire whisk for 1 minute. Put the butter in a small container and refrigerate.

2. When ready to prepare the corn, bring 3 quarts of water to a boil in a large pot. Add the corn and cook over high heat for 5 minutes.

3. Turn off the heat, cover the pot, and let stand for 5 minutes. Immediately remove the corn, drain it well, and place the corn on a serving platter. Serve with the Chili Butter. Pass the salt and the peppermill.

# Double Cranberry Mold

*Serves 8 to 10*
*(Preparation begins the night before)*

½ cup cold water
2 envelopes plain gelatin
3 cups cranberry juice
3 cups fresh cranberries
¼ cup sugar
1 cup drained canned
  crushed pineapple

1 cup diced celery
¾ cup chopped walnuts
1 head curly endive,
  washed and dried

1. Combine the water and gelatin in a small bowl. Let the gelatin soften for 5 minutes.

2. Meanwhile, bring the cranberry juice to a boil in a large saucepan. Add the cranberries and sugar, stir, and cook over medium-high heat for about 5 minutes, or until the cranberries begin to pop open. Remove from the heat and stir in the pineapple, celery, and walnuts. Add the softened gelatin and stir until it dissolves.

3. Pour the mixture into a 3-quart mold, cover, and refrigerate overnight. Unmold on a serving plate lined with curly endive leaves.

# Escarole with Onion–Mozzarella Topping

### Serves 4

6 tablespoons olive oil, plus extra for greasing the pan

1 medium-to-large onion, thinly sliced

1 teaspoon minced garlic

1 large head escarole, washed and broken into bite-sized pieces

½ cup seasoned dry bread crumbs

½ cup freshly grated Parmesan cheese

½ teaspoon dried basil

Freshly ground black pepper to taste

1 cup shredded mozzarella

1. Preheat the oven to 350 degrees.

2. Heat 4 tablespoons of the oil in a large frying pan. Add the onion and garlic and cook for 10 minutes over medium-low heat, stirring often.

3. Meanwhile, bring 1 quart of water to a boil in a large saucepan. Plunge the escarole into the boiling water, stir once, and immediately drain in a colander.

4. Combine the bread crumbs, Parmesan cheese, basil, and pepper.

5. Lightly grease a shallow 9- by 13-inch baking pan or dish and spread the escarole over the bottom. Top with the onion and garlic. Sprinkle the bread crumb mixture over the top and top with the mozzarella. Drizzle with the remaining 2 tablespoons of olive oil.

6. Bake for about 25 minutes, or until the cheese is golden brown. Run under the broiler, if necessary.

## Lentils with Oil and Vinegar

*Serves 6*

| | |
|---|---|
| 1 pound lentils | 3 tablespoons red wine |
| 1 medium-sized onion, | vinegar |
| minced | 2 teaspoons Dijon |
| 1 bay leaf | mustard |
| 2½ cups water | 1 teaspoon Worcestershire |
| 3 cups homemade chicken | sauce |
| stock or canned broth | Freshly ground black |
| ½ teaspoon salt | pepper to taste |
| ½ cup olive oil | |

1. Put the lentils in a colander and run your fingers through them, discarding any foreign matter or shriveled lentils.

2. Put the washed and drained lentils in a heavy 3-quart saucepan and add the onion, bay leaf, water, chicken stock, and salt. Bring the mixture to a boil. Immediately lower the heat to a simmer, and cook for about 45 minutes, or just until the lentils are tender.

3. Drain well and transfer to a large bowl.

4. Combine the remaining ingredients and pour the mixture over the hot lentils. Toss gently and check the seasonings. Serve immediately or cool, cover, and refrigerate for several hours until well chilled.

*Variation:* Serve the hot cooked lentils with 1 pound of thin sliced sautéed Italian sweet sausage or kielbasa.

## Lima Beans with Roast Red Peppers

*Serves 4*

| | |
|---|---|
| 2 10-ounce packages frozen | 2 tablespoons butter |
| lima beans (Frozen lima | ½ cup drained diced jarred |
| beans are very good in | roasted red peppers |
| flavor and texture; fresh | Salt and freshly ground |
| ones are hard to find.) | black pepper |

1. Cook the lima beans in a saucepan following the package directions, but just until tender.

2. Meanwhile, melt the butter in a medium-sized frying pan and set aside.

3. Drain the limas well and toss them in the butter over medium heat. Add the red peppers, toss gently, and cook for 1 minute. Season with salt and pepper to taste.

# Caponata

*Serves 10 to 12   Makes about 1 quart*
*(Preparation begins the night before)*

| | | | |
|---|---|---|---|
| 1 | medium-sized eggplant, unpeeled and cut into 1-inch cubes Salt | 2 | tablespoons well-drained capers |
| ½ | cup olive oil | 4 | anchovy fillets, drained and minced |
| 1½ | cups finely chopped onion | 1 | tablespoon fresh chopped parsley |
| 1 | large garlic clove, minced | ½ | teaspoon dried basil |
| ½ | cup diced celery | ½ | teaspoon dried oregano |
| 1½ | cups diced, peeled, and seeded tomatoes | 3 | tablespoons red wine vinegar |
| ½ | cup green olive slivers | 1 | teaspoon sugar Salt and freshly ground black pepper to taste |

1. Sprinkle the eggplant lightly with salt and drain in a colander for 30 minutes.

2. Heat ¼ cup of the olive oil in a large frying pan. Add the onion, garlic, and celery and cook for 10 minutes. Transfer the mixture to a bowl.

3. Add the remaining ¼ cup of olive oil and cook the eggplant over medium-high heat for about 10 minutes, stirring often. Add the cooked onion mixture and the remaining ingredients. Simmer for 20 minutes, stirring often.

4. Cool the mixture in a large bowl, cover, and refrigerate overnight.

## Breaded Fried Mushrooms

### Serves 4

16  medium-sized fresh
    mushrooms, stems
    removed
    All-purpose flour

3  eggs, lightly beaten
   Italian-style dry
   bread crumbs
   Peanut oil

1. Dust the mushroom caps with flour and coat evenly with the beaten eggs. Then roll the mushrooms in the bread crumbs.

2. Heat ½ inch of oil in a large frying pan. Fry the mushrooms for a few minutes on each side until they are golden brown, turning with tongs, not a fork. (Precaution: Because of the moisture content in the mushrooms, the oil may splatter, so wear an apron and stand well back when turning the mushrooms.) Drain and serve immediately.

## Marinated Mushrooms

### Serves 6

1  cup olive oil
1  cup dry white wine
¼  cup homemade chicken
   stock or canned broth
1  dozen whole black
   peppercorns
½  teaspoon dried thyme
½  teaspoon salt

1  bay leaf
4  sprigs fresh parsley
1  teaspoon chopped garlic
⅓  cup fresh lemon juice
1  pound small whole fresh
   mushrooms
2  tablespoons chopped fresh
   parsley leaves

1. Put the oil, wine, stock, peppercorns, thyme, salt, bay leaf, parsley sprigs, and garlic in a large enamel or nonstick saucepan and bring to a boil. Lower the heat and simmer for 10 minutes.

2. Strain through a fine sieve and return the liquid to a clean saucepan. Discard the solids. Add the lemon juice and mushrooms and bring to a boil, lower the heat, and simmer for 5 minutes.

3. Immediately transfer the ingredients to a bowl and cool. Cover and refrigerate for at least 4 hours before serving.

4. Just before serving sprinkle with the parsley. The mushrooms will keep in the refrigerator for 4 days in a tightly covered jar.

# Baked Onion Halves with Honey

*Serves 6*

6 medium-sized yellow
   onions
1/4 cup honey
2 tablespoons butter,
   melted, plus extra for
   greasing the foil

1/4 cup homemade chicken
   stock or canned broth

1. Preheat the oven to 350 degrees.
2. Cut the ends off the onions and peel them. Cut each onion in half crosswise.
3. In a small saucepan heat the honey, butter, and chicken stock and set aside.
4. Butter a sheet of foil just large enough to hold and fold over the onions. Center the foil in a shallow baking dish. Place the onion halves side by side on the foil.
5. Pour the warmed honey mixture over the onions. Fold the foil loosely over the onions and close securely. Bake for 25 minutes, or until the onions are tender. Baste the onions with the pan juices. Run under the broiler for 1 or 2 minutes to brown the onions.

# Marinated Red Onion Rings

*Serves 8*

4 medium-sized red
   onions, thinly sliced
1 1/2 cups red wine vinegar

1 cup ice water
1 tray ice cubes

Separate the onion slices into rings and put them in a large bowl. Combine the vinegar, water, and ice and pour the mixture over the onion rings. Let stand for 30 minutes and drain well before serving.

# Pearl Onions with Raisins

*Serves 4*

| | |
|---|---|
| 1 **pound fresh pearl onions** | 1 **large bay leaf** |
| 3 **tablespoons olive oil** | 1¼ **cups dry white wine** |
| 3 **ounces raisins** | 2 **tablespoons sugar (optional)** |
| 3 **sprigs fresh parsley** | |
| 1 **sprig fresh thyme, or ½ teaspoon dried thyme** | |

1. Bring 3 cups of water to a boil in a heavy enamel-coated or nonstick saucepan. Add the onions and boil for exactly 2 minutes. Drain.

2. When the onions are cool enough to handle, cut off the stem ends and slip off the outer skins. As the onions are peeled, put them on a double layer of paper towels. Blot the peeled onions dry.

3. Heat the oil in a large frying pan and sauté the onions over medium-high heat for about 5 minutes, or until lightly browned. Add the remaining ingredients, bring to a boil, and simmer, covered, over very low heat for 45 minutes.

4. Discard the herbs and bay leaf and transfer the onions and raisins to a serving dish with a slotted spoon.

5. Bring the liquid in the pan to a boil and cook over high heat for 5 minutes. Pour the liquid over the onions and raisins. Toss and serve immediately, at room temperature, or well chilled.

# Sautéed Whole Shallots

*Serves 4*

| | |
|---|---|
| 1 **tablespoon vegetable oil** | *Salt and freshly ground black pepper* |
| 3 **tablespoons sweet butter** | *Snipped fresh chives* |
| 2 **cups whole peeled shallots** | |

Heat the oil and butter in a large frying pan. Add the shallots and shake the pan to coat them evenly. Cover and cook over medium-low heat for 5 minutes. Uncover and toss and increase the heat to medium. Cook for 3 or 4 minutes, or until the shallots are tender and light brown. Season with salt and pepper to taste. Sprinkle with the chives and toss gently.

# Braised Scallions

*Serves 4*

For this dish, select thick fresh scallions about ⅓ inch in diameter in bunches that are individually as alike as possible to ensure even cooking.

| | |
|---|---|
| 4 bunches scallions | Salt and freshly ground |
| ¼ cup dry white wine | black pepper to taste |
| 2 sprigs fresh parsley | Fluted lemon half |
| 1 bay leaf | Chopped fresh parsley |
| 3 tablespoons butter | leaves |

    1. Trim the root ends from the scallions and all but 2 inches of the green stem ends.

    2. Put the scallions in a large frying pan and add the white wine. Bring to a boil and cook for 30 seconds. Add the parsley sprigs, bay leaf, and enough hot water to just cover the scallions. Dot with the butter and sprinkle with salt and pepper. Bring to a boil, lower the heat, cover, and simmer for 8 minutes, or until the white parts of the scallions are tender-crisp. Discard the parsley sprigs and bay leaf.

    3. Transfer the scallions with a spatula to a warmed serving dish, rectangular in shape, if possible, and garnish with a fluted lemon half sprinkled with chopped parsley.

# Minted Fresh Peas

*Serves 6*

| | |
|---|---|
| 3 pounds fresh peas, shelled | Salt and freshly ground |
| 3 tablespoons butter | black pepper |
| 1 tablespoon chopped fresh mint, or 1 teaspoon dried mint | |

    1. In a large saucepan, cook the peas covered with boiling water until tender, about 12 minutes. Drain well.

    2. Melt the butter in a clean saucepan and add the cooked peas and mint. Toss and cook for 1 minute. Season with salt and pepper to taste.

## Stir-fried Snow Pea Pods

*Serves 4*

¼ cup peanut or vegetable
oil
¾ pound snow pea pods,
stem ends and strings
removed

2 teaspoons soy sauce
1 teaspoon sesame oil

Heat the oil in a wok or large frying pan. Add the snow pea pods and stir-fry, tossing constantly, for 1 minute. Sprinkle with the soy sauce and sesame oil, stir, and cook for 30 seconds longer. Transfer to a warmed serving dish with a slotted spoon.

## Spinach Packets

*Serves 4*

1 pound fresh spinach,
stemmed and washed
3 tablespoons olive oil
1 large garlic clove,
quartered

Salt and freshly ground
black pepper

1. Blanch the spinach for 30 seconds in a large saucepan filled with 1 quart of boiling water. Drain immediately, and cool.

2. Divide the spinach into 8 portions and make neat layers of the leaves. Fold the leaves into square 2- by 2-inch packets and press with paper towels to extract as much water as possible. The packets should be thin and flat.

3. Heat the oil in a large frying pan. Add the garlic and the spinach packets. Cook over medium heat for 2 minutes on each side.

4. Remove the spinach and sprinkle with salt and pepper. Serve immediately.

# Spinach Soufflé Roll

*Serves 6*

3  10-ounce packages frozen
   chopped spinach, cooked
   and drained very well
5  tablespoons butter,
   softened, plus extra for
   the baking pan, wax
   paper, and foil
4  large eggs, separated
   Salt and freshly ground
   black pepper

3  tablespoons all-purpose
   flour
1  cup milk
   Pinch of nutmeg
3  tablespoons freshly grated
   Parmesan cheese, or to
   taste

1. Preheat the oven to 400 degrees.

2. Butter a 10- by 15-inch jelly roll pan and line it with buttered wax paper. Butter the top of the wax paper. Set aside.

3. In a large bowl, combine the spinach with 2 tablespoons of the butter, the egg yolks, and salt and pepper to taste.

4. Beat the egg whites until stiff and fold into the spinach mixture.

5. Spread the spinach mixture over the wax paper in the prepared pan. Bake for about 15 minutes.

6. Meanwhile, prepare the sauce: Melt the remaining 3 tablespoons of butter in a saucepan. Whisk in the flour and cook over medium heat for 1 minute, whisking constantly. Add the milk and whisk over high heat until the mixture is smooth and has thickened. Season with nutmeg, salt, and pepper. Stir in the Parmesan cheese.

7. Invert the cooked spinach onto a buttered piece of foil. Peel off the wax paper and spread the sauce evenly over the spinach soufflé. Pick up the long end of the foil and roll up the filled spinach. Transfer the roll to a warmed serving dish. Serve immediately.

## Creamed Spinach with Pine Nuts

*Serves 4*

3 tablespoons butter
¼ cup pine nuts
1 small onion, minced
1½ pounds fresh spinach,
  washed and stemmed

⅓ cup sour cream
  Salt and freshly ground
  black pepper

1. Melt the butter in a large frying pan. Add the pine nuts and shake the pan often until the nuts are lightly browned. Remove them with a slotted spoon and set them aside.

2. Add the onion to the frying pan and cook for 4 or 5 minutes, or until transparent. Remove the pan from the heat.

3. In a large saucepan, cook the spinach covered with boiling water for 3 or 4 minutes, or until it is just wilted. Drain immediately.

4. Press out all the excess water from the spinach with the back of a spoon and chop the spinach finely. Add the spinach to the skillet with the onions and stir. Add the sour cream and pine nuts and season with salt and pepper to taste. Stir and heat thoroughly.

## Sautéed Tomato Fillets

*Serves 4*

3 medium-to-large firm ripe
  tomatoes, peeled, halved,
  and seeded
2 tablespoons butter
2 tablespoons olive oil

Salt and freshly ground
black pepper to taste
Chopped fresh parsley
leaves

1. Cut each tomato half into ½-inch-thick strips and drain on paper towels.

2. Heat the butter and oil in a large frying pan and add the tomatoes. Cook over medium-high heat for 3 minutes, turning gently. Season with salt and pepper to taste and sprinkle lightly with parsley. Serve immediately.

*Variations:* Add herbs, such as fresh chopped basil, thyme, or tarragon.

# Grilled Stuffed Tomatoes with Fried Bread Crumbs and Herb Butter

*Serves 6*

6   medium-firm ripe tomatoes
¾   cup vegetable oil
1   cup unseasoned fresh bread crumbs
6   tablespoons butter, softened
1   large garlic clove, finely minced

1   tablespoon chopped fresh parsley leaves
1   teaspoon dried basil
¼   teaspoon dried oregano
¼   teaspoon dried savory
    Salt and freshly ground black pepper

1. Preheat the oven to 375 degrees.

2. Cut about ⅓ inch off the stem ends of the tomatoes. Scoop out the center of each tomato. Drain the pulp well and chop it coarsely. Put the pulp in a bowl.

3. Heat the oil in a frying pan and fry the bread crumbs until they are crisp. Remove the crumbs with a slotted spoon and drain in a fine sieve.

4. Meanwhile, combine the butter with the garlic and herbs. Add the herb butter to the chopped tomato pulp and combine. Season with salt and pepper to taste and fold in the fried bread crumbs. Spoon the mixture in equal amounts into the tomato shells.

5. Put the stuffed tomatoes in a lightly buttered shallow baking dish. Bake for 12 minutes and run under the broiler 1 or 2 minutes, or until the tops are golden brown.

# Tomatoes Provençale

*Serves 6*

12 ½-inch-thick slices firm ripe tomato

3 tablespoons butter, plus extra for greasing the pan

2 large garlic cloves, minced

½ cup unseasoned dry bread crumbs

2 tablespoons chopped fresh parsley leaves

½ teaspoon dried thyme

½ teaspoon dried rosemary Salt and freshly ground black pepper Olive oil

1. Preheat the oven to 400 degrees.

2. Arrange the tomato slices in a lightly buttered shallow baking dish.

3. Melt the butter in a frying pan and add the garlic. Stir and cook for 3 minutes. Turn off the heat and stir in the bread crumbs and herbs. Season well with salt and pepper.

4. Spoon the mixture, in equal amounts, over each tomato slice and smooth over the surface. Drizzle each with a little olive oil. Bake for about 8 minutes. Serve immediately.

# Creamed Zucchini

*Serves 4 to 6*

2 medium-sized zucchini, shredded Salt and freshly ground black pepper

3 tablespoons butter

½ cup heavy cream

1. Sprinkle the shredded zucchini with salt and pepper and let it drain in a colander for 30 minutes. Press as dry as possible in a clean dish towel.

2. Melt the butter in a frying pan and add the zucchini. Stir and cook over medium-high heat for about 5 minutes. Add the cream and bring to a boil. Cook for 3 minutes over high heat and season with salt and pepper to taste.

# Mrs. M. T. Wong's Steamed Stuffed Zucchini
### (with thanks to Ann and C. C. Wong)

*Serves 4*

2 medium-sized Chinese mushrooms, soaked in warm water for 30 minutes and drained
1 tablespoon soy sauce
2 tablespoons cornstarch
1 tablespoon water
Freshly ground black pepper to taste

1½ cups ground pork
2 medium-to-large zucchini, peeled and cut crosswise into ¾-inch-thick slices
4 tablespoons peanut oil
1 tablespoon sesame oil

1. Pat the mushrooms dry and discard the stems. Finely chop the mushrooms and put them in a mixing bowl with the soy sauce, 1 tablespoon of cornstarch, water, and pepper. Mix well and combine with the pork.

2. With a small sharp knife, cut out the seeds and pulp from the center of the zucchini pieces and discard or use in soup-making.

3. Stuff the center of each zucchini slice with the pork mixture.

4. Heat the peanut oil in a large frying pan and sauté the zucchini on each side for 2 minutes, in 2 batches.

5. Pour 3 tablespoons of the oil from the skillet onto a plate. Add the remaining tablespoon of cornstarch and the sesame oil and combine.

6. Put the stuffed zucchini pieces on the plate in 2 layers and cook in a steamer for 20 minutes. Serve immediately.

## Zucchini and Carrots Julienne

Serves 4

3  tablespoons butter
1  small onion, finely
chopped
2  medium-sized zucchini,
cut into thin julienne
strips
2  carrots, peeled and cut
into thin julienne strips

¼  cup homemade chicken
stock or canned broth
1  teaspoon fresh lemon
juice
Salt and freshly ground
black pepper to taste
1  tablespoon chopped fresh
parsley leaves

1. Melt the butter in a large frying pan and cook the onion over medium heat for 4 minutes, stirring often. Don't let the onion brown. Add the remaining ingredients, except for the parsley, stir, cover, and simmer for 5 minutes.

2. Uncover, toss gently, and cook for 3 or 4 minutes, or until the vegetables are cooked but still tender-crisp. Sprinkle with the parsley before serving.

## Cold Marinated Zucchini

Serves 6

4  medium-sized zucchini
½  cup olive oil, plus oil for
coating the baking dish
12  fresh basil leaves, or 1
teaspoon dried basil
3  tablespoons minced
shallots

3  tablespoons vinegar, or
to taste
Salt and freshly ground
black pepper
Chopped fresh parsley
leaves

1. Preheat the oven to 350 degrees. Scrub the zucchini well, peel them, and cut them into ¼-inch-thick slices.

2. Put the slices in a lightly oiled shallow enamel or nonmetal baking dish in overlapping rows. Sprinkle with 4 tablespoons of the olive oil. Bake for 20 minutes.

3. Remove the dish from the oven and place half a basil leaf between some of the slices or sprinkle the slices with dried basil.

4. Heat the remaining olive oil in a saucepan. Add the shallots

and cook over medium-low heat for 5 minutes, stirring often. Add the vinegar and salt and pepper to taste.

5. Spoon the mixture over the zucchini, cool, cover, and refrigerate for several hours or overnight. Sprinkle with the parsley just before serving.

*Variation:* Yellow squash can be substituted for the zucchini, but peel the squash before cooking them.

## Sautéed Stuffed Zucchini Medallions

*Serves 4*

| | |
|---|---|
| 1 large zucchini, scrubbed | 2 large eggs, lightly beaten |
| 8 thin slices prosciutto | Unseasoned bread crumbs |
| 4 ounces mozzarella, thinly sliced | Peanut or vegetable oil for sautéing |
| Freshly grated Parmesan cheese | Salt and freshly ground black pepper |
| Dried oregano | Chopped fresh parsley leaves |
| All-purpose flour | |

1. Cut the zucchini into 16 ¼-inch-thick slices. Cut the prosciutto and mozzarella ¼ inch smaller in diameter than the zucchini slices and put a slice of each on 8 of the zucchini slices. Sprinkle each with Parmesan cheese and oregano. Place the remaining zucchini slices on top of each stuffed zucchini. Carefully dust each side with flour and dip in the beaten eggs. Coat each with bread crumbs and set aside. Heat ¼ inch of oil in a large frying pan and sauté the zucchini until they are golden on both sides. Sprinkle with salt and pepper to taste and parsley.

*Variation:* Small eggplant slices can be stuffed and prepared in the same manner.

# Zucchini Robinson

*Serves 6*

6 small-to-medium
zucchini, ends trimmed
and cut in half
lengthwise

¼ cup butter, melted, plus
extra butter for greasing
the baking sheet

1 garlic clove, crushed

¾ cup diced, peeled, and
seeded tomato

½ cup homemade or canned
tomato sauce
Dried oregano
Salt and freshly ground
black pepper

4 ounces mozzarella,
shredded
Olive oil

1. Bring 2 quarts of water to a boil in a large saucepan. Add the zucchini halves and simmer for 6 minutes. Drain.

2. Preheat the broiler.

3. Arrange the zucchini, cut side up, on a lightly greased baking sheet.

4. Combine the melted butter and garlic and brush over the zucchini.

5. Mix together the tomato and tomato sauce and spoon over the zucchini in equal amounts. Sprinkle the zucchini with oregano, salt, and pepper. Top with the cheese and sprinkle a few drops of olive oil over the top.

6. Cook under the broiler until the cheese turns golden brown. Serve immediately.

# Ratatouille

*Serves 12*
*(Prepare the night before serving)*

½ cup olive oil
1 large onion, thinly sliced
2 large garlic cloves, minced
3 medium-sized zucchini, cut in half lengthwise and cut into ¼-inch-thick slices
2 medium-sized eggplants, unpeeled and cut into 1-inch cubes
4 large firm ripe tomatoes, peeled and cubed
3 large sweet green peppers, seeded and cut into ¼-inch strips

2 teaspoons chopped fresh thyme, or ½ teaspoon dried thyme
1 tablespoon chopped fresh basil, or 1 teaspoon dried basil
1 tablespoon chopped fresh parsley leaves
Salt and freshly ground black pepper to taste
¼ cup dry white wine

1. Heat the oil in a large heavy flameproof casserole. Add the onion and garlic and cook over medium heat for 5 minutes, stirring often.

2. Add the remaining ingredients, stir, cover, and simmer for 30 minutes. Stir twice during the cooking time.

3. Uncover, stir, and cook over medium-low heat for 15 minutes.

4. Cool, cover, and refrigerate overnight to bring out the full flavor of the vegetables and herb combination.

NOTE: Ratatouille will keep in the refrigerator for 2 or 3 days if well covered. An excellent simple meal is Ratatouille served with Perfect Butter-roasted Chicken, French Bread, and white wine.

# Mixed Vegetables with Fine Egg Noodles

*Serves 6*

| | | | |
|---|---|---|---|
| 1 | cup frozen green peas | | Salt |
| 2 | medium-sized zucchini, quartered and cut into ⅛-inch-thick slices | 2 | tablespoons butter Freshly ground black pepper |
| 2 | carrots, scraped and diced | | Finely chopped fresh parsley leaves |
| 1½ | cups fine egg noodles | | |

1. Bring 2 quarts of water to a boil in a saucepan.

2. At the same time, in another saucepan, bring 2 cups of water to a boil.

3. When both pans of water are boiling, add ½ teaspoon of salt to each. Cook the noodles in the pan with the quart of water and the vegetables in the other pan. Cook each for about 5 minutes, or until they are tender.

4. Drain each and combine in a bowl. Add the butter and season with salt and pepper to taste. Sprinkle with the parsley.

*Variation:* Add only 1 tablespoon of butter and ¼ cup Crème Fraîche (see recipe page 277) for a creamy dish.

# Salads

There seems to be a cycle in the changing popularity of salads around the world. Just when one noted food writer announces that salads are boring and should be omitted from fine dining, chefs in France begin concocting the most exotic salads ever: greens with such unexpected ingredients as duck breasts, sweetbreads, warmed Chèvre cheese, or sliced noisettes of lamb. At almost the exact moment when home economists launch their massive assaults against fast-food chains, the burger giants and supermarkets introduce consumers to salad bars. And after years of facing menus that offered the predictable choices of salads labeled *chef's, shrimp,* or *fruit,* the new diet-conscious generation now enjoy salads that are as fashionable in their selections as the latest in jogging outfits or jewelry.

To avoid being relegated to what is now defined as the "iceberg and Thousand Island" generation, take a new look at the produce section or the greengrocer's bins. Whether you serve salad to guests as a first course, alongside the main dish, before the cheese and dessert as they do in France, or as the main dish, you will marvel at the variety of tastes, colors, and combinations that salads bring to today's table.

# Main-Course Salads

---

## *Poached Chicken*

*Makes about 3 cups cubed cooked meat*

Here is the basic recipe for cooking chicken for salad-making.

| | |
|---|---|
| 1 | medium-to-large onion, chopped |
| 1 | garlic clove, chopped |
| 2 | celery stalks, chopped |
| 2 | carrots, sliced |
| 1 | turnip, peeled and chopped |
| 1 | bay leaf |
| 6 | sprigs fresh parsley |
| 6 | whole black peppercorns |

½  teaspoon dried thyme
1  tablespoon salt
2  quarts water, or enough to cover the chicken and other ingredients
1  3½- to 4-pound chicken, cut into serving pieces, or 4 to 5 large chicken breasts

1. Put all the ingredients, except for the chicken, in a large pot and bring to a boil. Stir and add the chicken pieces. Bring back to a boil, lower the heat, and simmer for 50 minutes.

2. Turn off the heat, cover, and leave the chicken in the pot for 1 hour.

3. Remove the chicken and skin and bone it. Cut the meat in cubes, slices, or strips, as desired.

# Classic Plain Chicken Salad
### Serves 4

3  cups cubed cooked
chicken breast
1  tablespoon chopped fresh
parsley leaves
¾  cup mayonnaise

2  tablespoons heavy cream
2  teaspoons fresh lemon
juice
Salt and freshly ground
black pepper

1. Put the chicken in a large bowl and sprinkle it with the parsley.

2. Combine the mayonnaise, cream, and lemon juice. Spoon the mixture over the chicken and toss gently. Season with salt and pepper to taste.

*Variations:* Two diced celery stalks and/or 2 thinly sliced scallions can be added. To make Tarragon Chicken Salad, add 1 tablespoon chopped fresh tarragon, or 1 teaspoon dried tarragon to the basic recipe.

# Senegalese Salad
### Serves 6

3  cups cubed cooked
chicken
2  unpeeled Delicious
apples, cored and cubed
2  celery stalks, thinly
sliced
1  cup mayonnaise

3  tablespoons heavy cream
1½  tablespoons curry
powder
Salt and freshly ground
black pepper to taste
Chopped fresh parsley
leaves (optional)

1. Put the chicken, apples, and celery in a large bowl.

2. Combine the remaining ingredients in another bowl. Spoon the mixture over the chicken mixture and combine well. Garnish with parsley if desired.

*Variations:* The following ingredients can be added in ¼- or ½- cup amounts (it will be necessary to add a few tablespoons more of mayonnaise): shredded coconut, raisins, walnuts or pecans, cubed pineapple, diced sweet green pepper, or peeled, seeded, and diced cucumber.

# Chicken, Avocado, and Endive Salad

*Serves 4*

2½ cups cooked cubed
   chicken
1 large ripe avocado,
   peeled, pitted, and cut
   into ½-inch cubes
½ cup pecan halves

2 tablespoons thinly sliced
   scallions
1 tablespoon chopped
   fresh parsley leaves
3 endives, cut into ½-
   inch-thick slices

### DRESSING

1 teaspoon Dijon mustard
1 large egg yolk
¾ cup vegetable oil
1 tablespoon white wine
   vinegar

Salt and freshly ground
black pepper to taste

1. Put the chicken, avocado, pecans, scallions, and parsley into a large bowl.

2. In a shallow bowl combine the mustard and egg yolk with a wire whisk. Beat in the oil, drop by drop. Add the wine vinegar and season with salt and pepper to taste, whisking well.

3. Pour the dressing over the chicken mixture and toss gently.

4. Line a salad bowl with the sliced endives and spoon the chicken salad over the top.

# Curried Chicken Salad with Sun-dried Tomatoes and Raisins

*Serves 4*

3 cups cubed cooked
   chicken
4 chopped sun-dried
   tomatoes (see Note)
⅓ cup raisins
1 small onion, minced
1 tablespoon chopped fresh
   parsley leaves
1 large egg yolk

2 teaspoons curry powder
¾ cup olive oil
2 tablespoons fresh lemon
   juice
Salt and freshly ground
black pepper
Whole Boston or Bibb
lettuce leaves

1. Put the chicken, sun-dried tomatoes, raisins, onion, and parsley in a large bowl.

2. Combine the egg yolk and curry powder and whisk in the olive oil, drop by drop. Whisk in the lemon juice and season with salt and pepper to taste. Pour the mixture over the salad ingredients and toss gently.

3. Spoon over the lettuce leaves and serve immediately.

NOTE: Sun-dried tomatoes are available in specialty food stores or Italian markets.

# Chinese Chicken, Broccoli, and Toasted Almond Salad

*Serves 4*

2½ cups cubed cooked chicken

2 large fresh broccoli stalks

3 tablespoons butter

½ cup blanched whole almonds

## DRESSING

½ cup peanut oil

1 tablespoon fresh lemon juice

1 teaspoon soy sauce

1 tablespoon sesame oil

Salt and freshly ground black pepper to taste

1. Put the chicken in a large bowl.

2. Cook the broccoli stalks covered with just-boiling water in a saucepan for 8 minutes. Drain and cool the broccoli.

3. Meanwhile, melt the butter in a frying pan and brown the almonds lightly over medium heat, stirring often. This will take about 4 minutes. Drain the almonds on paper towels, then add them to the bowl with the chicken.

4. Cut the broccoli into bite-sized pieces and add it to the bowl.

5. Combine the dressing ingredients thoroughly with a wire whisk and pour over the salad. Toss gently. Serve at once, or cover and chill in the refrigerator.

*Serving Suggestions:* Emily McCormack's Tomatoes and Chocolate Madeleines.

# Chicken Breast, Fennel, and Feta Cheese Salad

*Serves 6*

3½ cups cubed cooked chicken
1 cup thinly sliced fennel
1 cup crumbled feta cheese (approximately 4 ounces)

4 radishes, thinly sliced
2 scallions, thinly sliced
6 small sesame seed pitas, lightly toasted

### VINAIGRETTE DRESSING

¾ cup olive oil
3 tablespoons red wine vinegar
1 tablespoon Dijon mustard

½ teaspoon dried oregano
Salt and freshly ground black pepper

1. Put the salad ingredients in a large bowl and toss gently.
2. Mix the dressing ingredients well by whisking or shaking in a tightly sealed jar. Pour the dressing over the salad and toss gently. Serve with lightly toasted sesame seed pita bread.

# Frances Bangel's Hot Hong Kong Chicken Salad

### (with thanks to Kitty Freydberg)

*Serves 6*

3 cups cooked cubed chicken
½ cup sliced almonds
½ cup thinly sliced water chestnuts
½ cup chopped pimiento
2 celery stalks, thinly sliced

1 cup mayonnaise
2 tablespoons fresh lemon juice
Salt and freshly ground black pepper
1 cup grated Monterey Jack or Cheddar cheese

1. Preheat the oven to 350 degrees.
2. In a large bowl, combine the chicken, almonds, water chestnuts, pimiento, and celery.

3. In a small bowl mix together the mayonnaise, lemon juice, and salt and pepper to taste. Add the mixture to the chicken mixture and combine well.

4. Spoon the salad into a shallow 1½-quart baking dish or casserole and sprinkle with the cheese. Bake for about 25 minutes, or until the cheese melts and is golden.

*Variation:* Sprinkle a 2.8-ounce can of French fried onion rings over the salad before you add the cheese. Bake as directed above.

# Chicken and Mushroom Salad with Basil

*Serves 6*

3½ cups cubed cooked
    chicken breast
1 tablespoon Dijon
    mustard
1 large egg yolk
2 tablespoons olive oil
¾ cup vegetable oil
1 tablespoon chopped
    fresh basil, or 1
    teaspoon dried basil

2 tablespoons white wine
    vinegar
    Salt and freshly ground
    black pepper
12 ounces fresh mushrooms,
    cut into ⅛-inch-thick
    slices
2 tablespoons chopped
    fresh parsley leaves

1. Put the chicken in a large bowl.

2. In a shallow bowl, beat the mustard with a wire whisk for 30 seconds. Add the egg yolk and whisk until creamy. Add the olive and the vegetable oils, drop by drop, whisking constantly. Beat in the basil and vinegar. Taste for seasoning and add a few drops more vinegar, if desired. Season with salt and pepper to taste.

3. Put the mushrooms and the parsley in the bowl with the chicken. Spoon the dressing over the mixture and combine gently. Cover and refrigerate for at least 3 hours before serving. The salad will keep in the refrigerator for 2 days.

*Variations:* Two thinly sliced scallions and 1 chopped roasted red pepper may be added. For a French provençale flavor, add 4 finely chopped drained anchovies.

# Fried Chicken Salad

## Serves 4

3 large chicken breasts, skinned, boned, and halved
Salt and freshly ground black pepper
All-purpose flour
½ cup peanut or vegetable oil
3 tablespoons butter
1 cup cooked corn kernels
¼ cup diced sweet green pepper

1 teaspoon Dijon mustard
¼ cup vegetable oil
1 tablespoon white wine vinegar
1 tablespoon fresh lemon juice
½ pound spinach, washed, dried, stemmed, and broken into bite-sized pieces

1. Season the chicken halves well with salt and pepper, then coat with flour.

2. Heat the ½ cup peanut oil and the butter in a large frying pan and fry the chicken until tender and golden brown on each side. Drain.

3. Put the corn and green pepper in a large bowl.

4. Cut the chicken into bite-sized pieces and add to the bowl.

5. Whisk together the remaining ingredients, except for the spinach, and season with salt and pepper to taste. Pour the dressing over the salad and toss.

6. Line 4 salad plates with equal amounts of the spinach and spoon the salad in equal portions over the spinach. Serve immediately.

SPECIAL NOTE: Leftover fried chicken can be used in this recipe, but the salad must be eaten just after it is made.

# Chicken–Tonnato Salad

Serves 6

3½ cups cubed cooked
chicken breast, chilled

1 7-ounce can white meat
tuna, drained

6 anchovy fillets, drained
and chopped

2 teaspoons Dijon
mustard

½ cup mayonnaise

1 tablespoon fresh lemon
juice

½ cup olive oil

1 tablespoon chopped
fresh parsley leaves

1 tablespoon drained
capers

Freshly ground black
pepper

1 head romaine lettuce,
washed, dried, and
broken into bite-sized
pieces

12 cherry tomatoes

1. Put the chicken in a large bowl and set aside.

2. Put the tuna, anchovies, mustard, mayonnaise, and lemon juice in a food processor or blender container and purée. Slowly pour the olive oil through the feed tube or top of the blender with the machine running.

3. Pour the mixture over the chicken and add the parsley and capers. Combine gently and season with freshly ground pepper to taste.

4. Place equal amounts of the lettuce across 6 salad plates and top with equal amounts of the salad. Garnish each serving with 2 cherry tomatoes.

# Tossed Chef's Salad with Herb Mayonnaise

Serves 4

2 cups julienne strips
cooked turkey or chicken
1 cup julienne strips baked
or boiled ham
4 slices Swiss cheese, cut
into julienne strips

1 large tomato, seeded and
diced
½ cup black olive halves
8 large romaine lettuce
leaves, broken into
bite-sized pieces

### HERB MAYONNAISE

1 cup mayonnaise
1 teaspoon Dijon mustard
1 tablespoon white wine
vinegar
1 tablespoon chopped fresh
parsley leaves

1 teaspoon dried tarragon
½ teaspoon dried basil
½ teaspoon dried dill
Freshly ground black
pepper to taste

1. Put the salad ingredients, except for the lettuce, in a large bowl.

2. Combine the Herb Mayonnaise ingredients and spoon the sauce over the salad. Combine gently.

3. Divide the lettuce among 4 salad plates and top with equal portions of the salad.

# Egg, Watercress, and Swiss Cheese Salad

Serves 4

6 hard-boiled large eggs,
coarsely chopped
1 bunch watercress,
washed, dried, and
finely chopped
1½ cups ¼-inch cubes Swiss
cheese
2 scallions, thinly sliced
¾ cup mayonnaise

1 tablespoon chopped
fresh parsley leaves
1 tablespoon fresh lemon
juice
Salt and freshly ground
black pepper
4 large Boston lettuce
leaves

1. Put the eggs, watercress, cheese, and scallions in a large bowl.

2. Blend the mayonnaise, parsley, and lemon juice together. Add

the mixture to the salad ingredients and combine gently. Season with salt and pepper to taste.

3. Spoon the salad in equal amounts onto the 4 lettuce leaves.

*Variation:* To use the mixture for making canapés, finely chop the eggs.

## Beef Niçoise

### Serves 4

| | | | |
|---|---|---|---|
| 1 | quart crisp romaine lettuce pieces | 8 | cherry tomatoes |
| 2 | medium-sized potaotes, boiled, peeled, and cut into ¼-inch-thick slices | 1 | pound medium-rare roast beef cut into strips ¼ inch thick by 2 inches long |
| ¾ | pound crisp-cooked fresh whole string beans | 4 | anchovies, drained and chopped |
| 2 | hard-boiled large eggs, quartered | 2 | scallions, thinly sliced |
| 12 | black olives, Niçoise, if possible | 1 | tablespoon drained capers |

### VINAIGRETTE DRESSING

| | | | |
|---|---|---|---|
| ¾ | cup olive oil | ½ | teaspoon dried tarragon |
| 2 | tablespoons red wine vinegar | | Salt and freshly ground black pepper to taste |
| 1 | tablespoon Dijon mustard | | |

1. Put the lettuce in a large salad bowl. Arrange the potatoes, string beans, egg quarters, black olives, and tomatoes around the edge of the lettuce. Place the beef strips in the center of the lettuce. Sprinkle with the anchovies, scallions, and capers.

2. Whisk together the Vinaigrette Dressing, pour over the salad, and toss. Pass the peppermill.

*Serving Suggestions:* French Bread and red wine. For dessert, serve a good ripe Brie and firm ripe pears.

# Navy Bean and Tuna Salad

*Serves 6*
*(Preparation begins the night before)*

1   pound dried navy beans
1   large onion, halved
1   large garlic clove, minced
1   bay leaf
2   celery stalks, halved
    crosswise
2   carrots, peeled and
    halved lengthwise
1   large sweet red, yellow,
    or green pepper, seeded
    and diced (color in that
    order of preference)

3   6½-ounce cans white
    meat tuna, drained and
    flaked
¼   cup thinly sliced scallions
½   cup thinly sliced
    cornichons
½   cup thinly sliced fennel
    (optional)
¼   cup chopped fresh parsley
    leaves

## VINAIGRETTE SAUCE

1   tablespoon Dijon
    mustard
¼   cup red wine vinegar
½   cup olive oil
¼   cup vegetable oil

½   teaspoon dried thyme
    Salt and freshly ground
    black pepper to taste

1. Put the beans in a ceramic, glass, or stainless steel bowl and cover with 2 inches of cool water. Let the beans soak overnight. (The beans can also be boiled in water to cover them for 1 minute, then left in the hot water for 1 hour before being drained and cooked.)

2. Drain the beans and put them in a heavy pot with the onion, garlic, bay leaf, celery, and carrots. Cover the beans with 2 inches of cold water and bring to a boil slowly. Immediately lower the heat and simmer for about 2½ hours, or until the beans are tender. Stir occasionally to prevent the beans from sticking to the bottom of the pot.

3. Drain the beans well. Discard the onion, garlic, bay leaf, celery, and carrot.

4. Put the beans in a large bowl and add the remaining salad ingredients. Toss gently.

5. Use a wire whisk to combine the Vinaigrette Sauce ingredients in a bowl. Pour the sauce over the bean mixture and toss gently. Taste for seasoning; a little salt and pepper may be required. Cool, cover, and refrigerate for at least 2 hours before serving.

*Serving Suggestions:* A simple lunch of this salad and Crostini with a glass of French dry red wine is delicious.

# Shell and Lobster Salad with Creamy Dill Sauce

*Serves 6*

1 pound medium shell pasta
Salt
2 cups chopped cooked lobster meat
1½ cups mayonnaise
1 tablespoon fresh lemon juice

2 tablespoons finely chopped fresh dill, or 1 tablespoon dried dill
2 tablespoons olive oil
Freshly ground black pepper

1. Bring 3½ quarts of water to a rolling boil in a large pot. Stir in 1 tablespoon of salt and add the pasta. Stir and boil until the pasta is *al dente,* or just tender, stirring occasionally.

2. Meanwhile, put the lobster in a bowl and combine it with the mayonnaise, lemon juice, and dill.

3. Drain the cooked pasta and turn into a large bowl. Sprinkle with the oil and toss. Add the lobster mixture and combine. Season with salt and pepper to taste. Serve warm or chill thoroughly.

*Variations:* Cooked mussels, crabmeat, or chicken can be substituted for the lobster.

# Fresh Salmon and Green Pea Salad

*Serves 4*

1   8-ounce bottle clam
    juice
1   onion, coarsely chopped
1¾  pounds fresh salmon
    steaks
¾   cup fresh, or frozen
    green peas, cooked and
    drained

½   cup mayonnaise, or as
    needed
    Salt and freshly ground
    black pepper
4   Boston lettuce leaves
8   cherry tomatoes
8   large black olives

1. Bring the clam juice and onion to a boil in a large saucepan. Add the salmon, cover, and simmer for 15 minutes. Drain the salmon and remove the skin and bones.

2. Put the salmon in a bowl and flake it with a fork. Add the peas, mayonnaise, and salt and pepper to taste and combine well, but don't overmix. The mixture should be moist but not wet, so be careful about the amount of mayonnaise used.

3. Chill the salad, if desired, or spoon equal amounts of the salad over each of the lettuce leaves on each of 4 plates. Garnish the salads with 2 cherry tomatoes and 2 olives.

# Side-Dish Salads

## Emily McCormack's Tomatoes

*Serves 4 to 6*

4   medium-to-large firm
    ripe tomatoes
12  fresh basil leaves,
    coarsely chopped

1   medium-sized red onion,
    minced

### ITALIAN DRESSING

½   cup extra virgin oil
2   tablespoons red wine
    vinegar, or to taste
1   garlic clove, halved

½   teaspoon dried oregano
    Salt and freshly ground
    black pepper to taste

1. Slice the tomatoes thinly and place them in 2 overlapping rows in a serving dish.

2. Combine the basil and onion and spoon the mixture over the center of the rows of tomatoes.

3. Put the dressing ingredients in a jar and screw on the lid tightly. Shake vigorously until well combined. Discard the garlic halves and spoon the dressing over the tomatoes.

4. Cover and let stand at room temperature for 15 minutes before serving. Don't leave the dish longer or the tomatoes will become mushy.

*Variations:* In place of the basil you can use 2 tablespoons of capers or 3 tablespoons of sliced black and/or green olives.

# Hearts of Celery Salad with Phyllis' Dressing

*Serves 4*

### PHYLLIS' DRESSING

2/3   cup mayonnaise
1     tablespoon well-drained capers
1/2   teaspoon dried tarragon
1     tablespoon chopped fresh parsley leaves

1     teaspoon Dijon mustard
1/2   teaspoon sugar
      Pinch of cayenne pepper
      Freshly ground black pepper to taste

2 1/2   cups thinly sliced hearts of celery, sliced on the diagonal

4     Boston lettuce leaves
8     large black olives

1. In a large bowl, combine the dressing ingredients well with a wire whisk. Add the celery and toss.

2. Put equal amounts of the salad over each lettuce leaf. Garnish each salad with 2 black olives.

# Arugola and Endive Salad with Herb Dressing

*Serves 4*

1     bunch arugola, washed, dried, and stemmed

3     endives, separated and sliced

### HERB DRESSING

1/2   cup olive oil
1     tablespoon red wine vinegar
1/2   teaspoon dried tarragon

1/2   teaspoon dried dill
1/2   teaspoon dried basil
      Salt and freshly ground black pepper to taste

1. Put the arugola and endives in a bowl.

2. In a bowl, combine the Herb Dressing ingredients with a whisk and pour over the salad. Toss gently.

# Endive, Hearts of Palm, and Pimiento Salad

*Serves 4*

1 14-ounce can hearts of palm, drained

3 large endives, cut on the diagonal into 1/4-inch-thick slices and separated

1 2-ounce jar thinly sliced pimiento, well drained

1 tablespoon chopped fresh parsley leaves

## LEMON VINAIGRETTE

1 large egg yolk

2 teaspoons Dijon mustard

1/2 cup olive oil

1 tablespoon fresh lemon juice, or to taste

*Salt and freshly ground black pepper*

1. Put the salad ingredients in a salad bowl.

2. In a medium-sized bowl, beat the egg yolk and mustard together with a wire whisk for 15 seconds. Drop by drop, beat in the olive oil. Add the lemon juice and combine. Season with salt and pepper to taste.

3. Pour the dressing over the salad and toss gently.

NOTE: If desired, combine the hearts of palm, pimiento, and parsley with the dressing, cover, and refrigerate for up to 1 hour before serving. Just before serving, add the endive slices and toss.

## Endive and Snow Pea Pods with Lime Vinaigrette

*Serves 4*

¼ pound snow pea pods,
  ends trimmed and
  strings removed

3 endives, sliced on the
  diagonal
1 scallion, thinly sliced

### LIME VINAIGRETTE

½ cup vegetable oil
1 teaspoon soy sauce
2 tablespoons fresh lime
  juice

½ teaspoon grated lime
  rind
  Salt and freshly ground
  black pepper to taste

1. In a saucepan, blanch the snow pea pods in lightly salted boiling water to cover them for 1 minute. Drain well and cool.

2. In a large bowl, combine the snow pea pods, endives, and scallion.

3. Whisk together the Lime Vinaigrette ingredients and pour over the salad. Toss well.

## Three-Green Salad with Hazelnut Dressing

*Serves 4*

1 Bibb lettuce, washed and
  dried
1 bunch watercress, washed,
  dried, and stemmed

1 bunch arugola, washed
  and dried

### HAZELNUT DRESSING

1 large egg yolk
1 teaspoon Dijon mustard
4 tablespoons hazelnut oil
3 tablespoons olive oil

1 tablespoon white wine
  vinegar
  Salt and freshly ground
  black pepper

1. Put the greens in a salad bowl.

2. Beat together the egg yolk and mustard. Drop by drop, whisk in the oils. Whisk in the vinegar and season with salt and pepper to taste. Pour the dressing over the greens and toss.

# Caesar Salad

*Serves 4*

A good Caesar salad is a miraculous blend of aromatic velvet-textured dressing, crisp romaine lettuce, freshly made crunchy croutons, and pungent grated Parmesan cheese. My only two complaints about the classic recipe is the use of the 1-minute boiled egg, which doesn't enhance the flavor, and the usual overtossing of the salad, which wilts the lettuce. I've taken the liberty of eliminating the egg. The dressing ingredients are completely mixed together. This Caesar salad requires only two brief tossings. I'd like it for my final meal—as a first course.

1 *large head romaine lettuce, washed, dried, and broken into bite-sized pieces*

¾ *cup peanut or vegetable oil*

4 *slices firm white bread, crusts trimmed and bread cut into ½-inch cubes*

¾ *cup freshly grated Parmesan cheese*

### DRESSING

1 *teaspoon finely chopped garlic*

6 *anchovy fillets, drained and chopped*

1 *tablespoon Dijon mustard*

¾ *cup olive oil*

1 *tablespoon fresh lemon juice*

2 *teaspoons Worcestershire sauce*

*Freshly ground black pepper*

1. Store the lettuce in plastic wrap or clean dish towels in the refrigerator until you are ready to toss the salad.

2. Heat the oil in a large frying pan until hot, but not smoking. Add the bread cubes and cook over medium-high heat, turning often, until they are lightly browned. Remove the croutons with a slotted spoon and drain them in a single layer on paper towels.

3. Prepare the dressing: Put the garlic, anchovies, and mustard in a shallow bowl. Use a fork to combine the ingredients thoroughly. Begin adding the oil, drop by drop, whisking constantly until all the oil is used. Whisk in the lemon juice and Worcestershire sauce. Taste for seasoning, and add pepper. (Salt is not necessary because of the salt content in the anchovies and Parmesan cheese.)

4. Put the lettuce in a large salad bowl and pour the dressing over it. Toss only enough to coat the lettuce leaves. Add the croutons and Parmesan cheese and toss gently. Serve immediately.

# Romaine Strips Salad with Cucumber and Walnut Dressing

*Serves 4*

1    medium-sized head
     romaine, washed, dried,
     and cut crosswise into
     ½-inch strips

## CUCUMBER AND WALNUT DRESSING

1    teaspoon Dijon mustard
2    tablespoons white wine
     vinegar
⅓    cup olice oil
3    tablespoons walnut oil
     Salt and freshly ground
     black pepper

½    cup seedless diced
     cucumber
¼    cup chopped walnuts
8    whole walnut halves

1. Put the romaine strips in a salad bowl.

2. In a medium-sized bowl, whisk the mustard and vinegar together. Drop by drop, whisk in the olive and walnut oils. Season with salt and pepper to taste. Add the cucumbers and chopped walnuts and combine.

3. Spoon over the romaine and toss gently. Garnish each serving with 2 walnut halves.

# Romaine Salad with Croutons and Roquefort

## Serves 4

1 medium-sized head romaine lettuce, washed, dried, and broken into bite-sized pieces

½ cup vegetable oil

4 slices firm white bread, crusts trimmed and bread cut into ½-inch cubes

6 ounces Roquefort cheese, crumbled

### MUSTARD VINAIGRETTE DRESSING

¼ cup olive oil

¼ cup vegetable oil

2 tablespoons red wine vinegar

2 teaspoons Dijon mustard

1 garlic clove, quartered

Salt and freshly ground black pepper to taste

1. Put the prepared lettuce in a plastic bag or roll it up in a clean dish towel and refrigerate until you are ready to prepare the salad.

2. Heat the oil in a large frying pan. When it is hot, but not smoking, add the bread cubes. Cook over medium-high heat until they are lightly browned all over, turning frequently. Remove with a slotted spoon and drain in a single layer on paper towels. Cool.

3. Prepare the dressing by whisking the ingredients together in a bowl. Discard the garlic pieces.

4. Put the romaine lettuce in a salad bowl. Sprinkle with the croutons and Roquefort cheese. Pour the dressing over the salad and toss gently. Serve immediately.

# Romaine, Orange, and Red Onion Salad with Sherry Vinegar Dressing

*Serves 6*

1   large head romaine
    lettuce, washed, dried,
    and broken into bite-sized
    pieces
1   medium-sized red onion,
    thinly sliced and
    separated into rings

2   navel oranges, peeled
    (including white pith)
    and cut into segments

## SHERRY VINEGAR DRESSING

½   cup olive oil
1   tablespoon sherry
    vinegar, or to taste (see
    Note)

½   teaspoon dried oregano
¼   teaspoon salt, or to taste
    Freshly ground black
    pepper to taste

1. Put the lettuce, onion rings, and orange segments into a large salad bowl.

2. Combine the dressing ingredients well with a wire whisk and pour over the salad. Toss.

NOTE: Sherry vinegar adds a full-bodied sherry flavor to salad dressing. It is a potent vinegar, so begin by adding a small amount to the dressing, taste it, and add a little more if desired.

# Watercress and Orange Salad with Puréed Scallion Dressing

*Serves 4*

1 large bunch watercress, washed, dried, and stemmed

2 navel oranges, peeled and cut into segments

### PURÉED SCALLION DRESSING

⅓ cup olive oil
2 tablespoons vegetable oil
1 tablespoon red wine vinegar

½ teaspoon dried tarragon
2 scallions, sliced
Salt and freshly ground black pepper to taste

1. Put the watercress and orange sections in a bowl.
2. Combine the Puréed Scallion Dressing ingredients in a blender. Pour the dressing over the salad and toss gently.

# Pickled Cabbage Slaw

*Serves 12*

5 cups finely shredded cabbage, save 3 large whole leaves for serving (wrap in plastic wrap)
1 medium-sized sweet green pepper, seeded and diced
1 medium-sized sweet red pepper, seeded and cut into julienne strips

3 scallions, thinly sliced
⅔ cup cider vinegar
¼ cup water
1 teaspoon celery seeds
1 teaspoon light mustard seeds
1 teaspoon salt
Freshly ground black pepper to taste

1. Put the cabbage, peppers, and scallions into a large bowl.
2. Combine the remaining ingredients and pour the mixture over the vegetables. Toss well, cover tightly, and chill thoroughly.
3. To serve, overlap the 3 large cabbage leaves in a serving bowl and spoon the slaw mixture into the center of the leaves.

# Breads, Muffins, Biscuits, and a Savory

My mother was not a baker, but back in Kansas our neighbor, Mrs. Quinn, baked half a dozen loaves of French bread every Saturday morning. At noon on many Saturdays my sister and I were invited to the Quinns' kitchen for a lunch of warm fresh-baked bread served with butter, fruit jellies, and preserves and accompanied by milk or hot chocolate. The menu never varied, yet we couldn't imagine a richer meal. Years later when traveling through Europe I realized that those memorable meals were my first continental breakfasts. Mrs. Quinn's only competition in those years were my grandmother's hot buttermilk biscuits, slathered with butter and stuffed with a fried sausage patty, a grilled ham slice, or strips of crisp cooked bacon.

We all are bread lovers. The bread and baking specialities of every region of every country of the world are the highlights of any cuisine.

Included here are my recipes in the bread and baking category that have stood the test of serving to company time and time again.

# French Bread

*Makes 2 loaves*

| | | | |
|---|---|---|---|
| 3½ | cups all-purpose flour | 1 | (1 tablespoon) envelope |
| 1¼ | cups water | | yeast |
| 1 | teaspoon salt | | Oil |
| 1 | tablespoon sugar | 1 | large egg white |
| 2 | tablespoons butter, plus | | |
| | extra for greasing the | | |
| | bowl and pans | | |

1. Put the flour in a large mixing bowl or the bowl of an electric mixer fitted with a dough hook.

2. In a small saucepan, heat ¾ cup of the water with the salt, sugar, and butter until the butter melts. Stir often, but do not boil. Remove from the heat and cool for 5 minutes.

3. Meanwhile, pour the remaining ¼ cup of water into a small bowl and add the yeast; stir until it dissolves. Add the yeast mixture and the milk and butter mixture to the flour. Stir with the dough hook at medium speed or mix with a wooden spoon.

4. Knead with the dough hook for 5 minutes, or turn the dough onto a lightly floured board and knead it by hand for approximately 10 minutes, or until it is satin and smooth in texture.

5. Lightly grease a large mixing bowl with a little oil and place the ball of dough in the bowl. Turn the dough to coat with the oil. Cover the bowl with a dish towel and place it in a warm area (80 to 85 degrees is most desirable). Allow the dough to double in size, about 2 hours.

6. Lightly butter 2 baguette pans.

7. Punch the dough down with your fist and knead it twice. Cut the dough in half.

8. With the palms of your hands, roll each piece of dough into the shape of a loaf, rolling each piece back and forth until uniform in shape. The loaves should be about 2 inches shorter than the length of the baguette pans. Center each piece of the dough in the baguette pans.

9. With a very sharp knife make ¼-inch-deep slashes, on the diagonal, at 2-inch intervals in the top of the dough.

10. Beat the egg white for 15 seconds and brush the tops of the loaves with it. (This makes the bread brown, shiny, and crusty.)

11. Cover the pans and let the loaves rise in a warm place for about 30 minutes, or until the loaves fill the pans.

12. Fifteen minutes before baking the bread, place 6 quarry tiles on the lower rack of the oven and heat the oven to 450 degrees. (The tiles assist in producing crustier bread.)

13. Place the baguette pans on the tiles or on the lower rack and bake for 15 minutes. Lower the oven temperature to 350 degrees and bake for 30 minutes, or until the bread is golden brown and produces a hollow sound when tapped on the bottom.

14. Remove the loaves from the oven and cool across the pans or on a rack. The bread should be eaten within 2 hours. If not, wrap each cooled loaf securely in aluminum foil and freeze.

15. To reheat the frozen bread take the foil-wrapped bread directly from the freezer and put it in a preheated 350-degree oven for about 20 minutes. Remove the bread from the oven and unwrap it. Let the bread cool for 5 minutes before slicing and serving it.

NOTES:

More Loaves: To make 4 loaves of bread, double the recipe and follow the same procedure.

Storage: For easier storage, cut the baked bread loaves in half and wrap securely in foil and freeze. The limited area in freezers makes the smaller loaves a more convenient and manageable size. Half a loaf of bread will serve 2 or 3.

# Crostini

### Serves 6 to 8

The recipe can be easily doubled or tripled.

| | |
|---|---|
| 1 fresh loaf French bread (ficelle, the thin loaf, is best), cut into 1/4-inch-thick slices | 4 tablespoons butter, softened  Freshly grated Parmesan cheese |

1. Preheat the broiler.

2. Spread the butter lightly over one side of the bread slices. Sprinkle each buttered side with the cheese and put the slices on a baking sheet.

3. Run under the broiler until golden brown.

# Skillet Corn Bread

*Serves 8*

1½ cups yellow cornmeal
½ teaspoon salt
2 teaspoons baking powder
2 eggs, lightly beaten
⅔ cup vegetable oil, plus extra for greasing the skillet

1 cup sour cream
1 cup cream-style canned corn
¼ cup diced sweet green pepper
½ cup Cheddar cheese

1. Preheat the oven to 350 degrees.
2. Combine the cornmeal, salt, and baking powder in a bowl.
3. In another bowl, mix together the remaining ingredients and stir the cornmeal mixture into it.
4. Grease a 10-inch heavy ovenproof iron or heavy aluminum skillet and heat in the oven for 3 minutes. Pour the batter into the hot pan and bake for about 30 minutes, or until the corn bread is lightly golden on top. Let stand 10 minutes before slicing into wedges.

# Miniature Corn Bread Muffins with Bacon

*Makes 24 miniature muffins*

1 cup yellow cornmeal
1 cup sifted all-purpose flour
1 tablespoon sugar
1 large egg
1 tablespoon baking powder

½ teaspoon salt
4 tablespoons butter, melted, plus butter for greasing the muffin tins
1 cup milk
6 strips crisp-cooked bacon, coarsely chopped

1. Preheat the oven to 425 degrees.
2. In a large bowl, combine all the ingredients.
3. Liberally grease 12 muffin tins with butter and fill them with equal amounts of the mixture. Bake for 12 to 15 minutes, or until the muffins are golden on top. Cool for 10 minutes before serving.

# Norman Hodgson's Blueberry Muffins

*Makes 24 muffins*

For years, Norman Hodgson and his wife Dorothy owned and ran Aimhi Lodge, a summer resort in Little Segago, Maine. Each morning their happy guests looked forward to Norman's hot fresh Blueberry Muffins. The Hodgsons have retired to Cape Elizabeth, but Norman's still "foolin' around making muffins."

Here's the recipe he sent me for a birthday one year, with the admonition: "Don't change a thing, you can't improve them."

| | | | |
|---|---|---|---|
| | *Butter for greasing the muffin tins* | *1* | *teaspoon salt* |
| | | *2* | *large eggs* |
| *1* | *cup sugar* | *½* | *cup vegetable oil* |
| *5* | *tablespoons powdered milk* | *1⅓* | *cup water* |
| | | *3¼* | *cups all-purpose flour* |
| *2* | *tablespoons baking powder* | *2* | *cups fresh or frozen blueberries* |

1. Preheat the oven to 400 degrees. Butter 24 muffin tins.

2. Combine the sugar, powdered milk, baking powder, and salt in a large bowl. Mix well.

3. Add the eggs and vegetable oil and mix well. Stir in ⅔ cup of the water and combine well.

4. Mix in the flour and combine well. Add the remaining ⅔ cup water and mix in well.

5. Stir in the blueberries and combine them thoroughly with the batter.

6. Spoon equal amounts of the batter into the prepared muffin tins and bake for 16 minutes. Serve warm.

*Variations:* For Bran Muffins, follow the directions for the Blueberry Muffins, substituting 1¾ cups of All Bran for the blueberries and decreasing the flour to 2½ cups.

For Corn Muffins, follow the directions for the Blueberry Muffins, using ½ cup cornmeal and decreasing the flour to 2½ cups. Omit the blueberries and substitute 1½ cups of thawed and drained frozen whole corn kernels. Bake the muffins for 18 minutes.

# Banana, Coconut, and Macadamia Nut Muffins

*Makes 12 muffins*

½ cup (1 stick) butter, softened
½ cup sugar
1 large egg
2 medium-sized ripe bananas
1 teaspoon vanilla extract
2 cups sifted all-purpose flour
1 tablespoon baking powder

¼ teaspoon ground cinnamon
¼ teaspoon freshly grated nutmeg
½ teaspoon salt
½ cup sweetened shredded coconut
½ cup chopped macadamia nuts

1. Preheat the oven to 375 degrees.

2. In a large bowl, cream together the butter and sugar until light and fluffy. Beat in the egg.

3. Mash the bananas on a plate with a fork and add to the mixture with the vanilla. Combine well.

4. Add the combined flour and baking powder, cinnamon, nutmeg, and salt. Mix only until the dry ingredients are incorporated into the batter.

5. Add the coconut and nuts. Again, mix only until the ingredients are thoroughly combined.

6. Grease 12 muffin tins and fill each with an equal amount of the mixture.

7. Bake for 25 minutes, or until a cake tester comes out clean. Let the muffins rest in the pan for 5 minutes. Then invert the pan and tap them out. Serve immediately. (They are excellent served with honey butter and guava jelly.)

# Buttermilk Biscuits

*Makes about 1 dozen biscuits*

2½ cups sifted all-purpose
flour, plus extra flour
for rolling out the
biscuits
1 tablespoon baking
powder

1 teaspoon salt
6 tablespoons shortening,
plus extra for greasing
the baking sheet
¾ cup buttermilk

1. Preheat the oven to 400 degrees.

2. In a large bowl, combine the flour, baking powder, and salt. Cut in the shortening. Make a hole in the center and add the buttermilk. Stir lightly until the dough is combined.

3. Knead for about 30 seconds. Roll the dough into a circle 1-inch thick on a lightly floured surface.

4. Cut out the biscuits with a 2-inch round cutter. Put the biscuits on a lightly greased baking sheet and bake for about 12 minutes, or until they are golden brown.

# Sweet Potato Biscuits

*Makes about 1 dozen biscuits*

1¾ cups sifted all-purpose
flour
1 tablespoon baking
powder
¼ cup sugar
1 teaspoon salt

6 tablespoons shortening,
plus extra for greasing
the baking sheet
3½ cups warm mashed
cooked sweet potatoes

1. Preheat the oven to 400 degrees.

2. Mix together the flour, baking powder, sugar, and salt.

3. In another bowl, mix together the shortening and mashed sweet potatoes. Combine the 2 mixtures and knead for 2 or 3 minutes.

4. Roll out the dough on a lightly floured surface to about a ¾-inch thickness.

5. Cut the biscuits with a buscuit cutter and place on a lightly greased baking sheet. Bake for about 12 minutes, or until done.

# Buttered Cinnamon Sugar Fingers

*Serves 6*
*Makes 18 fingers*

Adults and children gobble up these simple and quick savories. Buttered Cinnamon Sugar Fingers are tasty accompaniments to a breakfast or brunch of omelets or other egg dishes and sausage patties.

| | |
|---|---|
| 6 slices firm white sandwich bread, crusts trimmed | ¼ cup sugar |
| | 1 teaspoon ground cinnamon |
| 4 tablespoons butter, melted | |

1. Preheat the broiler.
2. Cut each trimmed bread slice into 3 equal-sized pieces.
3. Brush each finger liberally with the butter and sprinkle with the combined sugar and cinnamon.
4. Put the coated fingers on a baking sheet without letting the pieces touch each other.
5. Run under the broiler until they are lightly browned. Transfer to a basket lined with a napkin.

NOTE: The bread can be cut into any shape: triangles, circles, hearts, stars, etc.

*Variations:* A quarter cup of finely chopped pecans, almonds, or walnuts can be sprinkled over the butter-brushed fingers before the cinnamon–sugar mixture is added. Whole wheat bread can also be used.

# Desserts

Thoughtless restaurateurs have spoiled many dinners for me by proudly displaying their dessert carts for nearby tables at the exact moment that I am selecting my first course and main dish. The confusion that results when the sight of mousses and tarts reaches a brain pondering pâtés and roasts is paralyzing. Selecting from an elaborate menu is chore enough, but when you suddenly have to begin making room for desserts to be consumed an hour or so later, the temptation to reverse the order of serving is hard to resist.

One diet-conscious doctor friend has spent the last ten years startling restaurant staffs and fellow diners by beginning his meal with a dessert course. He says it reduces his intake of calories, provides unique taste experiences, and saves money. I say that his main concern is having a slice of the Gateau St. Honoré before it has all been sold to the other patrons.

There is no solution to this weighty issue. The dessert course is a final treat for company, and it should surprise and satisfy. Knowing in advance what the final touch to the meal is going to be does heighten expectations—but there is always the risk that once you have ordered the soufflé forty-five minutes in advance, as requested, you won't be able to think about anything else throughout the meal. For myself and my guests I prefer to surprise, and not necessarily with the most elaborate confections. With the proper menu, a bowl of fresh figs and peaches, fresh grapefruit sorbet, or the simplest custard can be as delightful as dramatic crêpes, soufflés, and pastries.

# Cookies

## *Tuiles*

*Makes about 2 dozen*

Almost no meal ends in a good restaurant in France without these delicately crisp cookies. And, it seems that the farther south from Paris one travels, the larger the cookie becomes.

The cookies in this recipe are about 4 inches in diameter, but that size can be increased by using 2 teaspoons of the batter instead of 1. Be sure to leave 5 or 6 inches between each cookie if you are making the larger ones.

| | | | |
|---|---|---|---|
| 6 | tablespoons butter, plus extra for greasing the baking sheet | $\frac{1}{3}$ | cup sifted all-purpose flour |
| $\frac{1}{2}$ | cup sugar | 1 | cup sliced almonds |
| 2 | large egg whites, lightly beaten | 1 | teaspoon vanilla extract |

1. Preheat the oven to 400 degrees.

2. Cream the butter and sugar until light and fluffy. Add the egg whites, flour, almonds, and vanilla and combine thoroughly.

3. Drop by rounded teaspoons onto a buttered baking sheet at least 2 inches apart, and spread slightly.

4. Bake for about 6 minutes, or until the cookies are golden brown around the edges.

5. Remove each cookie with a spatula and drape it over a rolling pin or a baguette pan. Leave for a minute or 2, until they harden and retain the curved shape. Then cool them on a rack. Because of the size of the cookies, several batches will have to be baked. Serve the cookies within 1 hour, or store in a tightly sealed container.

# Ruglach

### Makes 24

¼ pound (1 stick) butter,
  softened
4 ounces cream cheese,
  softened
4 tablespoons granulated
  sugar
1 teaspoon ground
  cinnamon

1 cup sifted all-purpose
  flour, plus extra for
  rolling out the dough
6 tablespoons dark brown
  sugar
½ cup chopped walnuts
½ cup currants or raisins

1. Mix the butter and cream cheese together thoroughly. Add half of the combined granulated sugar and cinnamon and mix well. Add the flour and stir until well combined. Divide the dough in half and make 2 balls. Flatten each ball to 1-inch thickness and wrap each in plastic wrap. Refrigerate for 1 hour.

2. Preheat the oven to 350 degrees.

3. On a lightly floured board, roll out each ball to a 10-inch circle. Sprinkle the dough evenly with the brown sugar and the remaining cinnamon and granulated sugar mixture and top with the chopped nuts. Sprinkle the currants along a 2 inch border of the outer edges of the dough.

4. Cut each piece of dough into quarters and each quarter into thirds, making 12 pieces from each circle of dough.

5. Starting at the wide end of each piece of dough, roll up and transfer to an ungreased baking sheet. Turn each end of the ruglach toward you, making a crescent shape. Repeat the procedure for the remaining 23 pieces of dough.

6. Bake for 20 to 25 minutes, or until golden brown. Cool on racks. Store in tightly covered containers.

# Cakes

---

## Chocolate Mousse Cake with Chocolate Glaze

*Serves 12*

12 ounces semisweet
    chocolate
½ pound (2 sticks) butter,
    plus butter to grease the
    pan

1 cup sugar
1 teaspoon vanilla extract
8 large eggs, separated
1 cup all-purpose flour
½ teaspoon salt

### CHOCOLATE GLAZE

8 ounces semisweet chocolate
2 tablespoons butter

1 tablespoon Kahlua

1. Preheat the oven to 350 degrees.

2. Grease the bottom and sides of a 9-inch springform pan.

3. Melt the chocolate in the top of a double boiler over simmering water. Stir often.

4. Meanwhile, cream together the butter and sugar. Add the vanilla and egg yolks and combine well.

5. Cool the chocolate for 5 minutes, then add it to the butter mixture with the flour and salt. Mix well.

6. Beat the egg whites until stiff and fold into the chocolate mixture. Pour the batter into the prepared springform pan and bake for about 1 hour, or until a cake tester comes out clean.

7. Cool the cake in the pan on a rack. Remove the cake from the pan. The top of the cake will puff up and crack a little. Cut off the top evenly, and discard.

8. Make the glaze: Melt the chocolate with the butter and Kahlua in the top of a double boiler over simmering water. Cool the glaze completely.

9. Place the cake on a rack and spread the glaze over the top and sides of the cake. Chill the cake well before serving.

# Grandmother Evans' Devil's Food Cake
## (with thanks to Clita Illene Allen)

*Serves 8*

Here is the only recipe that I have from my father's mother, Bertha Berg Evans. She died when I was a toddler, but all who knew her well praised her cooking talents. She had five children, and I'm told that they rarely let this cake cool long enough for her to frost it. Since no chocolate frosting recipe of hers exists, I've included one of my own.

½ cup shortening or butter, plus extra for greasing the pan
1 cup sugar
3 large eggs
½ cup cocoa powder

1 teaspoon vanilla extract
1 cup buttermilk
2 cups sifted all-purpose flour
1 teaspoon baking soda
½ teaspoon salt

### CHOCOLATE FROSTING

6 ounces semisweet chocolate
2 tablespoons butter

2 tablespoons heavy cream

1. Preheat the oven to 350 degrees.
2. Grease the bottom and sides of a 9-inch-square cake pan.
3. In a large bowl, combine the shortening and sugar well. Add the eggs, cocoa, vanilla, and buttermilk and combine thoroughly. Add the flour, soda, and salt and mix.
4. Pour the batter into the prepared cake pan and bake for about 35 minutes, or until a cake tester inserted into the middle of the cake comes out clean.
5. Cool the cake on a rack for 10 minutes, then remove it from the pan and cool it completely on a rack.
6. Make the frosting: Melt the chocolate with the butter in the top of a double boiler over simmering water. Stir often. Add the heavy cream and combine. Remove from the heat and cool for 5 minutes, then spread over the cake.

# Lili Barr's Brownie Cake
## (with thanks to Jeff Barr)

*Serves 8 to 10*

4   ounces unsweetened
    chocolate
½   pound butter, plus butter
    to grease the pan
4   large eggs

2   cups granulated sugar
1   cup sifted cake flour
1   teaspoon vanilla extract
1   cup chopped walnuts

### TOPPING

½    cup confectioners' sugar
1½   teaspoons cocoa powder
3    tablespoons butter,
     melted

3   tablespoons heavy cream

1. Preheat the oven to 325 degrees.

2. Melt the chocolate and butter in the top of a double boiler over simmering water. Remove the top pan from the heat.

3. Beat the eggs and granulated sugar together in a large bowl. Add the chocolate mixture, cake flour, vanilla, and nuts. Mix well.

4. Turn the batter into a buttered 9-inch-square cake pan and bake for 45 minutes. Let the cake cool in the pan 10 minutes.

5. Meanwhile, combine the topping ingredients well with a wire whisk.

6. After the cake has cooled for 10 minutes, spread the topping over the warm cake. Cool for 30 minutes longer, cover, and refrigerate for at least 3 hours (overnight is best). If desired, serve with French vanilla ice cream.

# Vanilla Cake with Vanilla and Butter Pecan Frosting

*Serves 12*

As a child I always asked for a vanilla ice cream cone. This recipe was developed because of my continuing love affair with the flavor of vanilla, and for a friend's child, who also requests vanilla cones.

## VANILLA CAKE

½ pound (2 sticks) butter, softened, plus extra for greasing the pans
1½ cups granulated sugar
4 large eggs, separated
1½ cups sifted all-purpose flour

1 teaspoon baking powder
¼ teaspoon salt
1 tablespoon vanilla extract

## BUTTER PECAN FROSTING

2½ cups sifted confectioners' sugar
¾ cup butter, softened

1 teaspoon vanilla extract
1 cup chopped pecans
12 whole pecans

1. Preheat the oven to 325 degrees.
2. Cream together the butter and sugar with an electric mixer or by hand until lemon-colored and fluffy. Beat in the yolks one at a time. Add the flour, baking powder, and salt. Beat until smooth. Add the vanilla and mix well. Beat the egg whites until stiff and fold into the cake batter.
3. Pour the batter into a greased 10-inch tube pan. Bake for 1 hour, or until a cake tester inserted near the center of the cake comes out clean.
4. Cool the cake on a rack.
5. Prepare the frosting: Beat the sugar, butter, and vanilla together until creamy and smooth. Use a spatula to spread the frosting evenly over the cooled cake.
6. Press the chopped pecans against the outer edge of the cake, reserving 2 tablespoons of the nuts. Press the whole pecans in a circle at even intervals on the top of the cake near the outer edge and sprinkle the 2 tablespoons of chopped nuts over the top. Cover and refrigerate for at least 3 hours before serving.

*Variation:* Substitute 2 cups of fresh grated coconut for all the pecans and press the coconut into the sides and top of the cake.

# Cheesecake

### Serves 12

Butter for coating the
pan

1/3 cup ground hazelnuts
or almonds

2 pounds cream cheese,
softened

1/2 cup heavy cream

1 1/4 cups sugar

1 teaspoon vanilla extract

5 large eggs

1 tablespoon fresh lemon
juice

1. Preheat the oven to 325 degrees.

2. Rub butter over the sides and bottom of a 9-inch springform pan. Add the ground hazelnuts and shake the pan to coat it evenly.

3. Put the remaining ingredients into the bowl of an electric mixer and beat on low speed for 1 minute. Increase the speed to medium-high and run until the mixture is smooth. The mixing can be done by hand, too.

4. Turn the mixture into the prepared pan and bake on the center rack of the oven for 1 hour.

5. Turn off the oven and leave the cake in the oven for 45 minutes.

6. Remove the cake and cool it on a rack. When cool, cover and refrigerate for several hours or overnight. Serve with fresh raspberries, blueberries, or strawberries.

# Peach Cobbler

### Serves 8

1/4 cup shortening, plus
extra for greasing the
pan

1/2 cup sugar, plus 2
tablespoons for the
topping

1 cup all-purpose flour

2 teaspoons baking powder

1/4 teaspoon salt

1/2 cup milk

2 cups sliced peeled fresh
peaches

3/4 cup canned peach nectar

1/2 teaspoon ground
cinnamon

Whipped cream or ice
cream (optional)

1. Preheat the oven to 350 degrees.

2. Grease a 9-inch-square baking pan and set it aside.

3. In a large bowl combine the shortening and sugar until creamy. Add the flour, baking powder, salt, and milk. Combine well.

4. Pour the batter into the greased pan. Spoon the peach slices over the batter in neat rows. Pour the peach nectar over the top and sprinkle with the combined 2 tablespoons of remaining sugar and the cinnamon.

5. Bake for about 45 minutes, or until done. Serve warm with whipped cream or ice cream.

*Variation:* Blueberries and cranberry juice can be substituted for the peaches and peach nectar.

# Lemon Cake

### Serves 12 to 14

This cake is moist and light. It's a perfect tea cake or a dinner dessert served with small scoops of raspberry sherbet.

| | | | |
|---|---|---|---|
| ½ | cup butter, softened, plus extra butter for greasing the pan | 1 | tablespoon baking powder |
| 1 | cup granulated sugar | ½ | teaspoon salt |
| 2 | large eggs, lightly beaten | 1 | tablespoon grated lemon rind |
| ¾ | cup milk | ½ | cup fresh lemon juice |
| 2½ | cups sifted all-purpose flour | | Confectioners' sugar |

1. Preheat the oven to 350 degrees.

2. Cream the butter and sugar together until light and fluffy. Beat in the eggs and milk.

3. Combine the flour, baking powder, and salt and beat into the butter mixture. Add the lemon rind and juice and combine well.

4. Pour the batter into a greased 10-inch tube pan. Bake for about 1 hour, or until a cake tester inserted in the center of the cake comes out clean.

5. Cool in the pan on a rack for 15 minutes. Turn out the cake and cool for 1 hour. Sprinkle with confectioners' sugar before serving.

# Prize-winning Carrot Cake

*Serves 12*

| | |
|---|---|
| 1 cup granulated sugar | ½ teaspoon grated nutmeg |
| 1 cup light brown sugar | 2 teaspoons baking powder |
| 1 cup vegetable oil, plus extra for greasing the pan | 2 teaspoons baking soda |
| | 1 teaspoon salt |
| | 2 cups shredded carrots |
| 1 cup ricotta | ½ cup drained canned |
| 3 large eggs | crushed pineapple |
| 2 cups all-purpose flour, plus extra for the pan | ½ cup chopped walnuts |
| | ½ cup raisins |
| 2 teaspoons ground cinnamon | |

## FROSTING

| | |
|---|---|
| 2 tablespoons butter, softened | 1 teaspoon vanilla extract |
| 4 ounces cream cheese, softened | 2 cups sifted confectioners' sugar |
| ½ cup ricotta | 12 walnut halves |

1. Preheat the oven to 350 degrees.

2. Lightly grease a 10-inch tube pan with oil and add 2 tablespoons of flour. Tilt and shake the pan to coat it evenly and tap out any excess flour. Set aside.

3. In a large bowl, beat together the sugars, vegetable oil, and ricotta. Beat in the eggs one at a time.

4. Sift together the dry ingredients and stir into the first mixture. Fold in the carrots, pineapple, walnuts, and raisins.

5. Pour the batter into the prepared pan and bake for 1 hour.

6. Cool the cake in the pan on a rack for about 20 minutes. Turn the cake out and place on a plate and cool completely.

7. Prepare the frosting: Combine the butter, cream cheese, ricotta, and vanilla in a food processor or by hand. Transfer the mixture to a bowl and beat in the confectioners' sugar.

8. Frost the top and sides of the cake. Decorate the top with the walnut halves.

# Orange-flavored Gingerbread

Serves 8 to 10

½ pound (1 stick) butter, softened, plus extra for greasing the pan
½ cup packed dark brown sugar
1 large egg, lightly beaten
½ cup molasses
½ cup buttermilk
1 tablespoon grated orange rind
2½ cups sifted all-purpose flour

1 teaspoon ground ginger
1 teaspoon ground cinnamon
½ teaspoon ground allspice
1½ teaspoons baking soda
½ teaspoon salt
1 cup heavy cream
3 tablespoons sugar
2 tablespoons Grand Marnier
1 teaspoon vanilla extract

1. Preheat the oven to 350 degrees.

2. In a large bowl, beat together the butter and brown sugar until light and fluffy. Add the egg and beat for 15 seconds. Stir in the molasses, buttermilk, and orange rind and blend thoroughly.

3. Combine the remaining ingredients in a large bowl. Add the first mixture to the dry ingredients and stir until well combined.

4. Pour the batter into a greased 9-inch-square baking pan. Bake for about 40 minutes, or until a cake tester comes out clean.

5. Cool the cake in the pan for 5 minutes, then remove it and thoroughly cool it on a rack before slicing. Serve with whipped cream flavored with 3 tablespoons sugar, 2 tablespoons of Grand Marnier, and 1 teaspoon of vanilla extract.

# Nancy Dussault's Deluxe Monkey Bread

### Serves 8 to 12

This delightful sweet bread is convenient for outdoor gatherings, such as picnics, tailgate parties, and backyard barbecues, because no plates are needed to serve it. You simply pull off a piece and savor it. It's also a hit with children . . . they love to help prepare the bread.

| | | | |
|---|---|---|---|
| 2 | 13¾-ounce boxes hot roll mix | 2 | cups sugar |
| ½ | pound (2 sticks) butter melted, plus extra for greasing the pan | 2 | tablespoons ground cinnamon |
| | | 1½ | cups chopped walnuts |

1. Prepare the hot roll mix following the package directions. Cover in a large bowl and let rise for 45 minutes in a warm place.

2. Meanwhile, grease a 10-inch tube pan with a removable bottom.

3. Preheat the oven to 350 degrees.

4. Press the dough down and knead it for 1 minute. Shape the dough into 1½-inch balls.

5. Put the butter, combined sugar and cinnamon, and nuts in separate bowls. Coat each ball of dough with the butter, cinnamon sugar, and the nuts.

6. Place the coated balls side by side, layer upon layer, in the prepared pan.

7. Put the pan on a baking sheet and bake for about 45 minutes, or until the top is golden brown.

8. Remove the pan from the oven and cool for 15 minutes on a rack before removing carefully from the pan.

# Madeleines

*Makes 12 madeleines*

2  tablespoons butter,
softened, plus 3
tablespoons butter,
melted
3  tablespoons unseasoned
dry bread crumbs
1  large egg
2  large egg yolks

½  teaspoon vanilla extract
¼  cup sugar
½  cup sifted all-purpose
flour
¼  teaspoon salt
2  teaspoons grated lemon
rind

1. Preheat the oven to 375 degrees.

2. Grease the 12 shell-shaped molds in a madeleine pan with the softened butter. Sprinkle each mold with bread crumbs and shake out any loose crumbs. Set aside.

3. In a large bowl, beat the egg, egg yolks, vanilla, and sugar with an electric mixer on high speed for about 8 minutes, or until the mixture is thick and creamy. On low speed, gradually add the flour and salt. Fold in the melted butter and lemon rind.

4. Spoon the batter in equal amounts into the coated molds. Bake for about 15 to 18 minutes, or until the madeleines are firm to the touch.

5. Invert the madeleines onto a baking sheet and then place on a rack to cool.

*Variation:* For Chocolate Madeleines, add 1 ounce of melted semisweet chocolate to the batter with butter and eliminate the lemon rind.

# Frozen Piña Colada Ice Cream Cake

*Serves 10 to 12*

1   quart vanilla ice cream, softened
1   cup canned cream of coconut
1   8-ounce can crushed pineapple, chilled and well drained

½   cup chopped macadamia nuts, pistachios, or walnuts
1   cup shredded sweetened coconut

1. In a large bowl, beat together the ice cream, coconut cream, pineapple, and nuts. Turn the mixture into a 9-inch springform pan, cover, and freeze it overnight.

2. Toast the coconut on a baking sheet under the broiler. Watch the coconut carefully, because of its sugar content it browns in about 1 minute. Cool the coconut thoroughly and sprinkle it over the top of the cake.

3. Remove the cake from the pan and cut it into wedges.

# Tarts

## Chocolate Tart

*Serves 6 to 8*

1  10-inch tart pastry shell
   (see recipe page 276)
6  ounces semisweet
   chocolate
6  tablespoons butter
½  cup sugar
4  tablespoons all-purpose
   flour

3  large eggs
1  teaspoon vanilla extract
   Crème Fraîche (see recipe
   page 277)
   Chestnuts in syrup or
   candied violets

1. Prepare the tart shell and refrigerate.

2. Melt the chocolate with the butter in the top of a double boiler over simmering water. Cool.

3. Preheat the oven to 375 degrees.

4. In a bowl combine the sugar, flour, eggs, and vanilla well. Add the chocolate mixture and beat with an electric mixer for about 5 minutes, or until very creamy.

5. Pour the mixture into the prepared tart shell and bake for about 25 minutes, or until the crust is golden brown and a cake tester inserted into the center of the tart comes out clean. Serve with Crème Fraîche and decorate with chestnuts in syrup or candied violets.

# Fresh French Apple–Hazelnut Tart with Frangelico Whipped Cream

*Serves 8*

## PASTRY

1½  cups sifted all-purpose
   flour
½  teaspoon salt

6  tablespoons cold butter
3  or 4 tablespoons ice
   water

## TART FILLING

6  to 8 large Delicious
   apples, peeled and very
   thinly sliced
2  tablespoons fresh lemon
   juice
2  teaspoons all-purpose
   flour

¾  cup ground hazelnuts
2  large egg yolks
5  tablespoons sugar
½  teaspoon vanilla extract
2  tablespoons butter

## APRICOT GLAZE

1  10-ounce jar apricot
   preserves (peach or
   pineapple can also be
   used)

2  tablespoons sugar
2  tablespoons water

## FRANGELICO WHIPPED CREAM

1  cup heavy cream
3  tablespoons sugar

3  tablespoons Frangelico
   liqueur

1. Prepare the pastry: Combine the flour, salt, and butter with a pastry blender or in a food processor until it is a coarse crumb texture. Add the water and combine. Shape into a ball, cover with plastic wrap, and refrigerate for 30 minutes.

2. Meanwhile, put the sliced apples in a large bowl. Sprinkle with the lemon juice and toss very gently.

3. Preheat the oven to 425 degrees.

4. Roll out the pastry on a lightly floured surface until you have a circle ⅛ inch thick to fit a 10-inch tart pan. Fit the pastry into the pan and trim off the extra pastry by running the rolling pin over the top of the pan.

5. Brush the flour over the bottom of the pastry.

6. Combine the hazelnuts, egg yolks, 3 tablespoons of the sugar, and the vanilla. Spread the mixture evenly over the pastry.

7. Beginning at the rim of the pan, overlap a circle of the apple slices over the hazelnut filling. Make another circle of the apples and fill the center with a circle of apple slices. Each apple slice should overlap the next by about half the width of a slice because the apples shrink during cooking. Sprinkle the tart filling with the remaining 2 tablespoons of sugar and dot with the butter.

8. Bake on a baking sheet for about 40 minutes, or until the apples are golden brown.

9. Remove the cooked tart and cool it on a rack.

10. Meanwhile, combine the glaze ingredients in a saucepan and bring to a boil. Lower the heat and simmer for 5 minutes, stirring often. Strain the glaze and carefully brush it over the apples. Cool the tart and serve, or cover and refrigerate it for a few hours.

11. Whip the cream until soft peaks form. Gradually add the sugar and whip until fully peaked. Whip in the Frangelico and serve with the tart. (The cream can be prepared several hours ahead of time and kept covered and chilled in the refrigerator until needed.)

# Coconut–Buttermilk Tart

*Serves 10*

## PASTRY

1½  cups all-purpose flour
1  tablespoon sugar
½  teaspoon salt

6  tablespoons cold butter, cut into 6 pieces
4  tablespoons ice water

## FILLING

½  cup (1 stick) butter, softened
1  cup sugar
3  large eggs, lightly beaten
1¼  cups buttermilk

1  cup flaked sweetened coconut
1  teaspoon vanilla extract
3  tablespoons all-purpose flour

1. Make the pastry: Put the flour, sugar, salt, and butter in a food processor fitted with a steel blade. Run the food processor until coarse crumbs form. Immediately add the water through the feed tube. When the dough forms and rolls off the sides of the container, remove it and shape it into a ball. Cover the dough and refrigerate for 30 minutes. (The pastry can also be made by combining the flour, sugar, salt, and butter with a pastry blender to a coarse crumb consistency. Add the water and mix well. Shape into a ball, cover, and refrigerate as directed above.)

2. Preheat the oven to 350 degrees.

3. Roll the dough out to a ⅛-inch thickness and fit it into a 10-inch tart pan. Pass the rolling pin across the top of the pan to trim off the extra dough. Refrigerate.

4. In a large bowl, beat together the butter and sugar until creamy. Add the eggs and beat with an electric mixer until thoroughly combined and fluffy. Add the buttermilk, coconut, vanilla, and 2 tablespoons of the flour and beat by hand until well combined.

5. Sprinkle the bottom of the pastry with the remaining tablespoon of flour (this helps prevent the dough from becoming soggy).

6. Pour the buttermilk mixture into the tart shell and bake on a baking sheet for 55 minutes to 1 hour, or until the top is golden brown and firm to the touch.

7. Cool on a rack for 30 minutes before serving, or cool thoroughly, cover, and refrigerate.

# Crème Fraîche

Here are two different recipes for homemade crème fraîche. Both are respectable substitutes for France's thick double cream, but the recipe made with the buttermilk has a flavor more like the authentic cream. When buttermilk isn't available or when buying it to use only 1 tablespoon seems wasteful, the second recipe is very good indeed, and it yields 2 cups. Both recipes can be successfully doubled, and both keep well in the refrigerator for one week. After a week the cream begins to develop a sour taste.

## Crème Fraîche I

*Makes about 1 cup*

1   cup heavy cream                    1   tablespoon buttermilk

In a jar with a tight-fitting lid, combine the cream and buttermilk with a wire whisk, beating vigorously for 30 seconds. Cover tightly and leave at room temperature for about 8 hours, or until the cream has thickened. Refrigerate and use as needed.

## Crème Fraîche II

*Makes 2 cups*

1   cup heavy cream                    1   cup sour cream

In a jar with a tight-fitting lid, combine the cream and sour cream with a wire whisk, beating vigorously for 1 minute. Cover and leave at room temperature for about 8 hours, or until the cream has thickened. Refrigerate and use as needed.

# Pies

## Lime Pie with Gingersnap Crust

*Serves 8*

### CRUST

| | |
|---|---|
| 2 cups finely crushed gingersnaps | 3 tablespoons sugar |
| ½ cup (1 stick) butter, melted | |

### LIME FILLING

| | |
|---|---|
| 1 14-ounce can sweetened condensed milk | 1½ cups heavy cream |
| ¼ cup fresh lime juice | 1 lime, thinly sliced |
| 1 tablespoon grated lime rind | |

1. Preheat the oven to 350 degrees.

2. In a bowl, combine the crushed gingersnaps, butter, and sugar well. Put in a 9-inch pie pan and press evenly over the bottom and sides of the pan. Bake for 10 minutes. Remove and cool completely.

3. Pour the sweetened condensed milk into a bowl and add the lime juice and lime rind. Stir until well combined and thickened.

4. Whip the cream and fold into the mixture. Turn the mixture into the pie shell and smooth the top. Cover and freeze for several hours or overnight.

5. Transfer to the refrigerator 1 hour before serving. Garnish each serving with a lime slice.

*Variations:* Substitute lemon juice, lemon rind, and lemon slices for the lime juice, lime rind, and lime slices in recipe.

# Ellie Ashworth's Rum–Pecan Pie

*Serves 8*

## PASTRY

1½ cups sifted all-purpose
flour
½ teaspoon salt
¼ cup cold butter, cut into
small pieces

¼ cup solid shortening
3 tablespoons ice water

## RUM–PECAN FILLING

3 large eggs
⅔ cup sugar
1 cup light corn syrup
¼ cup butter, melted
¼ light rum

1¼ cups chopped pecans
12 whole pecan halves for
garnish
Whipped cream or ice
cream, if desired

1. First prepare the pastry for the pie shell.

2. Combine the flour, salt, butter, and shortening in a food processor or with a pastry blender until the mixture reaches a coarse crumb consistency. Add the water and combine in the food processor or stir into a ball. Cover the ball of dough in plastic wrap and refrigerate for 30 minutes.

3. Roll out the dough to a circle ⅛ inch thick on a lightly floured surface. Fit the dough into a 9-inch pie plate. Cut off the extra dough and crimp the edges. Refrigerate until needed.

4. Preheat the oven to 375 degrees.

5. In a large bowl, combine all the filling ingredients, except the pecans. Beat with a wooden spoon for 3 or 4 minutes. Fold in the chopped nuts.

6. Pour the mixture into the pie shell and garnish the top with the pecan halves. Bake for 45 minutes. Cool before slicing. Serve with whipped cream or ice cream, if desired.

# Mousses

## Chocolate Mousse

### Serves 8

8 ounces semisweet chocolate, cut into small pieces
1 tablespoon butter
3 large eggs, separated
½ cup sugar

2 tablespoons Cognac or brandy
2 teaspoons grated orange rind
2 cups heavy cream

1. Melt the chocolate with the butter in the top of a double boiler over simmering water.

2. Meanwhile, in a large bowl, beat the egg yolks with the sugar until light and fluffy. Add the Cognac and orange rind and combine well.

3. Whip the cream and stir in half. Fold in the remaining half of the cream.

4. Beat the egg whites until stiff, but not dry, and fold into the mixture.

5. Turn the mousse into a large chilled dessert bowl, cover, and chill thoroughly.

# Cold Lemon Mousse with Raspberry Sauce

*Serves 6*

1 cup heavy cream, whipped
1 envelope unflavored gelatin
½ cup cold water
4 large eggs, separated

¼ cup fresh lemon juice
1 cup sugar
Pinch of salt
2 teaspoons grated lemon rind

## RASPBERRY SAUCE

1 10-ounce package frozen raspberries, thawed

1 tablespoon fresh lemon juice

1. Refrigerate the whipped cream until needed.

2. Put the gelatin in a small bowl with the cold water to soften it.

3. Put the egg yolks, lemon juice, ½ cup of the sugar, and the salt in the top of a double boiler. Cook over simmering water, stirring constantly, until the sauce thickens, about 8 minutes. Remove from the heat and stir in the gelatin mixture and the lemon rind. Combine well. Turn the mixture into a large bowl and cool, stirring constantly over a larger bowl or container half-filled with ice, for about 5 minutes. Don't allow the mixture to begin to set. Fold the whipped cream into the lemon mixture.

4. Beat the egg whites until they begin to peak. Gradually beat in the remaining ½ cup of sugar and continue beating until stiff, but not dry. Fold the beaten egg whites into the lemon mixture and turn into a dessert bowl.

5. Cover and refrigerate for several hours, or until firm.

6. Meanwhile, purée the raspberries with the lemon juice in a food processor or blender. Force the mixture through a food mill or fine mesh strainer. Cover and chill thoroughly. Serve with the mousse.

*Variation:* A Lime Mousse can be made by substituting fresh lime juice and grated lime rind for the lemon juice and rind in the recipe.

# Prune and Orange Whip

*Serves 4*

| | | | |
|---|---|---|---|
| 1 | 12-ounce package pitted prunes | ¼ | cup light brown sugar |
| ½ | cup fresh orange juice | 2 | teaspoons grated orange rind |
| ½ | cup water | 3 | large egg whites |
| 1 | cup chilled heavy cream | | |

1. Put the prunes, orange juice, and water in a saucepan and bring to a boil. Lower the heat and simmer for 15 minutes.

2. Meanwhile, whip the cream in a bowl and refrigerate it.

3. Stir the brown sugar and orange rind into the prune mixture and purée in a food processor fitted with a steel blade or in the blender. Turn into a bowl and cool for 15 minutes.

4. Fold the prune mixture into the whipped cream.

5. Beat the egg whites until stiff, but not dry, and fold them into the prune mixture.

6. Turn into 4 dessert bowls and refrigerate for several hours or overnight.

# Dessert Soufflés

## Perfect Chocolate Soufflé

*Serves 6 to 8*

¾  cup plus 2 tablespoons
 sugar
10  tablespoons butter
 4  tablespoons all-purpose
 flour
1½  cups milk
 9  large eggs, separated
 (Set aside 6 egg yolks
 and use the remaining
 yolks for another
 purpose.)

6  ounces unsweetened
 chocolate
 Chocolate Sauce (see
 recipe page 284)
 Confectioners' sugar
 (optional)

1. Rub 1 tablespoon of the butter over the bottom and sides of a 2-quart soufflé dish. Measure aluminum foil to fit around the soufflé dish with 3 inches overlapping. Fold the foil in half lengthwise and butter one side with 1 tablespoon of the butter. Fit the foil around the soufflé dish, buttered side in, making a 3-inch collar and secure the foil to the dish with kitchen string. Put 2 tablespoons of the sugar in the dish and rotate it until the sugar coats the dish and foil. Set aside.

2. In a saucepan, melt 4 tablespoons of the butter and add the flour. Whisk and cook over medium heat for 1 minute. Whisk in the milk, stirring constantly, until the mixture boils, is smooth, and has thickened. Remove from the heat and cool.

3. Preheat the oven to 350 degrees.

4. Beat together the 6 egg yolks and ¾ cup of the sugar until light and fluffy. Stir into the sauce and cover.

5. Melt the chocolate with 2 tablespoons of the remaining butter in the top of a double boiler over simmering water. Cool the melted chocolate for 5 minutes and stir it into the sauce. Pour the sauce into a large bowl.

6. Beat the egg whites until stiff and fold them into the chocolate mixture. Turn the soufflé mixture into the prepared dish and bake for about 45 minutes, or until the top is firm.

7. Remove the soufflé from the oven and remove the string and collar. Serve at once with the sauce. If desired, the top of the soufflé can be dusted with confectioners' sugar.

# Chocolate Sauce

*Makes about 1 cup*

6  ounces semisweet chocolate
3  tablespoons sweet butter

4  tablespoons heavy cream

Fifteen minutes before the soufflé has finished cooking, begin to prepare the sauce: Put the chocolate and butter in the top of a double boiler over simmering water. Stir occasionally until the chocolate melts. Whisk in the heavy cream. Pour into a small warmed pitcher or sauceboat.

# Frozen Grand Marnier Soufflé

*Serves 6 to 8*

6  large egg yolks
⅔  cup sugar
1½  cups heavy cream
⅓  cup Grand Marnier
1  teaspoon grated orange rind

1  navel orange, peeled and cut into segments and drained well

1. In a bowl, beat together the egg yolks and sugar with an electric mixer until ribbons form when the beaters are raised, about 5 minutes.

2. Whip the cream and fold the egg mixture into it. Fold in the Grand Marnier and orange rind.

3. Turn the mixture into a 1½-quart soufflé dish or individual soufflé dishes or bowls and freeze overnight. Just before serving garnish the top with the well-drained orange sections.

# Puddings

---

## Susan Angel's Raspberry and Strawberry Summer Pudding

*Serves 8*
*(Preparation begins the night before)*

12  *slices firm white bread,*      1  *cup sugar*
    *or as needed*                  2  *tablespoons water*
 3  *cups fresh raspberries,*          *Whipped cream*
    *plus a few extra for*
    *garnish*
 3  *cup sliced strawberries,*
    *plus a few extra for*
    *garnish*

1. Cut off the crusts from the bread and cut each slice in half crosswise.

2. Line the bottom and sides of a 2-quart soufflé dish with the bread slices, overlapping them slightly. (Save enough bread slices to cover the top.)

3. In a heavy saucepan, heat the berries, sugar, and water over high heat, stirring for 3 minutes. Transfer the mixture to a bowl and cool.

4. Spoon the berry mixture into the bread-lined soufflé dish. Cover the top with the remaining bread slices.

5. Cover the bread loosely with plastic wrap. Put a plate that just fits inside the rim of the dish on the pudding and place a 1-pound can of food on it as a weight. Refrigerate the pudding overnight.

6. Unmold the pudding onto a serving dish. Cut into slices and serve plain or with whipped cream. Garnish each serving with a few raspberries and strawberries.

# Blueberry Pudding

### Serves 4 to 6

6   ½-inch-thick slices
    French bread
    Softened butter
1   cup milk
1   cup heavy cream

3   large eggs, lightly beaten
1   teaspoon vanilla extract
½   cup granulated sugar
1   cup blueberries
    Confectioners' sugar

1. Preheat the oven to 350 degrees.

2. Butter a 1½-quart baking dish.

3. Lightly butter one side of each slice of bread and cut them into ½-inch cubes.

4. In a bowl, mix together the milk, cream, eggs, vanilla, and sugar. Strain the mixture and pour it into the prepared dish. Sprinkle with the bread cubes and blueberries.

5. Bake for about 35 minutes, or until set. Dust with confectioners' sugar and serve warm.

# Dessert Crêpes

## *Crêpes with Cream Filling Flamed in Cointreau*

### Serves 4

### BASIC DESSERT CRÊPES:

| | |
|---|---|
| 3 eggs | 2 tablespoons sugar |
| ¾ cup water | ½ teaspoon salt |
| ⅔ cup milk | 3 tablespoons butter |
| ⅔ cup all-purpose flour | |
| 2 tablespoons butter, melted | |

### CREAM FILLING

| | |
|---|---|
| 1½ cups heavy cream | ½ teaspoon vanilla |
| ¼ cup sugar | extract, or to taste |

### TO FINISH

| | |
|---|---|
| 3 tablespoons sugar | ¼ cup Cointreau |

1. Prepare the crêpes first: Combine all the ingredients in a blender, except for the 3 tablespoons of butter, or whisk them together thoroughly in a large bowl.

2. Heat 1 teaspoon of the butter in a 6- to 7-inch crêpe pan and roll it around in the pan. The pan should be hot but not smoking. Wipe out most of the butter with a paper towel. Pour about ¼ cup of the batter into the pan and immediately tilt the pan in a circle to distribute the batter evenly. When the crêpe edges begin to brown and come away from the sides of the pan, loosen the edges and turn the crêpe with a cake spatula (this implement is essential). Cook only about 20 seconds on the second side, or until lightly browned.

3. Transfer the crêpe to a plate. Add ½ teaspoon of the butter, let it melt and roll it around in the pan, and repeat the crêpe-making process until all the batter is used. It will be necessary to beat the batter

occasionally between crêpe-making. The batter will yield at least 12 crêpes. (At this point the crêpes can be cooled, covered, and refrigerated overnight, if desired.)

4. Prepare the Cream Filling: Bring the cream to a boil in an enamel or nonmetallic saucepan. Boil for about 6 minutes, whisking frequently until the filling thickens to the consistency of fresh-made mayonnaise. Whisk in the sugar and vanilla.

5. Spread a tablespoon or so of the filling over the surface of each crêpe and fold in half; fold in half again, making a triangle.

6. Place the filled and folded crepes overlapping in a large au gratin or shallow baking dish. Sprinkle with the sugar and cook for 5 minutes under a hot broiler, or until the sugar sizzles. Immediately remove and pour the Cointreau over the crêpes. Standing well back, ignite the liqueur with a long kitchen match and, when the flame goes out, serve immediately.

*Variations:* One tablespoon of grated orange or lemon rind can be added to the thickened cream sauce. One teaspoon of chopped toasted almonds or hazelnuts can be sprinkled over each crêpe spread with the cream sauce. Grand Marnier can be substituted for the Cointreau.

## Fruit-stuffed Crêpes with Honey Butter

Place half a small sliced banana and ¼ cup sliced strawberries or blueberries in a dessert crêpe. Sprinkle with a little confectioners' sugar and fold into square package. Make 1 per person. Brush the tops with softened Honey Butter (see recipe page 124). Sprinkle lightly with granulated sugar and run under the broiler for a few moments, or until the tops sizzle and are golden brown. Serve with Crème Fraîche (see recipe page 277) or whipped cream.

# Beignets

## Apple Beignets

### Serves 4

2 firm unpeeled Delicious
  apples
  Peanut or vegetable
  oil for frying

Confectioners' sugar

### BATTER

1 cup all-purpose flour
1 cup beer

Pinch of salt

1. In a large skillet, heat ½ inch of oil to 375 degrees.

2. Combine the batter ingredients in a deep shallow bowl.

3. Slice each apple crosswise into 4⅓-inch-thick slices. Cut out the seeds in the center of each slice with an apple corer or cut out the centers with the sharp point of a small knife.

4. Dip an apple slice into the batter on both sides and let the excess batter drip back into the bowl.

5. Gently lower the coated apple slice into the hot oil. Repeat the procedure, cooking 4 apple slices at a time. Cook until golden brown on each side. Drain on paper towels and cook the remaining apple slices. Drain. Sprinkle with confectioners' sugar and serve immediately.

*Variation:* Fresh pear slices can be cooked in exactly the same manner.

# Fritters

---

## Banana Batter Banana Fritters

### Serves 6

### BATTER

| | |
|---|---|
| 2 medium-sized ripe bananas | 2 large eggs |
| 1 tablespoon fresh lime juice | ¾ cup milk |
| | 2 cups sifted all-purpose flour |
| 2 tablespoons peanut or vegetable oil | 2 teaspoons baking powder |
| 3 tablespoons granulated sugar | ¼ teaspoon ground cinnamon |
| | ¼ teaspoon salt |

### FRITTERS

| | |
|---|---|
| Peanut or vegetable oil for deep frying | 4 large ripe bananas Confectioners' sugar |

1. Place the first 6 ingredients for the batter into a blender container and purée for 15 seconds, or mix by hand by mashing the bananas well and combining with the other ingredients.

2. Pour the mixture into a large bowl and add the combined flour, baking powder, cinnamon, and salt. Mix well.

3. Heat 2 inches of oil to 375 degrees in a large heavy saucepan.

4. Meanwhile, cut the bananas crosswise into 1-inch lengths. Dip a piece of banana into the batter and lightly drop into the hot fat. (Cook 4 or 5 at a time in the oil.) Turn the fritters with a slotted spoon until golden brown all over. The fritters will be cooked in 3 to 4 minutes.

5. Transfer the cooked fritters to paper towels and drain. When all the fritters are cooked and drained sprinkle with confectioners' sugar.

*Variation:* For a delightful combination of flavors, substitute whole strawberries for the banana slices.

# Rosettes

## Rosettes
## (Beer Batter Recipe)
*Makes about 36*

A few years ago at a Kentucky Derby day luncheon that I attended, appreciative guests were served Rosettes for dessert. I was reminded of how surprisingly delicious these delicacies are; light and airy, they were sweetened by a dusting of confectioners' sugar. Rosettes have now become a traditional dish at my own Fourth of July luncheon. I cook them early in the day.

| | | | |
|---|---|---|---|
| 1 | cup sifted all-purpose flour | 1 | egg |
| ½ | cup evaporated milk | | Vegetable oil |
| ½ | cup beer | | Confectioners' sugar |
| ½ | teaspoon salt | | Ice cream (optional) |
| 1 | teaspoon granulated sugar | | |

1. Put the flour in a large bowl.

2. In another bowl, mix together the remaining ingredients, except for the oil and confectioners' sugar. Pour the liquid mixture slowly into the flour, stirring constantly until smooth.

3. Heat 2 inches of oil to 375 degrees in a heavy saucepan.

4. First, dip the Rosette iron in the hot oil for 10 seconds and suspend over the oil, shaking off any excess. Dip the hot mold into the batter, taking care not to let the batter reach over the top of the iron. (If this happens a perfect Rosette cannot be made. Clean the iron and begin the procedure again.)

5. Completely immerse the batter-coated iron in the hot oil for about 5 seconds. Still in the oil, shake the iron back and forth slightly and the Rosette will drop from the iron. If this doesn't happen easily, use the tip of a butter knife to help release the Rosette. Brown the Rosette lightly on each side. It should be completely cooked in a little less than a minute. Repeat the process until all the batter is used.

(Remember to dip the iron into the oil each time before coating it with the batter.) Beat the batter between making each Rosette, as the oil will collect on the top and prevent the batter from coating the iron evenly.

6. As the Rosettes are cooked, drain them in a single layer on paper towels. When all the Rosettes have been made dust them with confectioners' sugar. (Store the Rosettes loosely in a covered container and reheat in a warm oven. They will keep for 2 days, but are always better freshly made.) If desired, serve with the ice cream of your choice.

# Fruit Desserts

## Fresh Cantaloupe and Cherries
### Serves 6

This dish is more of a presentation than a recipe. It made a striking impression on me when I first saw it served for dessert in Sirmione, Italy, and subsequently in several other Italian cities.

Friends have improvised the presentation by using honeydew and small purple plums, which is also delightful after a hot morning in the sun.

| | | | |
|---|---|---|---|
| 1 | *large ripe cantaloupe* | 2 | *or 3 trays of ice cubes* |
| 1½ | *pounds fresh cherries,* | | *Gorgonzola cheese* |
| | *stems left intact* | | *Italian bread* |

1. Cut the cantaloupe in half lengthwise. Scoop out the seeds with a spoon.

2. Cut each half into 6 equal-sized pieces, making crescent shapes. With a small sharp knife cut just under the cantaloupe's skin halfway up each slice.

3. Fit the slice of cantaloupe onto the rim of a large glass bowl by placing the skin side of the slice over the outside rim of the bowl and the flesh side over the inside of the bowl. Repeat the procedure with the remaining slices, placing them equal distances apart around the bowl.

4. Fill the center of the bowl with the ice and top with the cherries. If desired, serve with Gorgonzola cheese and Italian bread.

# Cantaloupe, Raspberries, and Oranges with Framboise

*Serves 4*

| | |
|---|---|
| 1 large ripe cantaloupe | 2 navel oranges |
| 1 pint fresh raspberries | 8 tablespoon framboise |

1. Cut the cantaloupe in half lengthwise and scoop out the seeds with a spoon.

2. Peel each half. Cut each half into 6 even crescent-shaped slices.

3. Place 3 slices around the edges of 4 dessert plates with the cut sides of the slices facing the center, making a circle.

4. Spoon equal amounts of the raspberries into the center of the cantaloupe slices.

5. With a sharp knife, peel the oranges including the white pith. Slice each orange into ¼-inch-thick slices. Cut the slices in half and place 4 or 5 halves across the raspberries on each dish.

6. Spoon 2 tablespoons of the framboise over the orange sections.

*Variations:* Substitute blueberries or sliced strawberries for the raspberries. Grand Marnier or Cointreau can be used in place of framboise. If desired serve with Crème Fraîche.

# Orange Slices with Strawberry Purée

*Serves 4*

| | |
|---|---|
| 4 large navel oranges, peeled, including white pith, and cut into ¼-inch-thick slices | 1 10-ounce package frozen strawberries, thawed and drained |

1. Arrange each of the sliced oranges across a dessert plate.

2. Purée the strawberries in a blender or food processor and spoon the purée over the oranges in equal amounts.

## Broiled Fresh Peaches with Strawberry–Crunch Filling

*Serves 6*

6  large ripe peaches
6  tablespoons strawberry
    preserves
6  small macaroons,
    crumbled
1/3  cup chopped hazelnuts
2  tablespoons butter, plus
    extra for greasing the
    baking sheet

6  teaspoons Frangelico or
    Grand Marnier (both
    producing different
    flavors, each excellent)

1. Bring 1 quart of water to a boil in a saucepan. Dip each peach in the boiling water for 10 seconds and remove with a slotted spoon. Peel the peaches, cut them in half, and remove the pits.

2. Combine the preserves, crumbled macaroons, and hazelnuts.

3. Put the peaches on a lightly greased baking sheet. Spoon equal amounts of the mixture over the pitted sides of each peach half. Spoon 1 tablespoon of the liqueur over each and dot with equal amounts of the butter.

4. Broil about 6 inches from the flame for about 5 minutes, or until the tops sizzle. Serve immediately.

## Strawberries in Cream

*Serves 6*

1  quart fresh hulled
    strawberries
4  tablespoons granulated
    sugar
3  tablespoons fraise des bois
    liqueur

1  cup heavy cream
3  tablespoons confectioners'
    sugar
1  teaspoon vanilla extract

1. Slice the strawberries and put them in a large bowl. Sprinkle them with the sugar and liqueur. Toss gently and set aside.

2. Whip the heavy cream and add the confectioners' sugar and vanilla. Combine well and spoon over the strawberries. Fold together and refrigerate until served.

# Special Desserts

## Buñuelos

### Serves 4

4 flour tortillas
  Peanut or vegetable oil
3 tablespoons sugar
½ teaspoon ground
  cinnamon

4 scoops chocolate Hägan
  Daz, or other good
  quality brand (1 pint)

1. Heat ¼ inch of oil in a medium frying pan and brown the tortillas lightly, one at a time, on each side.

2. Sprinkle the combined sugar and cinnamon over each hot cooked tortilla and place 1 scoop of ice cream on the center of each. Serve immediately.

## Zabaglione Coupes

### Serves 6

6 scoops vanilla ice cream
1 pint fresh raspberries
  (strawberries can be
  substituted)
6 large egg yolks

¼ cup sugar
½ cup Marsala (Madeira or
  a good dry sherry can
  also be used.)

1. Place a scoop of ice cream in each of 6 balloon wineglasses and top with an equal portion of the raspberries. Refrigerate until needed.

2. Heat the egg yolks with the sugar in the top of a double boiler over simmering water, stirring constantly with a whisk. (Don't allow the water in the lower pan to touch the bottom of the top pan.) Whisk the mixture until it becomes frothy. Add the Marsala and whisk until the Zabaglione is foaming and slightly thickened.

3. Spoon equal amounts over the ice cream and raspberries in the glasses. Serve at once.

# Cooking for Crowds

Whether we cook for crowds only once a year or every week, it is an activity that requires careful planning and organization and that is the formula for *fearless* cooking in general. Planning for 12 or 24 guests at home will generally mean serving a buffet meal. Because people will be eating "lap style," the dishes selected for the menu should comprise those that are easily cut—no thick cuts of meat, corn on the cob, and so forth. Here are the guidelines for menu planning: Pass two or more hors d'oeuvres, and eliminate a first course. Select the entrée and balance out the menu with fresh seasonal vegetables, a rice or potato dish, and always a tossed green salad. Serve at least two breads: French, Italian whole wheat, pumpernickel, hot rolls, biscuits, corn muffins, etc. Complete the meal with two or three desserts. This offers guests a choice and makes it possible to cook the desserts in normal amounts. Select as many dishes that can be partially or totally prepared in advance as possible.

Offer both coffee and tea. Because I'm a tea drinker, I'm always relieved when a hostess or host offers me coffee *or* tea, rather than rushing off to the kitchen to boil the water.

Here are some small tasks that can be done in advance of mealtime:

1. Stock and arrange the bar with glasses and cocktail napkins. Arrange chilled white wine, apéritifs, red wine, and liquor with setups of club soda, tonic, ginger ale, and a pitcher of ice water. Have lemon and limes in the refrigerator ready to set out with a small cutting board and knife and a corkscrew for opening the wines. Arrange for twice as much ice as you think you will need, and set out a large ice bucket or container.

2. Arrange the buffet table with a cloth, a centerpiece, dinner plates, and forks and knives rolled up in napkins, which makes it easier for guests to manage. Position the required numbers of trivets and serving spoons, with serving dishes selected and ready in the kitchen.

Line bread baskets with cloth napkins and set out the butter dish and knife.

3. Meanwhile, back in the kitchen, fill the sugar bowl and set out the creamer. Have the coffee and tea ready to prepare and have lemon slices cut. Set out cups and saucers, spoons and dessert plates and forks. Set out the dessert serving dishes if the desserts are not already on them and the required serving spoons or knives.

The few extra minutes devoted to arranging the bar, buffet table, utensils, and backup service items in the kitchen in advance of dinner will minimize the traffic and logistical problems that are almost unavoidable when more than a dozen hungry people gather to dine at the same time and place. And you will have a much better chance of enjoying your own party.

*Note:* In some instances, it will be necessary to double or triple the Serving Suggestion recipes included with the following recipes, depending upon the number of people being served.

# Entrées for Twelve

## Bestilla

*Serves 12*

Bestilla is the miraculous aromatic Moroccan multi-layered chicken (traditionally pigeon) pie cooked in a flaky crust of filo pastry. It is lusty, delicate, spicy, and sweet all at once. Unlike the traditional version, I do not turn the pie over after it has baked half-way.

| | | | |
|---|---|---|---|
| 1 | cup Oriental sesame oil | 3 | tablespoons sesame seeds |
| 1½ | teaspoons ground cumin | 1 | cup raisins |
| 1½ | teaspoons ground turmeric | 1 | cup slivered almonds |
| 1 | teaspoon paprika | ½ | cup confectioners' sugar, plus extra for coating the pie |
| 1¼ | teaspoons ground ginger | | |
| 1 | teaspoon powdered saffron | 1 | teaspoon ground cinnamon |
| ½ | teaspoon freshly ground black pepper | ¼ | cup fresh lemon juice |
| 1 | whole 3-inch cinnamon stick | 9 | large eggs, lightly beaten |
| 2 | 3½-pound chickens, cut into 8 serving pieces each | 12 | filo pastry leaves (available in specialty food stores) |
| 4 | cups homemade chicken stock or canned broth | 1 | cup (2 sticks) butter, melted |
| 1 | large onion, finely chopped | | |

1. Heat ¼ cup of the sesame oil in a large heavy casserole or pot. Add the spices and cinnamon stick. Stir well and add the chicken pieces. Turn the chicken to coat it evenly. Add the chicken stock and stir. Cover and simmer for 1 hour and 20 minutes.

2. Meanwhile, heat 4 tablespoons of the remaining sesame oil in a large frying pan. Add the onion and simmer for 15 minutes. Stir in the sesame seeds and raisins and set aside.

3. Heat 2 tablespoons of the oil in a frying pan and lightly brown the almonds. Drain. Grind the cooled nuts in a food processor. Turn into a bowl and combine with the ½ cup confectioners' sugar and ground cinnamon. Set aside.

4. Remove the cooked chicken to a plate with a slotted spoon. Reduce the liquid in the pan to 1½ cups over high heat.

5. As the liquid reduces, remove the chicken meat discarding the skin and bones. Tear the meat into thin shreds and put them in a large bowl. Add the lemon juice to the reduced liquid, and add ¾ cup of the combined mixture to the chicken. Stir and set aside.

6. Add the other cup of liquid to a large frying pan and stir in the eggs. Cook over low heat, stirring constantly, for about 10 minutes, or until the eggs are set and have absorbed all the liquid. They will have the consistency of curdled scrambled eggs. Set aside.

7. A paella pan or 14-inch pizza pan are best for baking the Bestilla.

8. Set out the melted butter and filo leaves. Keep the filo leaves that aren't being worked with covered with a damp dish towel at all times. Butter the pan and arrange 6 overlapping sheets of buttered filo leaves over the bottom of the pan, one at a time, with part of the leaves hanging over the edge of the pan. Work quickly as the filo breaks easily.

9. Spread the mixtures over the buttered filo in the following order: eggs, almond and sugar mixture, onion and raisin mixture, and top with the chicken mixture. Fold the ends of the filo leaves up over the center.

10. Preheat the oven to 400 degrees.

11. Brush a filo sheet with melted butter and place over the top to cover it, overlapping, with 6 more buttered leaves. Fold all the edges under the pie.

12. Bake for 25 minutes, or until the top is golden brown and puffy.

13. Sprinkle confectioners' sugar over the surface of the pie and sprinkle cinnamon, in a geometric pattern, over it. Decorate with whole toasted almonds, if desired. Cut into wedges and serve hot or at room temperature.

*Serving Suggestions:* Crudités with lemon mayonnaise, Shrimp Toast Coins, mixed green salad, toasted sesame seed bread, and Sliced Oranges with Strawberry Purée and assorted cookies.

# Nancy Dussault's Ground Beef and Noodle Casserole

## Serves 12

Nancy Dussault, the talented actress-singer, is an old friend from my theater days. When I was visiting her in California last year, she threw a lively birthday party for her friend Karen Morrow. The celebration menu included hot sautéed almonds as an appetizer, then her Ground Beef and Noodle Casserole, Roast Turkey Breast, eight vegetable salad of romaine and Bibb lettuce, cherry tomatoes, green peppers, red onion rings, julienne of carrot, cucumber, and sliced olives with a vinaigrette dressing, hot crusty French bread with whipped butter, and a double chocolate cake.

About 20 people were to attend the party, so she made 2 double casseroles for the party. She looked forward to lots of leftover casserole that she could savor for the next few days, but not a morsel remained. "I made it *too* good," Nancy laughed. She said, "It's a very ordinary dish, but every time I serve it, people gobble it up and want the recipe" . . . and so did I.

| | | | |
|---|---|---|---|
| 4 | tablespoons olive oil | 2 | 3-ounce packages cream |
| 1 | large onion, chopped | | cheese, softened |
| 2 | large garlic cloves, minced | 6 | scallions, thinly sliced |
| 3 | pounds lean ground beef | | (about 1 cup) |
| 2 | 16-ounce cans tomato | 3 | cups cottage cheese |
| | sauce | 1 | cup sour cream |
| | Salt and freshly ground | 1 | cup grated Cheddar |
| | black pepper | | cheese |
| 2 | pounds medium egg | | |
| | noodles | | |

1. Bring 3½ quarts of water to a rolling boil in a large pot.

2. Meanwhile, heat the oil in a large frying pan. Add the onion and garlic and cook for 5 minutes, stirring often. Add the ground beef and crumble with a wooden spoon as it cooks, stirring, occasionally, until the beef loses the red color. Stir in the tomato sauce and season with salt and pepper to taste. Set aside.

3. Add 1 tablespoon of salt to the boiling water, stir, add the noodles, stir, and cook until tender, about 8 minutes.

4. Meanwhile, preheat the oven to 350 degrees.

5. In a large bowl, beat the cream cheese until light and fluffy. Stir in the scallions, cottage cheese, and sour cream and combine.

6. Drain the cooked noodles and turn into the bowl with the

cottage cheese mixture and toss. Season well with salt and pepper.

7. In a 3- or 4-quart casserole, place a layer of the meat sauce, then a layer of the noodles. Continue making layers until all is used, ending with a layer of the meat sauce. Sprinkle the Cheddar cheese over the top and bake, uncovered, for 30 minutes.

*Serving Suggestions:* Serve Nancy's menu listed above.

## Cold Lamb and Flageolet Salad

*Serves 12*
*(Preparation begins the night before)*

1½  pounds dried flageolets
1  7-pound leg of lamb
2  large garlic cloves, cut into slivers
  Salt and freshly ground black pepper
1  teaspoon dried thyme
1  large onion, quartered
1  cup olive oil

½  cup white wine vinegar
2  tablespoons Dijon mustard
2  teaspoons dried tarragon
1½  cups diced fresh fennel
¼  cup chopped fresh parsley leaves

1. Put the flageolets in a large bowl and cover with 3 inches of cold water. Soak overnight.

2. Preheat the oven to 450 degrees.

3. Cut small incisions in several places in the meaty part of the lamb near the bone. Insert the garlic slivers. Season the lamb with salt and pepper and sprinkle with thyme.

4. Put the lamb in a roasting pan and roast for 10 minutes. Lower the oven temperature to 350 degrees and roast for about 1½ hours. The lamb should be just pink at the bone when cooked.

5. Meanwhile, drain the flageolets and put them in a large flame-proof casserole. Cover them with 1 inch of water. Add the onion and 1 tablespoon of salt. Stir and bring to a boil. Lower the heat and simmer for about 1½ hours, or until the beans are tender, but not mushy. Add a little more water, if necessary, to keep the beans covered, and stir occasionally.

6. When the lamb is cooked, remove it from the oven and cool it completely.

7. Drain the cooked beans and discard the onion. Transfer the beans to a large bowl to cool.

8. Meanwhile, combine the oil, vinegar, mustard, and tarragon and season with salt and pepper to taste.

9. When the lamb is cool, carve it into very thin slices. Cut each slice into bite-sized pieces. Add the lamb, fennel, and parsley to the flageolets.

10. Whisk the sauce mixture again to combine it well and pour it over the salad. Toss gently and taste for seasoning. Serve at room temperature or cover and chill thoroughly. Toss again before serving.

*Serving Suggestions:* Salmon Mousse and Red Salmon Caviar with Dill, Gougère, Emily McCormack's Tomatoes, green beans vinaigrette, Cheesecake, and a fruit salad of fresh pineapple cubes and blueberries.

# Shrimp, Mushroom, and Leek Casserole

## Serves 12

| | | | |
|---|---|---|---|
| 3½ | pounds medium shrimp, shelled and deveined | 2 | tablespoons all-purpose flour |
| 1 | lemon, cut into slices and seeded | 2 | teaspoons Dijon mustard |
| 8 | tablespoons (1 stick) butter, or as needed | 2 | cups heavy cream |
| 2 | tablespoons olive oil | 1 | cup milk |
| 2 | pounds fresh mushrooms, thinly sliced | 1 | tablespoon brandy |
| | | 1 | tablespoon fresh lemon juice |
| 6 | leeks (white parts only), cleaned, washed, and thinly sliced | ¼ | cup chopped fresh parsley leaves |
| | | 1 | cup grated Gruyère cheese |

1. Put the shrimp and lemon slices in a large pot. Add water to cover them and bring to a boil. Cook over high heat for 1 minute, stirring often. Remove from the heat and drain. Discard the lemon slices and transfer the shrimp to a large bowl.

2. Heat 2 tablespoons of the butter and the olive oil in a frying pan. Add half the mushrooms and cook for 5 minutes, stirring often. Drain the mushrooms in a colander and cook the second batch of mushrooms in the frying pan, adding a little more butter and oil, if necessary. Drain the second batch of mushrooms.

3. Melt 3 tablespoons of the butter and sauté the leeks for 5 minutes over medium heat.

4. Preheat the oven to 400 degrees.

5. Butter a large baking pan—a paella pan is perfect.

6. Add the leeks and mushrooms to the bowl with the shrimp and combine gently. Turn the mixture into the baking pan.

7. Melt the remaining 3 tablespoons of butter in a heavy saucepan. Add the flour, whisking constantly for 1 minute over medium heat. Add the mustard, heavy cream, milk, brandy, lemon juice, and parsley. Whisk until the sauce boils and is smooth and creamy.

8. Pour the sauce over the shrimp mixture and sprinkle with the Gruyère. Bake for 10 minutes. Run under the broiler until the top is golden brown, just a minute or 2.

*Serving Suggestions:* Fried Chicken Breast Cubes with Marmalade Dip, buttered green peas, Lemon Rice, Madeleines, and Swiss chocolate almond ice cream.


# Whole Roast Turkey Salad
### Serves 12

Roasting a whole turkey and turning it into a salad allows the hostess or host to cook early in the day and be free to be with guests during the meal.

I often serve a dinner of salads for a large group, especially in the spring, summer, or fall. The rest of the menu might be composed of a tossed green salad, Ratatouille, and a fresh fruit salad served with a freshly made sherbet. The basic recipe that follows can be easily changed into many different salads as you will see in the *variations* that are listed after the recipe. Whichever salad you decide to prepare can depend on the season, theme, or the mood of the moment. For more ideas on converting this salad into a more unusual one, check the section on chicken salads.

| | | | |
|---|---|---|---|
| 1 | 13- to 14-pound ready-to-cook turkey | 1/4 | cup heavy cream |
| | Salt and freshly ground black pepper | | Juice of 1 lemon |
| | | 1 1/2 | cups thinly sliced celery |
| 1 | large onion, quartered | 1/4 | cup chopped fresh parsley leaves |
| 3 | tablespoons vegetable oil | | |
| 1 1/2 | cups mayonnaise, or as needed | | |

## GARNISHES

*Whole endive leaves, cherry
tomatoes and/or black
olives, watercress, cooked
string beans or cooked
carrot sticks tossed in a
vinaigrette dressing, or
halved orange slices*

## SERVE WITH

*French bread and/or
pumpernickel bread slices
or rolls or Riviera toast*

1. Preheat the oven to 325 degrees.
2. Remove the giblets and save for another use, such as stock-making. Season the turkey inside and out with salt and pepper. Place the onion quarters in the body cavity. Tie the legs together.
3. Put the turkey in a roasting pan and rub it all over with the oil. Roast for 3½ to 4¼ hours, or until it is tender, approximately 18 minutes per pound. When done, the turkey's legs should move easily, and the juices from the thickest area of the thigh should run clear when it is pricked with a fork.
4. Remove the turkey from the oven and roasting pan and let cool on a platter for 1 hour.
5. Peel off all of the skin. Remove the legs and thighs and each breast half and the wings. Cut the meat into bite-sized pieces.
6. Put the turkey in a large bowl and add the remaining ingredients. Combine gently and season with salt and pepper to taste. Turn the salad into a serving bowl or platter.

*Variations:* For an Herb Turkey Salad, add 1½ tablespoons dried tarragon or dill. You may also add ½ cup thinly sliced scallions and/or 1 cup of chopped sun-dried tomatoes and 1½ tablespoons dried basil. To make a Curried Turkey Salad, mix 2 tablespoons of curry powder with the mayonnaise before combining it with the other ingredients. ¾ cup each of raisins, green grapes, diced cucumbers, and toasted slivered almonds can be added with the curried mayonnaise for a Polynesian Turkey Salad. More mayonnaise will be required for the latter salad. The salad should be moist to creamy, but not mushy.

# Entrées for Twenty-four

## Twin Cold Roast Fillets of Beef
### Serves 24

Cook 2 whole tenderloins of beef exactly as in the recipe for Roast Fillet of Beef (see recipe page 142). Cook one fillet 5 minutes longer for varying degrees of doneness. Let the cooked roasts cool completely. Cover and chill the roasts until shortly before serving. Slice the beef very thinly and arrange it on a large platter. Serve with Quick Béarnaise Sauce.

### QUICK BÉARNAISE SAUCE

8 ounces cream cheese, softened  
2½ cups mayonnaise  
3 tablespoons tarragon wine vinegar  
1 tablespoon chopped fresh tarragon, or 1 teaspoon dried tarragon  
3 tablespoons finely chopped shallots  
3 tablespoons finely chopped fresh parsley leaves

In a bowl thoroughly combine the cream cheese and mayonnaise. Use the food processor if desired. Add the remaining ingredients and mix well. Turn into a serving bowl, cover, and chill until ready to be served.

*Serving Suggestions:* Anchovy and Apple Tidbits, Jumbo Black Olives Stuffed with Walnut Cream Cheese, Chicken Liver Pâté with Cognac with a Parsley Topping, Ratatouille, Potato Salad with Dill Dressing, mixed cold vegetables, Chocolate Mousse Cake, and Fruit-stuffed Crêpes with Honey Butter.

# Bigos
## (Polish Hunter's Stew)

*Serves 24*

8 strips bacon, chopped
2 tablespoons butter, and
  as needed
2 pounds boneless lean
  pork, cut into 1-inch
  cubes
2 pounds stew beef, cut
  into 1-inch cubes
1½ pounds boneless veal
  shoulder, cut into
  1-inch cubes
1 large onion, chopped
1 large cabbage, cored
  and shredded

2 quarts homemade beef
  stock or canned broth
2 cups chopped prunes
6 large Delicious apples,
  peeled, cored, and
  cubed
3 pounds kielbasa
  sausage, cut into ¼-
  inch-thick slices
  Salt and freshly ground
  black pepper

1. Put the bacon in a large 6- to 8-quart ovenproof casserole or pot and fry it until it is crisp. Remove the bacon, drain, and set aside.

2. Pour off all but 2 tablespoons of the bacon drippings and add the butter to the casserole. Brown the pork, beef, and veal in several batches. Transfer the browned meat to a bowl. Occasionally wipe out the pan and add more butter.

3. Add the onions and cabbage to the casserole, stir, and simmer for 5 minutes. Add the stock and bring to a boil.

4. Return the meat to the pot and simmer for 1½ hours, stirring occasionally.

5. Add the prunes, apples, sausage, and bacon and combine. Cover and simmer for 30 minutes, or until the meat is fork-tender. Season with salt and pepper to taste.

*Serving Suggestions:* Sun-dried Tomato and Mozzarella Canapés with Fried Capers, Sardine and Chutney Canapés, hot cooked buttered noodles, mixed green salad, hot cooked string beans, Chocolate Tarts, and Fresh French Apple–Hazelnut Tarts with Frangelico Whipped Cream.

# Stuffed Chicken Breasts

*Serves 24*

| | |
|---|---|
| 8 tablespoons (1 stick) butter | 2 teaspoons dried tarragon |
| 4 leeks (white parts only), chopped | 12 large chicken breasts, skinned, boned, and halved |
| 1 8-ounce package herb-seasoned stuffing mix | 4 tablespoons butter, melted |
| ¾ cup hot water | 1½ cups homemade chicken stock or canned broth |
| ½ cup chopped fresh parsley leaves | ½ cup dry white wine |

1. Melt the butter in a frying pan and cook the leeks for 5 minutes, stirring often. Remove from the heat and add the stuffing mix, hot water, parsley, and tarragon and combine well.

2. Spoon 2 rounded tablespoons of the mixture on the boned side of each chicken breast half and roll up, tucking the ends underneath.

3. Preheat the oven to 350 degrees.

4. Put the stuffed breasts in a very large roasting pan or 2 large ones. Brush each breast with melted butter and sprinkle lightly with paprika.

5. Pour the combined chicken broth and wine into the 1 pan or half the mixture into the 2 pans. Bake for 1 hour.

*Serving Suggestions:* Shrimp Wrapped with Prosciutto, Sliced Eggs and Caviar Canapés, Celery Sticks with Roquefort–Cream Cheese Spread, Wild Rice Minnesota-style, Three-Green Salad with Hazelnut Dressing, Chocolate Mousse, and Rosettes.

# Seafood and Pasta Ragout

### Serves 24

¾ cup olive oil
3 cups chopped onion
2 teaspoons minced garlic
1½ cups chopped sweet
   green pepper
3½ cups canned imported
   Italian plum tomatoes,
   drained
3 tablespoons tomato
   paste
1½ cups dry red wine
3 cups bottled clam juice
1½ teaspoon dried basil
1½ teaspoons dried oregano
   Salt and freshly ground
   black pepper

2½ pounds penne, ziti, or
   rigatoni
2 pounds medium shrimp,
   shelled and deveined
2 pounds sea scallops, cut
   into quarters
1 pound king crabmeat
1 pound mushrooms,
   thinly sliced
1 16-ounce can chick-peas,
   well drained
   Freshly grated
   Parmesan cheese (about
   3 cups)

1. Heat the olive oil in a 6- or 8-quart pot. Add the onion, garlic, and green pepper and cook over medium-low heat for about 15 minutes, stirring often. Add the tomatoes, tomato paste, red wine, clam juice, basil, oregano, and salt and pepper to taste. Bring to a boil and boil for 1 minute. Lower the heat and simmer for 15 minutes.

2. Meanwhile, bring 6½ quarts of water to a rolling boil in an 8-quart pot. Add 2 tablespoons of salt, stir, and add the pasta. Immediately stir for about 20 seconds. Cook until the pasta is *al dente,* just until tender. It will be necessary to stir the pasta often to prevent it from sticking together because of the large amount; especially at the beginning of the cooking time.

3. Add the seafood, mushrooms, and chick-peas to the sauce, stir, and simmer for 8 minutes, or until the pasta is cooked.

4. Drain the pasta well and put it in one very large pot. Ladle the seafood sauce over the pasta and toss. Serve in 1 or 2 large serving dishes with freshly grated Parmesan cheese on the side.

*Serving Suggestions:* Antipasto Kebabs in a Bread Basket, Smoked Chicken Canapés, buttered string beans, mixed green salad, Cheesecake, two of Ellie Ashworth's Rum–Pecan Pies, and assorted cookies.

# Italian Hero Sandwiches for 24

For casual gatherings, a picnic, beach party, or tailgate party, hero sandwiches are great for crowds.

6 medium-sized red onions, thinly sliced and separated into rings

4 1½-foot loaves crusty Italian or French bread

8 tablespoons (1 stick) butter, softened

1 large head iceberg lettuce, shredded

2 pounds Provolone, thinly sliced

2 pounds mortadella, thinly sliced

2 pounds Genoa salami, thinly sliced

Dried oregano

Dried basil

1½ cups jarred roasted red peppers, drained and cut into thin strips

Olive oil in a cruet

Red wine vinegar in a cruet

1. Put the onion rings in a large bowl of ice water and let stand for 30 minutes. Drain well and pat dry with paper towels.
2. Cut each loaf of bread in half lengthwise. Scoop out the loose bread and discard. Butter the insides of the bread halves.
3. Arrange the shredded lettuce across the bottom halves of the bread loaves. Top with the onion rings, cheese, and meat, cut to fit the width of the bread. Sprinkle the herbs lightly over the top. Place the pepper strips across the filling and sprinkle the sandwiches very lightly with the oil and vinegar.
4. Cover with the bread tops and cut each loaf into 8 pieces. Secure the sandwiches with toothpicks and arrange on a large platter.

*Variations:* Any complimenting variety of cheese and meat can be used, such as Munster, Swiss, mozzarella, or Fontina or roast beef, chicken breast, turkey, or ham. If you know that some of your guests might not like the onions, either omit them or place them across only 2 loaves. In that event, slice only 3 onions.

*Serving Suggestions:* Fruit Crudités with Caribbean Curried Mayonnaise, Pasta Primavera, Caponata, two of Lili Barr's Brownie Cakes, Prize-winning Carrot Cake, and Ruglach.

# Index